Sweet Carolina

Sweet

Carolina

Favorite Desserts *and* Candies
from the Old North State

FOY ALLEN EDELMAN

THE UNIVERSITY OF NORTH CAROLINA PRESS
CHAPEL HILL

Manufactured in the
United States of America
Designed by Kimberly Bryant
Set in Whitman and Zapfino
by Rebecca Evans

Unless otherwise noted,
the photographs in this
book have been taken by
the author.

Map by Michael Newhouse
and illustrations by David
Jackson, all courtesy of
Deborah Wolfe, Ltd.

The paper in this book meets the guidelines for
permanence and durability of the Committee on
Production Guidelines for Book Longevity of the
Council on Library Resources.

The University of North Carolina Press has been a
member of the Green Press Initiative since 2003.

Library of Congress Cataloging-in-Publication Data
Edelman, Foy Allen.
Sweet Carolina: favorite desserts and candies from the
Old North State / Foy Allen Edelman.
     p. cm.
Includes index.
ISBN 978-0-8078-3294-3 (cloth: alk. paper)
1. Desserts—North Carolina. 2. Candy—North Carolina.
I. Title.
TX773.E332 2009
641.8′609756—dc22   2009016595

CLOTH   13 12 11 10 09   5 4 3 2 1

For my mother,

SARAH SAWYER ALLEN,

and for

IDA MAE BLOUNT,

my other mother

Contents

Acknowledgments

I am indebted to all the cooks who shared their recipes and stories with me. I was a stranger, and they welcomed me. Their generosity of spirit humbled me, and this collection would not be possible without their contributions. My deepest appreciation goes to my daughter, Harper Lazo, and my husband, Jerry Edelman. I also appreciate Dr. Anne Phillips, my North Carolina history professor, who taught me the basics of oral history and encouraged me every step of the way; and Elaine Maisner, who guided me through the process of organizing the material. Victoria Medaglia, Kate McKinney Maddalena, and Janet Silber provided editorial assistance; Brad Goodwin, graphics support; and Debbie Moose, guidance and encouragement in the publishing process. Thanks, too, to the North Carolina Cooperative Extension Service agents for Family and Consumer Education, who led me to meet many of the cooks; Vanette McKinney, an inspiration to me and to everyone who knows her; Ava Murgia and Sam Staples in Camden County, and Laura Herbert, Allison Best, David Teague, Brenda Zimmerman, and the Blankenship family in Cherokee, who hosted me as I traveled west; Sharon Stroud, Helen and Mickey Cochrane, Dr. Christine Mallinsen, Theresa Jack, Kathy Revels, Dr. Valerie Yow, Barbara Boney, Terry McManus, Brandon Donaldson, and Dwan Upchurch, who introduced me to cooks and sometimes traveled with me; North Carolina State professors Dr. Walt Wolfram, Dr. James Clark, and Dr. Carmine Prioli; Karen Gottovi, director of the North Carolina Council on Aging; Carolyn Shankle, librarian for Special Collections and Rare Books, Jackson Library, University of North Carolina at Greensboro; descendents of Loucinda Wilson in Yancey County and the Porter Family of Bladen County who let me visit their reunions; my good friends who helped me test the recipes, including Mary Charles Pawlikowski, Dr. Gail Mahnken, Peggy Lanier, Rachel Wilde, and Cecelia and Dr. Michael Flickinger.

In Memoriam

Julia Maxwell Allen

Sarah Sawyer Allen

Martha Barnes

Ammie Best

Ida Mae Blount

Susan Carson

Mary Deal

Leone Epperson

Marguerite Hughey

Margaret Barnes MacNeill

Harriet Robson

Hattie Smith

Ruby Teague

Nolie Ridenhour Zimmerman

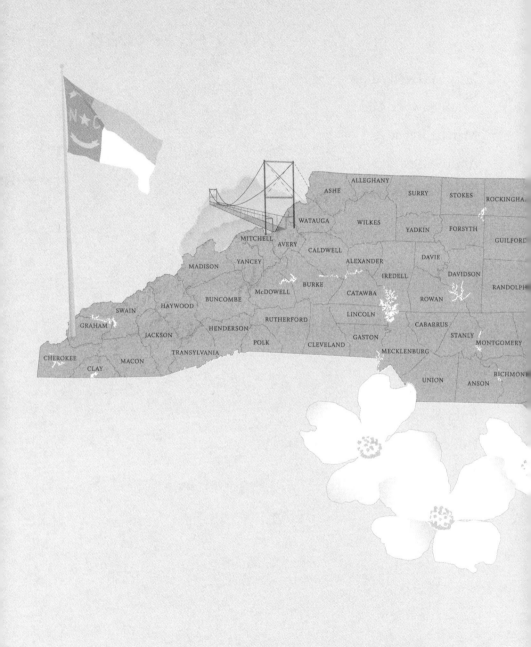

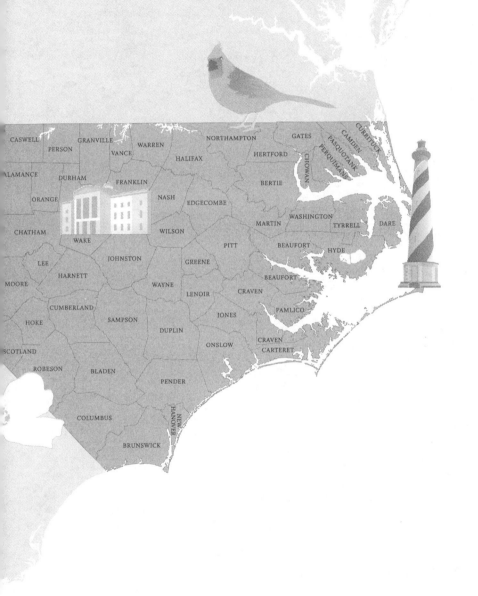

Sweet Carolina

Introduction

Exploring North Carolina and its food traditions has been a happy, life-long adventure. Recently, I've been on a treasure hunt: I've been seeking out local cooks and recording their recipes, cooking experiences, and stories. With a map of North Carolina as my guide and a recipe box as my treasure chest, I set off to find adventure, meet intriguing people, try new foods, and dig up forgotten recipes and homegrown stories in all corners of the state. All that I sought I found, and more.

My goal was to visit every county in the state, to taste food in the kitchens of local cooks, and to see the vast range of life in the area through their eyes. You might say I have been putting together a culinary jigsaw puzzle of North Carolina, where each county was a distinctive and delicious piece.

We all have a favorite food and often a particular recipe related to home. During my treasure hunt, I've asked people for recipes that connect them with family and friends, recipes that are dependable, wholesome, and appealing. Doors opened as easily as cookie jars; recipes and related stories flowed out like honey. In this book, you'll find easy-to-follow recipes for these and other tried-and-true goodies that generation after generation of North Carolinians have loved, copied, and recopied.

Who are the cooks who prepare these delectable treats? While they are as varied and remarkable as our state, all are united in their love of home and country. They are friendly, generous, and resourceful, using relatively few ingredients to create a vast assortment of desserts and candies. Fruits, vegetables, eggs, and dairy products mingle together in mouthwatering combinations that are fairly simple to create. Traditional ingredients such as berries, apples, pumpkins, and pears find their way into rich pies, cakes, cobblers, and ice cream.

Because I am particularly gratified when friends and family sigh "mmmm" and "ah" and "oh" after consuming a special sweet I've prepared, I decided to feature desserts and candies in this volume. Later collections will include main dishes, vegetables, and everything else good that lands on a North Carolina table. I also plan, in future volumes, to feature cooks from the other forty-nine states who have moved to North Carolina and brought their culinary traditions with them, and to find new citizens from around the world who came here to make their homes and brought different and exciting ways of preparing foods with them.

I was born in Lenoir County. There, as in many places in North Carolina, the earth is rich and will grow almost anything. The land and natural seasons gave, and still give, rhythm to our lives and our diets. During the 1950s, when I grew up, the region was economically depressed. Food in Lenoir County was a source of abundance in a culture of scarcity. Preparing it, serving it, and sharing it were important parts of the lives of people in town, regardless of economic status. How we ate, when we ate, and what we ate were all part of our collective identity. If we were happy or sad; if we graduated, failed, married, lost a loved one; if we got a raise or just arrived home from school, something edible marked the occasion. Food was so important in Kinston, where I grew up, that it seemed to provide an unspoken language. Each meal and event was somehow a script that people understood, and a quality of reverence imbued each occasion no matter how casual.

As soon as I could walk, my small feet were quickly transplanted to the outdoor world, which was one of my playhouses; it provided awesome beauty, the full range of our climate, and creative experience through make believe. Each summer, I was free to roam the neighborhood barefooted, collecting leaves, grasshoppers, and June bugs that I tied thread to and made my own personal toys for the day before freeing them. While squishing mud between my toes in puddles, I watched tadpoles grow tiny legs and become minute frogs. Summer nights sparkled with fireflies that lit up our backyards like fairies. My lullabies were the rhythms of bullfrogs, cicadas, and crickets. I played with toy pans in a sand pile, turning out wedding cakes decorated with bachelor buttons, dandelions, zinnias, and camellia blossoms, then fed slices of them to my dolls. Once a year my family vacationed at the coast or in the mountains. Sometimes I roamed the beaches, caught, cleaned, and ate fish, crabs, and oysters; other years

I explored trails near Blowing Rock and on Grandfather Mountain. In the fall, cool winds shook the branches of pine trees, scattering straw over the yard so that it looked like it was covered with drops of caramel candy. I felt like I was scratching the back of the earth as I raked the fragrant pine needles into huge stacks, and then jumped into them. Autumn was the season of apple desserts, pecan pie, and popcorn balls.

Another playhouse was our kitchen. Both my mother, Sarah Sawyer Allen, and our housekeeper, Ida Mae Blount, welcomed me into what seemed to be an enchanted world, where white powders, exotic flavorings, and raw eggs were transformed into beautiful cakes and handsome pies. Ida Mae, I realize now, taught me a lot about the African American contributions to traditional southern cooking. Looking back on those times, I also see that I was enthusiastically included in the kitchen, mostly for the extra set of hands I provided. Around age four I received a blunt, aluminum GI surplus knife and learned how to scrape the skin off potatoes. Soon I climbed on a chair to reach the kitchen table, where I cut out biscuits by turning an orange juice glass upside down over dough that had been flattened with a rolling pin. Around age five, I accumulated a variety of small Blue Willow porcelain plates, cups, and saucers. My younger brother used to sit across from me at our school table for tea parties during which we sipped kettle tea (a mixture of mostly milk and sugar with a tiny bit of real hot tea) from the cups and ate cookies dipped into the concoction. Those were happy days when I began to feed people. I'm still feeding my brother and many others and use those same Blue Willow cups after dinner, though now they are filled with espresso.

My culinary career took a more sophisticated turn when my eighth birthday was celebrated with a dinner party; my girlfriends came dressed as their mothers. My mother laid out the dining room table with her best linen cloth and napkins, a centerpiece of homegrown zinnias, silver flatware, and porcelain plates. Each elegant guest was served a fried chicken leg accompanied by our unique variation on Toad in the Hole (mashed potatoes indented in the top and filled with green peas), hot biscuits with honey, and a grown-up drink: sweetened iced tea. The final course was a spectacular white layer cake with boiled icing and a side of ice cream.

By the time I was ten I owned two cookbooks. My great-aunt Martha Barnes handwrote her recipes in a notebook she gave to me for Christmas one year. Her cookbook is one of the material treasures that remain from my childhood. I use it to this day. I also had a copy of *Betty Crocker's Cook Book for Boys and Girls*. I was elated as I cooked, preparing butterscotch brownies, whiz cinnamon rolls, and cheese dreams (a hot sandwich made with an English muffin covered with tomatoes, bacon, and melted cheese) for my small group of regulars.

In the 1950s, Kinston was the commercial center for farms in the area. Lifestyles then were more basic than they are today; many people knew hardship. I vividly remember seeing mule-drawn wooden wagons downtown on Saturday afternoons. The drivers were often sharecroppers who came to town once a week to buy supplies. I also remember seeing a beggar on Queen Street playing an accordion. A monkey, perched on his shoulder, danced in front of McClelland's Five and Dime to attract tips to the beggar's tin cup. Unpaved roads ran through many neighborhoods.

Communities located close the Neuse River frequently flooded during summer cloudbursts.

Waste in our part of the world was unacceptable. Clothes were worn until they didn't fit anymore, then handed down, patched, and used in quilts and potholders until they became dust rags. Seed sacks and fertilizer bags were made into clothes and aprons. At most dinner tables, all were encouraged to "clean their plates"; leftover foods either were consumed or became food for animals. I grew up on Highland Avenue, where I saw two neighborhood boys, Joe Carey and Dee Taylor, argue over and drop a large watermelon probably weighing fifteen to twenty pounds while helping Dee's mother, Alice, unload groceries from her car. Alice made them sit down on the ground and eat the entire melon while the local children watched so they could benefit from the lesson.

Though the economy was meager, the natural world, despite the whims of nature such as droughts, hurricanes, tornados, and pests, produced bountifully. We were poor in goods, but we were rich in foods. The spoils of gardens and fields were widely enjoyed and inspired talented cooks to develop their own recipes. My father was a lawyer, and many of his clients were farmers who brought wooden boxes of dusty potatoes, country hams, juicy tomatoes, and homemade sausage by our house in partial payment for his services. Town dwellers who owed him money sometimes brought beautiful and delectable cakes, pies, and candies.

Pastimes were limited, and those in which we did indulge were most likely tied to productivity. We often shelled peas, popped beans, and cracked pecans in bowls on our laps as we visited with each other. People collected things like shells, rocks, and recipes. Men and women hunted, fished, and raised backyard gardens; they canned and dried what foods they did not consume. When Scheryl Cannon and Brenda Cannon Bowers of Burke County were children, they went out to local fields to pick berries that their grandmother used to make sonker, a sweet pastry that can be made with a variety of fillings. Improvised tools were popular. Few people competed for status with houses, cars, and clothes, but those who could make something out of otherwise useless articles such as bottle tops, popsicle sticks, canceled stamps, out-of-date license plates, discarded buttons, or empty tin cans were revered. Last year's Christmas cards became next year's package tags; scraps of cloth became lively rugs; empty coffee cans turned into cookie jars. It was the age of the garage inventor who spent Saturday afternoon using simple tools to make a better birdhouse or mousetrap.

Family entertainment, mostly homemade, cost little or nothing. Telling family stories after dinner offered tremendous amusement practically for free. In our home, hard candies were stored in a pretty dish on a coffee table in the living room. We used the candy to keep our mouths moist while we talked. The jar had to be filled regularly because when we had guests, we talked a lot. Good conversation and food, history, and nature were, and remain, family values. Visiting historical sites, going for walks, repeating stories of wars and the aftermath, working in the yard, and picnicking in many areas of the state were collective pastimes.

As I became a teenager and then a young woman, no matter where we came together, whether fancy house or farmhouse, I gathered with the cooks in the kitchen after dinner. Here we scraped dishes, drained tea glasses, made coffee, took another bite of dessert, licked icing off our fingers, talked, and exchanged recipes. We often discussed menus for family dinners, church events, luncheons, funerals, and other social gatherings. Newcomers quickly joined our circle of close friends in this warm environment. The intimacy and tenderness of recipe exchanges transcended many differences and spilled over into other discussions of secret desires, confidences, hurts, and questions that bound us together in deep ways. This experience—the communion that took place in the kitchen with shared recipes as its motivation and its lingering gift—is what my treasure hunt seeks to celebrate and, I hope, preserve.

I thought I knew the majority of traditional recipes throughout the state, but I found *many* surprises. In the far western corner of North Carolina, Cherokee County cooks make a thick pudding out of hominy and walnuts. Madison County is famous for apple stack cake. Stokes and Surrey Counties celebrate an annual festival that showcases sonker. Chocolate gravy poured over hot, homemade biscuits is a special treat in several places. Moravians are celebrated bakers who are just as likely to churn scrumptious ice cream. Egg custards and molasses cakes are popular in the Piedmont, along with more elaborate concoctions such as open face peach pie. Scuppernong grapes are used for a delicious pie in the eastern counties. Chocolate, though a relatively recent addition to our gastronomic history, is enjoyed statewide in dark, gratifying cakes, brownies, and icings. Peanuts, pecans, and walnuts add flavor and texture to alluring confections in every corner of the state. Many folks passed along heirloom recipes, such as the Atlantic coast cook who makes her mother's Christmas pie. These are recipes that have been made for generations and are precious to families. Some are even secret. When I visited Warren County, Lynn Pierce found a note in her mother's handwritten cookbook specifying that the recipe not be divulged to anyone outside the family. It was fine to share the resulting food, however, and I enjoyed every mouthful during my journey across the state.

In collecting these recipes, I especially looked for those that the cooks themselves enjoy, serve to everyone they can, and hand down to others. These are enduring, traditional recipes like pound cake, apple pie, egg custard, gingerbread, and cookies, recipes that are widely known and used across the state. Many of them were carefully recorded by hand in notebooks or files kept by North Carolina women during the nineteenth century, like these:

Lemon Pie

MRS. MARTHA T. COWLES, Elkville, Wilkes County, 1846

One lemon
One spoonful flour
Three spoonfuls sugar
A little butter and salt

GRATE the yellow outside peel to flavor your pie; then pare away the white skin which is apt to be bitter and slice your lemon pulp into a plate lined with paste [pastry]. Dissolve the flour and other ingredients in water enough to fill the paste, then cover with another. This is an excellent pie, the lemon being a good substitute for apple.

Ice Cream with Peaches

MARY K. WILLIAMS, Warren County, 1858

TAKE a quart of soft peaches well mashed & sweetened.
1 tablespoonful of peach or Rose water. 1 pint and a half good
cream with nutmeg.

Caramel Filling

MRS. MAGGIE UPCHURCH, Raleigh, Wake County, 1859

Nice Light Brown Sugar 2 pounds
Water 1/2 pint
Butter 2 table spoonful
Flavor with Vanilla

BOIL the sugar and water until it ropes, but not enough to pull.
Pour over the butter. Stir smooth and allow cool enough,
place between the layers and on top for icing.

During my quest, my first visit was to Mecklenburg County, where I met Essie Gilliard, a woman whom my daughter had met at a local Charlotte farmers market. Known to her friends as "Mom," Essie invited me to her small store, Mom's Carryout Kitchen, in an urban Charlotte neighborhood, where she told her story. She was the first African American teller at an NCNB bank in the late 1970s. Mom was successful at her job and was soon promoted to manage ATM machines. But another calling drew Mom away from the world of deposits and withdrawals. Her dream was to open her own business. Eventually, she saved enough money, retired from NCNB, and purchased a small café. "I worked for the bank for eighteen years until servicing ATM machines became dangerous," said Mom. "I started wanting to own my own business . . . this man wanted to sell his building . . . well, the only problem was I didn't know how to cook." She asked her 101-year-old mother-in-law, Mrs. Oralee Gilliard, known as "Miss Peach," to teach her. "I called her up one day," said Mom. "'You put a pinch of this and a handful of that,' [Miss Peach] said. I wanted to start making sweet potato pies. She said to keep it simple but always to use fresh potatoes and just try different things because you might come up with your own thing that you like that will make it a little different from everybody else's. So I started using Carnation evaporated milk." Later, Mom worked to perfect recipes for delicious pies and cakes. Her specialty is Miss Peach's sweet potato pie, found in the pie chapter.

Essie Guilliard

Another tradition reflected in this collection is simply practicality. The vast majority of recipes contain ten or fewer ingredients; many take less than thirty minutes to prepare. The kitchens I visited are sensible and basic. Appliances are prized as much for their longevity as for their usefulness. Marie Batchelor of Duplin County wrote to me that she has "been cooking on the same stove for more than fifty-one years with no repairs." The cooks I visited take advantage of each laborsaving gadget that makes them more productive, from egg separators, to various Ronco devices that slice, dice, and shred, to Tupperware storage containers. "I wouldn't take a pretty for my new spreader," Maverine Baker, of Johnston County, told me. These cooks are also inventive. The Speece and Rash families invited me to Sunday dinner in Iredell County. They gave me three homemade kitchen aids made from pieces of scrap wood: a jar opener, a fox-shaped tool to move pans around in the oven without burning yourself, and a tool for measuring pasta. Many others whom I met told me that they make ample use of time-saving devices like electric ice cream makers and blenders and that they use premade piecrusts and whipped toppings. Some use cake or pudding mixes as ingredients.

The ability to take anything you have, make something good out of it, and share it is perhaps the most characteristic tradition of all. I think that this custom is deeply rooted in our state's past; it seems to have grown up right in North Carolina's backyards, where ingenuity and need met local agriculture. "I remember my grandmother on my mother's side, Alice Williams [born about 1870], well," Flossie Clark Johnson of Clingman in Wilkes County told me. "She lived on a farm. They raised their own fruits and vegetables. Grandma grew herbs in the garden. She made sassafras tea, Spicewood tea. She knew the branches that grew out in the woods.

The one thing she always taught me was that you take the best of what you've got and make the best of it. [My mother] always picked out a pretty feedbag to make our dresses out of. She made dried-apple pies and little turnovers. She made peach pies, blackberry cobblers, anything she had."

The tradition of creating a tasty treat spontaneously is valued today just as it was in the past. Liberty Heath of Caldwell County told me that her grandmother bakes a basic cake in the morning as a breakfast pastry, adds a side of ice cream to it at lunch, and then perhaps covers it with a tasty sauce or some fresh fruit after supper. "Everything is made and remade," Liberty told me.

I am deeply contented in more than body when I think about cooks like Peggy Lanier of Onslow County, who shared a homemade video of her mother making what she calls a blueberry biscuit from flour, shortening, sugar, and blueberries; Flossie Johnson, whose mother fashioned apple roll-ups from biscuit dough, fresh apples, sugar, and spices; and Pat Carroll, who grew up savoring blackberry dumplings made from sweet and pungent wild berries. You'll find these humble but delicious desserts in the following pages. Like a patchwork quilt composed of familiar and colorful remnants, homegrown fruits, vegetables, and leftovers combined with sugar and biscuit dough become sweet and unique family foods.

In my quest, I gathered many treasures. Beyond the gift of her sweet potato pie recipe, Essie Gilliard gave me the first gem in my treasure chest—the gift of knowing her and her family. Soon after, relatives, friends, and neighbors contributed recipes from Cartaret, Lenoir, Washington, Duplin, Bertie, Durham, Nash, and Wilson Counties. Doors continued to open as I began to call on county agricultural extension agents, librarians, welcome center staff, senior center directors, churches, and historical societies to ask for suggestions for finding cooks.

I talked to strangers in farmers markets and churches whenever I thought I heard the dialect of a county in which I was looking for a local cook. Some friends spent days with me, traveling to remote counties and introducing me to their communities' renowned cooks. Each time I left home to explore another county, my heart skipped a beat in anticipation of the people I'd meet that day, the natural beauty of the rural countryside

I'd see, the varieties of cityscapes and towns I'd encounter, the tastes I would share, and the unique stories I'd hear.

In Jackson County, I was amazed to see Eula Mae Kilby's heirloom tomato vines wind around their stakes and reach way over my head toward the sky. Anne Radford Phillips's paternal grandfather built a family home near Dalton, Stokes County, in 1888. The house is imbued with the intrigue of history that drew me in to enjoy morning light; the huge old kitchen begged to whisper stories of the generations whose spirits linger around the breakfast table. Outside, tempting plump blueberries beckoned me to commune with them and indulge in the primitive pleasure of eating fresh, ripe fruit still warm from the sun. I was invited to make sorghum syrup with David Davis and his friends on his farm in Moore County. It seemed like a charmed world. The Queen Anne's lace grew all the way up to my shoulders, but then everything at David's house is either huge, including David, or prodigiously abundant—dozens of hummingbirds competed for his feeders; sunflowers, pole beans, and other vegetables grew with abandon—only Peanut, a tiny Jack Russell terrier, escaped the colossal scale of the place.

In Cartaret County, I watched the wild ponies, looking like magical creatures, emerge from the early morning mists of Shackleford Banks. They led their foals into the cooling waters of the sound to swim from one sandbar to another to munch the salty marsh grass that is exposed only when the tide is out. I rocked with Martha Blaine Wood and her husband on their front porch in Macon County while a covey of wild turkeys strolled through the yard. I attended powwows where I was dazzled by the colorful regalia of Native American dancers, and had my hunger satisfied with hot fry bread (recipe included) and sassafras tea. I was invited to a reunion in a beautiful valley in Yancey County where all the family members are descended from Loucinda Wilson, an emancipated slave, who is buried there. I attended a birthday party in Warren County where there is an unusual custom of shouting out the words to "Happy Birthday," tunelessly, to the honoree. One hundred and forty-nine family members invited me to attend the Porter houseparty, a family reunion at White Lake, where we took a hayride through the family farm and chowed down on watermelon and homemade cakes. Generous friends cooked me a wonderful supper of doves and seafood in Durham; another group invited me to a traditional Sunday dinner in Iredell County that ended with a spectacular devil's food cake decorated with tiny animals made from candy.

All of these people and scenes had called to me, and I answered them. Sharing foods and stories are some of the ways we bond with each other. I hope you will share in this sweet experience by trying the dishes in this book and using them to nourish the people you love.

Notes on the Recipes

I was lucky to be able to spend lots of time talking with the cooks whose recipes appear in this book, and you'll see their own words, taken from my recordings and notes of these conversations and interviews, sprinkled throughout. I hope my selections convey each cook's heritage and enthusiasm.

In developing this cookbook, I have altered some recipe titles slightly in order to describe as best I can the actual dessert or candy produced. The ages of recipes that compose this collection range from well over one hundred years old to fairly recent. Recording styles varied from cook to cook and over time. For example, the recipes that were recorded in the early nineteenth century often consist of a handwritten list of ingredients with measurements in pounds and no further instructions. Likewise, recipes from the early twentieth century frequently contain a handwritten list of ingredients with measurements in cups and spoons but no additional instructions.

In contrast, an early-twenty-first century recipe is often created with computer software and contains detailed instructions, measurements, and ingredients. I've taken the approach of combining the original style of the cook with the types of measurements and cooking terms in current use so that as a whole, the recipes are consistent and easy to understand and use today. Old-fashioned kitchen references—place a pot over the fire, put something on ice, prepare custard in a hot cause pan—have been replaced with modern phrases. Likewise, lard and oleo (margarine) are replaced with shortening and butter in some recipes.

In addition:

* This collection includes many recipes developed by cooks who inherited a basic recipe, then customized it in their own way. Sometimes this happened out of necessity when they had to substitute an available ingredient for one that was missing. Perhaps blackberries were available in great quantities and were used to replace blueberries in a pie filling; or the cook had no graham crackers but did have macaroons to make a crumb crust. Other times a cook simply didn't like an ingredient and substituted another. I hope you will follow this tradition by individualizing recipes to make them your own. If you prefer milk chocolate chips to semisweet, or crunchy peanut butter to smooth, or you like lemon zest in your meringue, please make the recipes your way. May you come up with new and tasty treats that will be enjoyed by future generations!

* Serving sizes for the recipes are arbitrary and based on the experiences of the testers.

* All the recipes have been tested in kitchens similar to those where they were collected and under similar conditions.

* Most chapters contain tips for successfully preparing recipes. These tips are just guidelines and suggestions that reflect simple kitchen wisdom gained by years of experience. If you have a better way of doing something, don't hesitate to use it!

* Cooking is part art and part science, but, most of all, it's just plain fun. If you're a beginner cook, as you gain experience and see how much those around you enjoy the results, you'll have more and more success and will discover your own version of kitchen wisdom.

* Butter and margarine are interchangeable unless otherwise noted. If you use margarine, however, be sure to *use solid stick*, not whipped.

* All spices are ground, unless otherwise noted.

* Nondairy whipped topping is interchangeable with whipped cream.

* If a specific type of milk is called for, it is noted. Otherwise, milk means whatever cow's milk you have in your refrigerator. If evaporated milk is specified, use it right out of the can, not diluted.

* Evaporated milk needs to be refrigerated for at least twelve hours when a recipe calls for it to be whipped.

* Ingredients generally combine better when all are at room temperature, unless otherwise noted.

* Food safety experts generally recommend that for recipes featuring raw or lightly cooked eggs, pasteurized eggs or egg substitute be used.

* Separating eggs carefully is a requirement for many desserts. You will need two bowls, one for the whites and another for the yolks. Pick up eggs one at a time. Crack the eggshell by gently knocking it against a hard surface like a counter edge. Finish breaking the eggshell into two halves over the bowl where you want to save the egg whites. Pour the yolk from one half of the eggshell into the other, allowing the white part to drop into the bowl. Be sure that no egg yolk drops into the white, as it will keep the eggs from becoming stiff when beaten. If a drop of yolk does fall into the egg whites, remove it with a spoon. If you have trouble mastering this technique, you can purchase a simple tool for separating eggs. It looks like a small cup with a curved slit cut into it, a little like a bowl with a smile; the egg white falls through the slit while the yolk is trapped inside.

Cakes

Plain Cake

One-Two-Three-Four Cake

Yellow Daisy Cake

Mae Wells's Gingerbread

Hot Milk Sponge Cake

Molasses Cake

Lazy Daisy Oatmeal Cake and Icing

Spice Cake

Yellow Cake and Chocolate Icing

Black Chocolate Cake and Icing

Lena Belle's Seven-Layer Chocolate Cake and Icing

Chocolate Velvet Cake and Frosting

Hot Chocolate Cake and Topping

Marble Cake

Chocolate Walnut Loaf

Brownie Cupcakes

The Amazing Cheesecake

Carrot Cake and Icing

F OR GENERATIONS, the crowning glory of the southern dessert table has been the cake. Expensive ingredients, elaborate icings, beautiful decorations, and its role as the perfect conclusion to any meal elevate the cake to its deserved status as the central focus for eye and palate. Special events—holidays, birthdays, weddings, funerals—are all marked by these elegant, sweet delicacies. Wherever I traveled, I found cakes as diverse as the regions; some are literally styled as "plain" while others are rich, lavished with nuts, chocolate, and fruit. All shapes and sizes are represented, from cupcakes to layer cakes, sheet cakes to stack cakes.

I strolled through Old Salem one December morning. Founded in 1766, this historic area of Forsyth County is a happy, thriving community. Enticing aromas of fresh baking captivated me as I neared the Winkler Bakery. Through the half-open door I saw the male bakers dressed in long white aprons, their matching cooking berets decorated with holly. They looked like holiday elves as they prepared the magnificent, rich cakes the bakery has offered since 1807.

Rebeccah Neff, a Moravian who grew up near Winston-Salem, told me about her culinary heritage. She, like many North Carolinians, thinks of baking as a family art, not a chore. "Before he owned a KitchenAid mixer, Dad sometimes made cake batter with his hands, because, he claimed, 'It makes a fine-textured cake.' And he was right. Until I inherited his Kitchen-Aid, which is still going strong, I sometimes used his technique of hand mixing, blending the butter and sugar, adding the eggs, the flavorings, flour, and leavening until I had created a soft, light batter that yielded springy, even-textured layers with as fine a crumb as you can imagine. Dad's 'Feathery Coconut Cake' began with these soft-textured layers."

Many bakers, including Tom Brown, another Forsyth County resident, favor locally grown ingredients. Tom has an unusual pastime. "My hobby is looking for old heritage apple varieties," he explained to me at his home in Clemmons. "These are varieties that people knew about a hundred years ago but can't find any more. I try to find them and then restore them to production, to get them into preservation orchards, and to get them to people who sell the heritage trees." Tom has located hundreds of rare apple varieties mostly in the Piedmont and Mountains. When asked about what motivates him, he answered, "I was fascinated by all the names and textures and colors and tastes." Tom puts his homegrown apples to good use in his mouth-watering Big Mama's apple cake.

Cakes don't have to be complicated to be good; some popular recipes are so simple they don't even need to be written down. Pound cake originally included a pound of sugar, a pound of flour, a pound of lard, and a pound of eggs, usually a dozen. Well liked for over two hundred years, the pound cake remains vastly popular today. Brown sugar, rum, lemon, chocolate, nuts, and fruit give this old standby renewed appeal. Another easy-to-remember recipe is the one-two-three-four cake contributed by Juanita Hudson, from Harnett County. It calls for one cup of butter, two of sugar, three of flour, and four eggs.

Other traditions are represented in the recipes included here. Colored cakes fascinated Americans of the nineteenth century; recipes for silver, gold, marble, and black cakes were popular across the country. Wanda Brooks prepared a yellow sheet cake for me when I visited her at the high school in Stanly County, where she teaches home economics. Cooks from Yancey, Guilford, Pitt, and Wake Counties bake brown, marble, black, and even red cakes. Like generations of bakers preceding them, residents of Rowan, Guilford, and Chowan Counties use locally produced dairy ingredients—cream cheese, buttermilk, whipped and sour cream—to make elegant cheesecakes, carrot cake icing, and coconut cake.

The cake recipes in this chapter contain more than flour and sugar. They are as loved and revered as the relatives and friends who handed them down. The confections are sweet, tangible connections with our past and tasty heirlooms for future generations who will also cherish our culinary heritage.

Tips for Baking Successful Cakes

∗ There are several ways to prepare pans quickly and easily to prevent cakes from sticking to them:

1) When I was growing up, we turned our baking pans upside down, fitted sheets of waxed paper over them, cut out the shape of the bottom of the pan, and placed the cut sheet into the pan before baking. We

used shortening and flour on the inside edge of the pan. The parchment paper sold for baking purposes works well this way, too.

2) Use a small piece of paper towel to spread a little softened butter, margarine, or shortening over the bottom and sides of the pan. Next, sprinkle a little flour into the center of the pan. Evenly distribute the flour by swishing it over the bottom and sides. Discard any excess flour. A tablespoon of shortening and 1/4 cup of flour for each 9-inch baking pan works well. Adjust amounts depending on the number and size of pans.

3) My cousin Katherine Sawyer Ward of Windsor combines softened butter, margarine, or shortening with flour and spreads it evenly around the cake pan with a small piece of paper towel in one step.

4) Spray the bottom and sides of the pan with cooking spray, such as Pam. Then sprinkle flour over bottom and sides as described in method 1.

* Make sure your oven is cleaned regularly; otherwise remnants from previously baked foods may lend unwanted flavors to your cake.

* Use fresh ingredients. Even flour loses moisture and flavor when stored for long periods.

* White refined sugar is most often used in cake baking. If other sugars, such as brown sugar, are called for, they are specified.

* Adding molasses to white sugar creates brown sugar. It is easy to make if you don't have any in your pantry. For light brown sugar, blend 1 cup of white sugar and 1 tablespoon of molasses. For dark brown sugar, combine 1 cup of white sugar with 2 tablespoons of molasses.

* The two basic flours used and tested in the cakes contained in this chapter are all-purpose or self-rising. Each is made from bleached wheat flour. All-purpose flour does not contain baking powder or salt. Self-rising flour contains both baking powder and salt. You can make your own self-rising flour by adding 1 1/2 teaspoons baking powder and 1/2 teaspoon salt to each cup of all-purpose flour and blending well. Making your own, of course, allows you control over how much salt you add. Many brands of flour, including White Lily and Swans Down, use winter wheat, which makes soft, light cake flours. I prefer these brands, but they are not necessary.

* Check your flour package. Most flour is now pre-sifted; thus you will only need to sift if your flour is not pre-sifted.

* You can use any cows' milk in your refrigerator unless a particular specification is made. Some recipes call for canned milks, such as evaporated milk or sweetened condensed milk. You can find these in the baking aisle of your grocery store.

* Begin testing for doneness at the minimum time indicated in the recipe. Cooks used to break off a straw bristle from a broom, rinse it, and insert it into the baking cake to see if it was done. Today most cooks use either a toothpick or a small needlelike cooking tool called a cake tester that can be used indefinitely. Test for doneness by inserting a clean toothpick or cake tester into the center of the cake. As soon as it comes out clean, with no batter clinging to it, the cake is done; so don't be shy about testing. You can always put a cake that isn't done back into the oven for a few minutes, but an overdone cake is usually dry. Another way to test for doneness is by gently pressing the center of the cake. If it springs back, it's done.

* When making a layer cake, you can use either 8-inch or 9-inch cake pans. If you use an 8-inch pan, you'll have a little thicker layer that will need to be cooked a few minutes (very few) longer than a 9-inch layer. If you use a 9-inch pan, be sure to start checking cake for doneness at the earliest cooking time.

* Let cakes cool until you can comfortably handle the pans. Don't let them cool completely or they are likely to stick. Running a knife blade between the edge of the cake and the pan before removing is also a good idea.

* Ice cakes when they have cooled completely, unless otherwise instructed. If icing a layer cake, place the least attractive layer on your serving plate first. Ice the top part only, then add the next layer and ice the top of it. When the all the layers and are stacked and iced in this manner, ice the sides. If the icing seems to stick to the cake and pull up crumbs, dip your knife or spatula in water before dipping it into the icing. This adds a little more moisture to the icing and makes it spread smoothly. When you're cutting the cake, you can dip the knife in water to prevent the icing from coming off onto the knife.

* A quick way to preserve iced cake without damaging the frosting is to cut it into slices, place them upright on an unbreakable plate in the freezer, and leave for a couple of hours until the icing is frozen. Wrap individual slices quickly in plastic wrap or aluminum foil, and return to freezer. When thawing, unwrap each frozen cake slice and place it on your serving plate. This method preserves flavor and leaves the frosting undamaged.

Plain Cake

MARTHA BARNES, Pitt County

Martha Barnes was born in 1890. She was my great aunt and lived at the time when cooks baked desserts at home every day. It only takes a few minutes to make plain cake, and it can be served warm or cold, with a filling, icing, fresh fruit, or ice cream. Like many recipes that have stood the test of time, plain cake is simply delicious.

2 1/4 cups all-purpose flour
3 1/4 teaspoons baking powder
1 1/4 cups sugar
2/3 cup shortening
1 cup milk, divided
2 eggs

PREHEAT OVEN to 350°. Grease and flour two 8- or 9-inch round cake pans, or a 9 × 13-inch baking pan. Combine flour, baking powder, and sugar. Add shortening and 2/3 cup milk. Beat 2 minutes. Add the eggs and the remaining milk. Beat hard for 2 more minutes. Pour the batter into the prepared pan(s). Bake for 25 to 30 minutes or until a toothpick inserted into the center of the cake comes out clean. Cool in pans for 20 minutes. Turn out and cool completely.

Serves 8 to 10

One-Two-Three-Four Cake

JUANITA OGBURN HUDSON, Harnett County

Juanita Ogburn Hudson was in high school in the early 1940s when the United States entered World War II. Food shortages were widespread in North Carolina and the whole country. As president of her high school 4-H Club in 1943, Juanita led a local effort called "Feed a Fighter" to raise food for members of the armed services. Participating students signed an annual pledge to do one of the following:

Juanita Hudson

    feed two baby beef animals
    feed six pigs
    feed sixteen lambs
    raise three hundred boiling chickens
    care for fifty hens
    feed and handle one milk cow
    grow 113 bushels of corn
    grow 110 bushels of tomatoes
    grow 135 bushels of sweet potatoes
    grow 135 bushels of Irish potatoes
    produce 270 gallons of cane syrup
    grow one acre of mixed vegetables
    can 500 quarts of vegetables.

Any one of these selections was calculated to be sufficient to feed a serviceman for one year. Juanita's club raised and contributed more food to the Feed a Fighter program than any other club in the state, enough to feed 132 American soldiers for a year. She was so proud of her club that she wrote to President Franklin Delano Roosevelt and told him of its contributions. FDR responded with a congratulatory letter and a referral to the Maritime Marine Commission, and on July 9, 1944, Juanita christened a war ship, the USS *Tyrell*, constructed in the Wilmington, North Carolina, shipyard, in honor of her club's achievement.

Juanita later moved to Bailey's Crossroads in rural Harnett County, where she has continued to be a civic leader serving as a National Cultural Arts chairman; she is also a lifetime member of the Associated Country Women of the World. She enjoys having company. Her husband, Mack, says, "If Juanita doesn't have company, she's out looking for it." Guests from around the world enjoy one-two-three-four cake at the Hudson's table. You can add Juanita's coconut filling (see the Icings, Fillings, and Sweet Sauces chapter) to the cake, pour fruit over it, make it into a sundae by adding ice cream, or just enjoy it by itself.

2 sticks (1 cup) butter, softened

2 cups sugar

4 eggs

1/2 teaspoon salt

3 cups all-purpose flour

3 teaspoons baking powder

1 cup milk

1 teaspoon vanilla extract

1/2 teaspoon almond extract (optional)

PREHEAT OVEN to 350°. Grease and flour three 8- or 9-inch round cake pans. With an electric mixer, cream the butter and sugar together until light and fluffy. Add the eggs and salt and blend until smooth. In a separate bowl, combine the flour and baking powder; add the mixture gradually to creamed mixture, alternating with milk. When well blended, add flavoring, beating until the batter is smooth. Divide batter evenly among the prepared pans. Bake for 25 to 30 minutes or until a toothpick inserted into the center of the cake comes out clean. Cool in pans for 20 minutes. Turn out and cool completely.

Serves 10 to 12

Yellow Daisy Cake

WANDA BROOKS, Stanly County

Bright and delicious yellow daisy cake tastes good by itself or combines well with fillings, icings, fresh fruits, or homemade ice creams.

2 cups self-rising flour
1 1/2 cups sugar
1/2 cup shortening
1 cup milk
1 1/2 teaspoons vanilla extract
3 eggs

PREHEAT OVEN to 350°. Grease and flour a 9 × 13-inch baking pan or two 9-inch round cake pans. In a large mixing bowl, cream the shortening. Add the sugar and beat well. Add the eggs, one at a time, blending well after each addition. Add the flour in thirds, alternating with the milk, blending well. Add the vanilla extract. Beat until smooth, but be careful not to overbeat. Pour the batter into the prepared pan(s). Bake for 25 to 30 minutes or until a toothpick inserted into the center of the cake comes out clean. Cool completely before serving.

Serves 8 to 12

Mae Wells's Gingerbread

Juanita Bailey

JUANITA BAILEY, Perquimans County

"I got this recipe from another extension agent," Juanita Bailey told me when I visited her in Hertford. Juanita is North Carolina Agricultural Extension agent for Family and Consumer Education. The agency was formed early in the twentieth century to provide support and education for rural families whose income depended on crops and animals that they raised. Agents live in the counties where they work so they can be close to the families they support. They provide demonstration projects that originally started with seed selection, planting, and canning processes. As needs changed, Agricultural Extension agents learned new skills, including how to offer advice on legal decisions and health issues as well as on how to purchase farm equipment. Juanita carries on this important legacy in the northeastern section of North Carolina between the Virginia border and the Albemarle Sound.

"Perquimans County was once the home of Native Americans," she told me. "The county is said to have taken its name from a Yeopim Indian word meaning 'land of beautiful women.'" That meaning was reiterated the day I visited, as Juanita had invited a number of local cooks to meet me, all "beautiful women." She served this spicy, traditional dessert for the meeting. "Young people and adults like gingerbread," she continued. "I use coffee cans or vegetable cans or fruit cans to bake it."

1/2 cup shortening, to grease a 46-ounce can or a 9 × 5-inch metal loaf pan	1 teaspoon cinnamon
	1/3 cup sugar
2 1/3 cups all-purpose flour	1 egg
1 teaspoon baking soda	1 cup molasses
3/4 teaspoon salt	3/4 cup hot water
1 teaspoon ginger	

PREHEAT OVEN to 300°. Remove the top of an empty, clean 46-ounce juice can (I use an empty V-8 can) and remove the label, or you can substitute a loaf pan for the juice can. Grease the bottom and sides of the can (or loaf pan). Combine all ingredients in a large mixing bowl. Beat with an electric mixer on low speed for 30 seconds, scraping the sides of the bowl constantly. Continue to scrape the sides of the bowl as you beat on medium speed for 3 more minutes. Pour the batter into the prepared can or loaf pan. Bake for 50 to 55 minutes, or until a toothpick inserted into the center of the cake comes out clean. Cool in pan for 20 minutes before removing.

Serves 8 to 10

Hot Milk Sponge Cake

WILL ALLEN, Wake County

Recipes for sponge cakes appear in cookbooks as early as the eighteenth century. Some early recipes contained eggs but no shortening. My grandmother, Alice Ward Allen, made this recipe frequently when my brother, Will Allen, now of Raleigh, and I were young. Will loved the way the butter melted into the milk, creating yellow puddles. He learned how to make it as a teenager and still enjoys it. Hot milk sponge cake has a rich, sweet aroma that puts me right back in my Grandmother Alice's kitchen.

Marie Solomon Kahn of Wilmington, New Hanover County, remembers using sponge cake for two desserts. "My grandmother's family sat down to dinner in the middle of the day every day," she told me. "You always had the whole thing. It was not an informal meal like today. It was dinner like we would be having it at night, but they had it in the middle of the day. One of the favorite desserts was a sponge cake baked in a tube pan; we used to call them steeple pans. When it was cooled, they sliced the top off, scooped out the middle of the cake, made a shell of the cake, and filled that with whipped cream, put the top back on it, and had this wonderful chocolate frosting, really dark and good, that went on the top of the cake. I guess you could call it chocolate cream cake. The filling that you took out of the cake was what you used with banana custard the next day." You can try these adaptations by using the chocolate frosting in the Icings, Fillings, and Sweet Sauces chapter, and Marie's banana custard in the Puddings and Custards chapter.

4 eggs, separated
1/2 cup sugar
2 cups all-purpose flour
2 teaspoons baking powder
1/4 teaspoon salt
1 cup milk
1 stick (1/2 cup) butter
1 teaspoon vanilla extract

PREHEAT OVEN to 375°. Grease and flour two 8- or 9-inch round cake pans. Drop the egg yolks into a bowl and beat with an electric mixer until smooth. In a separate bowl, combine the sugar, flour, baking powder, and salt. Use a wooden spoon to blend dry ingredients into the eggs. In another bowl, beat the egg whites until stiff, then gently fold them into the flour and egg mixture. In a saucepan, bring the milk just to the boiling point; add the butter, reduce heat, and stir until it is thoroughly combined with the milk. Remove from the heat and fold the mixture into the batter. Stir in the vanilla extract. Pour the batter into the prepared pans. Bake for 20 minutes or until the cake springs back when touched in the middle. Cool in pans for 20 minutes. Turn out and cool completely.

Serves 10 to 12

Molasses Cake

MYRTLE AND RICHARD FREEMAN, Montgomery County

"Few people make homemade sorghum molasses any more," Richard Freeman of Star told me. "We began by accident, when my brother decided to see what 'making syrup' was all about. Our parents and grandparents had grown up making syrup, but it was a new experience for us. This experience has continued for about ten years."

"The first step is growing the cane," Richard continued. "The seeds of sorghum cane are small. We plant ours either by hand or with a modified planter. The cane stalks grow quite tall, between five and six feet. In a good year, the cane stalk has an abundant supply of sap or juice. It is this juice that is cooked and becomes sorghum molasses. The cane plant has leaves similar to corn. These leaves are called fodder. The seeds grow on top of the plant like a tassel. In the fall, when the seeds are ripe and the cane is mature, the fodder is 'stripped' or pulled off and the stalks are cut down. This has to take place before a killing frost. Then the fun begins."

David Davis, a friend of the Freemans who owns the pans and equipment for making sorghum molasses and with whom the Freemans have been making the syrup for years.

"The cane is hauled to a friend's place. He has a mill and 'syrup pan' and has been cooking syrup for about fifty years. This mill is powered by a tractor. The cane stalks are fed into the mill, which has rollers to press the juice out, and the juice runs into a wooden tub. From there the juice goes into the syrup pan. This pan sits on top of an outdoor furnace. The pan is a sort of a maze. As the juice cooks and thickens, it runs into the next compartment. While the juice cooks, someone skims the foam off of the top. These 'skimmings' are best tasted with a spoon made from a fresh cane stalk. By the time it gets to the end of the pan, the juice has cooked into syrup. It is then drawn into a holding pot, where the final step of filling the jars takes place."

2 1/4 cups self-rising flour

1 1/4 cups sugar

1 teaspoon cinnamon

1/2 teaspoon cloves

1/2 teaspoon ginger

1/2 cup vegetable oil

3/4 cup sorghum syrup or molasses

2 eggs

1 cup nuts, chopped (optional)

PREHEAT OVEN to 350°. Grease and flour a 9 × 13-inch baking pan. Mix the flour, sugar, and spices together. Add the oil, sorghum syrup or molasses, and eggs. Beat until smooth. Add nuts, if desired. Pour the batter into the prepared pan. Bake until a toothpick inserted into the center of the cake comes out clean, 30 to 35 minutes.

Serves 10 to 12

Lazy Daisy Oatmeal Cake and Icing

HELEN COCHRANE, Guilford County

Lazy daisy oatmeal cake has a dense and satisfying texture. It's a good dessert and also a nice brunch dish.

Cake

1 1/4 cups boiling water

1 cup oats (quick or old-fashioned)

1 1/2 cups self-rising flour, sifted

1/2 teaspoon salt

3/4 teaspoon cinnamon

1/4 teaspoon nutmeg

1 stick (1/2 cup) butter, softened

1 cup white sugar

1 cup brown sugar

2 eggs

1 teaspoon vanilla extract

Icing

1/2 stick (1/4 cup) butter, softened
1/2 cup brown sugar
3 tablespoons light cream or evaporated milk
1/2 cup walnuts or pecans, chopped
3/4 cup flaked coconut

PREHEAT OVEN to 350°. Grease and flour an 8-inch-square cake pan. Pour the boiling water over the oats. Mix and let stand for 20 minutes. Combine the flour, salt, cinnamon, and nutmeg and set aside. In another bowl, mix the butter and both sugars together until smooth. Mix in the eggs and vanilla extract. Blend in oats. Gradually add the dry ingredients, stirring until well blended. Pour the batter into the prepared cake pan. Bake for 50 minutes or until the top of the cake springs back when lightly pressed. Remove from the oven and let stand while you prepare the icing.

To make the icing, combine the butter, brown sugar, and cream or milk. Fold in the nuts and coconut. Turn oven to broil. Ice the cake evenly. Place the cake under the broiler for 4 to 5 minutes or until the icing bubbles, watching carefully so that it doesn't burn.

Serves 9

Spice Cake

LUCIE LEA ROBSON, Mecklenburg County

"I love books," Lucie Lea Robson, now of Raleigh, told me. When she decided to move to a smaller home, Lucie Lea called me and asked if I would like to look through some cookbooks she had collected over the years. A multitude of dusty cardboard boxes greeted me when I walked into her living room. Inside the boxes was my definition of a treasure trove—old cookbooks. We spent hours rummaging through the collection, thumbing through the yellowed pages, reading, and drooling over the recipes. Handwritten notes, sometimes penned on old envelopes, hotel stationary, or the backs of receipts, often fell out. This recipe for spice cake was among them. You can eat this warm with ice cream, or ice it with caramel or seafoam icing found in the Icings, Fillings, and Sweet Sauces chapter.

1 stick (1/2 cup) butter, softened

2 cups brown sugar

2 eggs

1 egg white

2 1/2 cups all-purpose flour

1 teaspoon baking soda

1 teaspoon allspice

1/2 teaspoon cloves

1/2 teaspoon nutmeg

1 cup sour milk or buttermilk

PREHEAT OVEN to 350°. Grease and flour two 8-inch-square baking pans or two 8- or 9-inch round cake pans. Cream the butter well with the sugar until light. Add the eggs and egg white. Continue beating until smooth. Combine the flour, baking soda, and spices, then beat into the butter mixture. Continue beating as you add the milk. Blend until smooth. Pour the batter into the prepared pans. Bake for 20 to 25 minutes or until a toothpick inserted into the center of the cake comes out clean.

Serves 10 to 12

Yellow Cake and Chocolate Icing

MARGARET KING, Moore County

When I was a child and wanted a piece of chocolate cake, this was IT, a yellow cake with chocolate icing, and it proves that even uncomplicated cakes can be glorious.

Margaret King is from Vass. She learned this recipe from her grandmother, Laura. "I was born in her house, and I lived there until I was nine years old," Margaret said. "Whoever would be there when she finished making the cake got a chance to lick the bowl, so me and my two cousins, we waited till she got through so we could lick the bowl. So we'd watch what she was doing, and I could make the cake. We didn't have a whole lot of sugar to be wasted; she saved it for Saturday and Sunday when she made us cakes.

"She always had chickens; so she traded some eggs for some butter from a lady down the road. She would just make us the best cake, flour and sugar and vanilla. She didn't have a mixer 'cause she would mix the cake up with her hand and a spoon, a big old wooden spoon. She would mix the cake up, she would beat the eggs and sugar till it was so creamy you could take the spoon and flop it back down in the bowl. And then she would get the cake all made up, and she would bake like two or three layers.

"She worked at different houses taking care of people. Sometimes when she come home she'd bring different things they'd give her. One time she came home she had some Hershey's cocoa. We was about five 'cause I remember going to the one room schoolhouse in Vass. And Grandma dipped snuff; she always had a toothbrush and snuff in a can. So when she would go to work, we would get the Hershey's cocoa and put it in the snuff box, put some sugar in it, and we would walk around like we were dipping, put the stick in the snuff box, put it in our mouth, and walk around, and we would spit and act like she did while she was gone to work. But she soon found out that we was stealing the cocoa and eating up the sugar 'cause we didn't get much sugar back in that time; she saved it for Saturday and Sunday when she made us cakes.

"It was a yellow cake 'cause she didn't have nothing to go in it to make it turn colors. She would buy vanilla from the Watkins man [a peddler] when he came through the neighborhood. And then we didn't have powdered sugar. She would take granulated sugar, and she would cook it in the pot with the Hershey's cocoa and the vanilla, and she kept cooking it and cooking it until it was like a thick, what you might call sauce now. After the cake got done, she would take the bottom of the wooden spoon and poke holes in the bottom layer, and she would pour the chocolate all through it, and it would go all down inside of it. Then she would do it until she got to the top [layer], and then she would cover it all up so you couldn't see the holes until you cut into the cake and you could see that chocolate between all those layers all the way down to the bottom.

"When I make chocolate icing now I heat the powdered sugar and the butter and the milk so it'll be soft, kind of like a fudge. Don't taste as good as grandma's, but it's the same recipe what I revived from when I was a child that she used to make."

Cake
2 cups sugar
3 eggs
1/2 cup water
2 sticks (1 cup) butter, softened
2 1/2 cups self-rising flour
1 teaspoon vanilla extract

Icing
2 sticks (1 cup) butter, softened
4 cups 10X powdered sugar
1 cup Hershey's cocoa
2 teaspoons vanilla extract
1 cup milk (or more, as needed)

PREHEAT OVEN to 325°. Grease and flour three 8- or 9-inch round cake pans. Beat the sugar, eggs, and water with the butter until smooth. Continue beating while you stir in the flour. Stir in the vanilla extract. Pour the batter into the prepared pans. Bake for 30 minutes or until golden brown and a toothpick inserted into the center of the cake comes out clean.

Prepare icing while the cake is baking. Combine the butter, powdered sugar, cocoa, and vanilla extract in a double boiler and cook over medium heat, stirring, until the mixture is thick and smooth, like fudge sauce. Gradually blend in the milk until the icing is soft enough to spread. Keep the icing warm over low heat while the cake cools.

Place a cooled cake layer on a plate. Poke holes in it with the handle of a wooden spoon. Let the icing run into the holes as you ice the layer. Repeat for the next two layers, then ice the sides. Call me when you get to this point.

Serves 10 to 12

Black Chocolate Cake and Icing

MARTHA BARNES, Pitt County

Sarah Barnes Sugg is Aunt Martha's daughter and my first cousin once removed on my father's side. Sarah invited me to her home in Greenville, where she shared her copy of Aunt Martha's recipes. We sat in the kitchen, where a sampler on the wall read "Happy is the girl who learns to cook, from her mother or from a book." Despite the fact that Sarah's home burned to the ground at one point, her copy of Aunt Martha's handwritten cookbook is in perfect condition. The recipe for black chocolate cake and icing is recorded with a note that gives credit for the recipe to Mrs. C. Oettinger, a longtime friend of Aunt Martha's many years ago.

Sarah Barnes Sugg with her mother's and grandmother's cookbooks

Cake

2 sticks (1 cup) butter, softened
3 1/2 cups brown sugar, divided
1 cup milk, divided
4 eggs plus 2 egg yolks
4 cups self-rising flour
1 cup cocoa
2 teaspoons vanilla extract

Icing

5 egg whites
3 cups sugar
water, to cover sugar

PREHEAT OVEN to 350°. Grease and flour three 8- or 9-inch round cake pans. In a large mixing bowl, combine the butter, 2 cups brown sugar, 1/2 cup milk, 4 eggs, and flour until well blended; set aside. In another bowl, combine the cocoa, egg yolks, 1 1/2 cups brown sugar, 1/2 cup milk, and vanilla extract; blend until smooth. Add mixtures together. Blend well. Pour the batter into the prepared pans. Bake about 30 minutes or until a toothpick inserted into the center of the cake comes out clean.

To make the icing, beat egg whites until stiff. Set aside. In a small saucepan, combine the sugar with just enough water to cover the sugar. Bring to a boil. Reduce to a syrup that forms threads when lifted with a spoon. If you have a candy thermometer, the temperature should be 230°. Pour the hot syrup over the egg whites, and beat until mixture is white and creamy. Spread over the cake layers.

Serves 10 to 12

Lena Belle's Seven-Layer Chocolate Cake and Icing

BECKY PAUL, Cartaret County

Becky and Alton Paul with their dog, Xmas (pronounced "Christmas")

Becky Paul lives in Davis, one of the Down East communities in Cartaret County. Multilayer chocolate cakes, often cut in half so you can actually see the many thin layers, are famous icons of southern hospitality in North Carolina. Mrs. Paul's mother, Lena Belle Brown from Ocracoke, gave her this particular recipe, but variations can be found across the state.

Icing

1 cup cocoa
3 cups sugar
1 can (12 ounces) Carnation or other evaporated milk
1/2 stick (1/4 cup) butter
2 teaspoons vanilla extract

Cake

2 sticks (1 cup) butter, softened

2 cups sugar

5 eggs

3 cups all-purpose flour

3 teaspoons baking powder

1 cup milk

3 teaspoons vanilla extract

PUT THE ICING on the stove to cook before making cake. Mix all the ingredients together in the top of a double boiler. Cook over boiling water until the icing is thick and rich, at least 30 minutes. Let cool before icing cake.

In the meantime, make the cake. Preheat oven to 350°. Grease and flour seven 8- or 9-inch round cake pans. Cream the butter and sugar together. Add eggs, one at a time, beating well after each addition. In a separate bowl, combine the flour and baking powder; add to the wet mixture gradually, alternating with the milk. Beat until the batter is smooth. Stir in the vanilla extract. Pour the batter into the prepared pans. Bake until the layers are firm in the middle, about 8 to 10 minutes.

Fill layers one at a time with icing, then cover the sides.

Serves 8 to 10

Chocolate Velvet Cake and Frosting

JANET HAIRE MANUEL, Martin County

You can't go wrong when you make this luscious chocolate confection. It's one of Janet Haire Manuel's favorite family recipes.

Cake
2 1/4 cups all-purpose flour, sifted

1 teaspoon baking soda

3/4 teaspoon salt

1 package (6 ounces) semisweet chocolate chips

1 1/4 cups water, divided

1 3/4 cups sugar

1 1/2 sticks (3/4 cup) butter

1 teaspoon vanilla extract

3 eggs, beaten

Frosting
1 package (6 ounces) semisweet chocolate chips

3 tablespoons butter

1/4 to 1/2 cup milk

1 teaspoon vanilla extract

1/4 teaspoon salt

3 cups 10x powdered sugar, sifted

PREHEAT OVEN to 375°. Grease and flour two 8- or 9-inch round cake pans. Combine the flour, baking soda, and salt. Set aside. Place the chocolate chips and 1/4 cup of the water in a saucepan; stir over medium heat until smooth. Add sugar, butter, and vanilla extract to the melted chocolate; mix well and remove from heat. Blend some of the chocolate mixture into the eggs (to prevent the eggs from cooking), then add all back into the chocolate mixture, stirring continuously until smooth. Add the chocolate mixture to the flour mixture alternately with the remaining water, beating until well blended. Pour the batter into the prepared pans. Bake for 30 to 35 minutes or until a toothpick inserted into the center of the cake comes out clean. Remove from pans and let cool before frosting.

To make the frosting, melt chocolate chips and butter over low heat. Remove from heat. Add 1/4 cup milk, vanilla extract, and salt. Beat in the powdered sugar, a little at a time, until well blended. If the frosting is too thick to spread easily, add another tablespoon or two of milk.

Serves 10 to 12

Hot Chocolate Cake and Topping

WANDA BROOKS, Stanly County

"I thought you might like to see this," Wanda Brooks of Richfield told me as she displayed a notebook of recipes. "I started years ago to make a cookbook for each of my three daughters, Jenny, Kim, and Amanda. The first year I put in some of the things that our family likes and where they came from. The second year I included my mother's recipes and put some old pictures in with that. My daughters and I host an open house on Christmas Eve. We cook lots of food; so the third year I wrote up the open house recipes. We spend an entire day together cooking for the open house." The recipes for hot chocolate cake and the topping that goes with it are some of the family favorites recorded in the girls' cookbooks.

Cake
2 cups self-rising flour
2 cups sugar
1 stick (1/2 cup) butter
1/2 cup shortening
1 cup water
1/4 cup cocoa
1/2 cup buttermilk
2 eggs
1 teaspoon vanilla extract

Topping
1 stick (1/2 cup) butter
6 tablespoons milk
1/4 cup cocoa
2 cups 10x powdered sugar
1 teaspoon vanilla extract
1 cup pecans, chopped

PREHEAT OVEN to 350°. Grease a 9 × 13-inch baking pan. Mix the flour and sugar together thoroughly. Set aside. Combine the butter, shortening, water, and cocoa in a saucepan and bring to a boil. Remove the pan from the heat and pour the mixture over the flour mixture and beat well. Add the buttermilk, eggs, and vanilla extract; mix until well blended. Pour the batter into the prepared pan. Bake for 25 minutes or until a toothpick inserted into the center of the cake comes out clean.

While the cake bakes, prepare the topping. Combine the butter, milk, and cocoa in a saucepan. Bring to a boil. Remove from heat, add the powdered sugar, and beat until smooth. Mix in the vanilla extract and nuts.

Pour the topping over the hot cake as soon as it comes out of the oven.

Serves 12 to 15

Marble Cake

. . . .

WANDA BROOKS, Stanly County

"I have lots of good memories when I look over the recipes I've collected," Wanda Brooks told me. "This one came from a good friend, Annie Scott."

> *3 cups all-purpose flour*
> *1/2 teaspoon baking soda*
> *1/2 teaspoon salt*
> *1 cup shortening*
> *3 cups sugar*
> *6 eggs*
> *1 cup buttermilk*
> *1 teaspoon vanilla extract*
> *5 ounces chocolate syrup*

PREHEAT OVEN to 325°. Grease and flour a 10-inch tube pan. Combine the flour, baking soda, and salt. Set aside. Cream the shortening and sugar until smooth. Add the eggs, one at a time, beating well after each addition. Add the dry ingredients in thirds, alternating with the buttermilk, blending well. Add the vanilla extract. Pour half the batter into the prepared pan. Mix chocolate syrup into the remaining batter. Pour the chocolate batter over the plain batter. Then use a knife in a flowing back-and-forth motion to gently marble the two colors together. Bake for 1 hour and 15 minutes or until a toothpick inserted into the center of the cake comes out clean. Serve iced or plain.

Serves 10 to 12

Chocolate Walnut Loaf

WANDA BROOKS, Stanly County

"Happiness is not something you pursue for itself. It is a by-product of being useful," says Wanda Brooks. Making this sweet, chewy loaf is a good way to make yourself both happy and useful.

2 1/2 cups all-purpose flour
1 teaspoon baking soda
1/4 teaspoon salt
1 1/2 sticks (3/4 cup) butter, softened
2 cups sugar
5 eggs
2 squares (2 ounces) unsweetened chocolate
1 teaspoon vanilla extract
1 cup buttermilk
1 cup walnuts, chopped

PREHEAT OVEN to 325°. Grease two 9 × 5-inch loaf pans. Combine the flour, baking soda, and salt. Set aside. In a large mixing bowl, cream the butter. Gradually add the sugar and beat until fluffy. Add the eggs; mix thoroughly until the batter is smooth. Melt the chocolate in a small saucepan over medium heat and add it to the sugar mixture. Blend well. Add the vanilla extract. Add the dry ingredients in thirds, alternating with the buttermilk, blending well. Fold in the nuts. Pour the batter into the prepared pans. Bake for 50 to 60 minutes or until a toothpick inserted into the center of the cake comes out clean.

Serves 10 to 20

Brownie Cupcakes

. . . .

HELEN COCHRANE, Guilford County

Helen grew up in Greensboro but makes her home in Garner, Wake County, today. This recipe combines the richness of a brownie with the convenience of a cupcake. These yummy little cakes fit nicely into a school lunch box or are easily transported to work. I enjoy them with a cup of coffee. You might want to double the recipe, as they often disappear quickly.

4 ounces semisweet chocolate chips
2 sticks (1 cup) butter
1 3/4 cups sugar
1 cup self-rising flour
4 eggs
1 teaspoon vanilla extract
1/4 teaspoon butter flavoring
1 1/2 cups pecans, chopped

PREHEAT OVEN to 325°. Grease a muffin tin or line with muffin cups. Melt the chocolate chips in a saucepan over low heat. When melted, remove from heat and add the butter. Stir until butter is melted and blended with chocolate. In a mixing bowl, combine the sugar, flour, eggs, vanilla extract, and butter flavoring. Add the chocolate mixture; stir until smooth. Stir in the pecans. Fill the prepared muffin cups 2/3 full. Bake for 25 minutes, watching carefully to avoid overbaking.

Makes 20 to 24

The Amazing Cheesecake

BRENDA MALONE ZIMMERMAN, Rowan County

"I always thought this cake was amazing," Brenda Malone Zimmerman of Salisbury told me. "My roommate's mother used to send it to her when we attended Appalachian State University, but as time went by, we lost track of each other. That cake was so good that I spent a fortune on ingredients trying to duplicate it, but never could. After many years I bumped into another friend who knew my old roommate. She had obtained the recipe and shared it with me. It never fails to get happy sighs from all those who bite into it."

Crust
1 cup all-purpose flour
1/4 cup sugar
1 teaspoon grated lemon zest
1 stick (1/2 cup) butter
1 egg yolk, beaten
1/4 teaspoon vanilla extract

Filling
5 packages (8 ounces each) cream cheese, softened
3/4 teaspoon grated lemon zest
3 tablespoons all-purpose flour
5 eggs plus 2 egg yolks
1/4 teaspoon vanilla extract
1 3/4 cups sugar
1/4 teaspoon salt
1/4 cup heavy cream

PREHEAT OVEN to 400°. For the crust, combine the flour, sugar, and lemon zest. Cut in the butter with a pastry blender or fork until the mixture is crumbly. Add the egg yolk and vanilla extract; blend well. Pat 1/3 of the dough into the bottom of a 9-inch springform pan.

Bake for 16 minutes or until golden. Let the pan cool until you can grease the sides. Press the remaining dough about 2 inches up the side of the pan, then smooth it down to attach it to the precooked bottom.

Turn the oven up to 500°. Beat the cream cheese until fluffy. Add the vanilla extract and lemon zest. In another bowl, combine the sugar, flour, and salt, then gradually blend them into the cheese mixture. Add the eggs and yolks one at a time, beating well after each addition. Gently stir in the heavy cream until the mixture is well blended. Pour the batter into the crust-lined pan. Bake for 5 to 8 minutes or until the crust is golden. Reduce heat to 200°. Bake for 1 hour. Cool for 3 hours before removing sides of pan. Refrigerate any leftovers.

Serves 10 to 12

Carrot Cake and Icing

RENE SADLER AMICK, Chowan County

"This recipe is from my mother," Rene Sadler Amick of Edenton told me. "I love the moistness. It's from scratch. My family has it often for holidays and birthdays. My husband makes the cake, and I make the icing."

Carrot cake has been a southern tradition since it became popular during World War II, when eggs and butter were in short supply. It never lost its popularity, even after the war. Grated carrots combined with oil make the cake dark and dense. Cream cheese icing is a tangy companion to the sweet cake. This is one of those cakes that is even better the day after it's made, if it lasts that long.

Cake

2 cups sugar	*2 teaspoons cinnamon*
1/4 cup canola oil	*1 teaspoon salt*
4 eggs, well beaten	*3 cups carrots, grated*
2 cups all-purpose flour	*1 cup nuts, chopped*
2 teaspoons baking powder	

Icing

2 cups 10X powdered sugar

1/2 stick (1/4 cup) butter, softened

1 cup cream cheese, softened

1 cup of crushed pineapple, drained

PREHEAT OVEN to 325°. Grease and flour two 8- or 9-inch round cake pans. In a large bowl, mix the sugar and oil well. Add the beaten eggs, flour, baking powder, cinnamon, salt, and carrots. Blend until smooth. Fold in the nuts. Pour the batter into the prepared pans. Bake for 30 minutes. Let layers cool for 10 minutes, then remove and ice.

Prepare the icing by combining the powdered sugar, butter, cream cheese, and crushed pineapple. Blend until smooth. Ice between the layers, top, and sides. Store in refrigerator.

Serves 10 to 12

Paul's Feathery Coconut Cake and Filling

REBECCAH KINNAMON NEFF, Forsyth County

"Dad [Paul] always used fresh coconut," Rebeccah confided when describing her Moravian father's coconut cake recipe, "from which he drained the milk and then grated the meat into fine flakes. Each cake layer received a spoon or two of coconut liquid and a generous spread of whipped cream, followed by a hearty allowance of fresh coconut. Dad used Avocet cream from a well-known local dairy. By the time he had finished assembling one of his creations, it was about nine or ten inches tall: a snowy white confection any cook would be proud to acknowledge. Dad liked to serve homemade ice cream with his cake."

Cake

1 scant cup shortening (Dad used Crisco)
1 1/2 teaspoons vanilla or lemon extract
2 cups sugar
3 eggs
3 cups all-purpose flour
3 teaspoons baking powder
1/4 teaspoon salt
1/2 cup milk
1/2 cup coconut milk (liquid from the coconut or canned)
additional coconut liquid for assembling cake
1 cup grated coconut (optional)

Filling

1 cup sugar, divided
1 large coconut, grated fine
16 ounces heavy cream
1/2 teaspoon vanilla extract

PREHEAT OVEN to 375°. Grease and flour four 8- or 9-inch round cake pans. Using your hands (or a stand mixer), cream the shortening with the flavoring. Add the sugar gradually, blending well. Add the eggs, one at a time, blending well after each addition. Combine the flour, baking powder, and salt and add to the creamed mixture alternately with regular milk and coconut milk. Blend until smooth. If using grated coconut, mix it in evenly. Divide the batter equally among the prepared pans. Bake for 20 to 25 minutes or until each layer is lightly brown and has pulled away from the sides. Let the cake cool in pans for 10 minutes, then turn out onto racks and cool completely before frosting.

To make the filling, combine 1/2 cup of the sugar and the coconut. Set aside. Whip the cream until soft peaks form; add the vanilla extract. While beating, gradually add the second 1/2 cup of sugar until the cream is stiff. Stop beating as soon as the sugar is incorporated and the cream is stiff or you will have butter.

To assemble the cake: Place a cake layer on a cake plate and spoon a small amount of the reserved coconut liquid over the cake just to moisten it (not too much, or you'll make the cake soggy). Spread whipped cream over the layer. If coconut was not added to the batter, sprinkle the layer with some of the finely grated coconut. Repeat for all layers, frosting the sides of the cake last. Finish off with a dusting of grated coconut.

Serves 10 to 12

Orange Rum Cake

LUCIE LEA ROBSON, Mecklenburg County

"I think that my family's tradition of using fresh food from the land began with my great-grandfather, a country doctor in Anson County," Lucie Lea Robson told me. "It was an era when he was grateful to be paid in fresh eggs, chickens, pecans, or fresh vegetables from one of his patients who was a farmer."

"I'm originally from Charlotte," Lucie Lea continued. "When I was a child, I spent a lot of time with two of my maiden aunts at an old house in Charlotte called Rosedale. I have a recollection from my childhood of a dinner held in a garden there. I had the task of helping prepare desserts when I visited them. One time, I brought out Grandmother Lucie Lea Dunlap's recipe for pecan pie. It called for all sorts of ingredients that were measured in 'a pinch, a handful and something else the size of a walnut.' When it was time for dessert, my presentation turned out first as piecrust holding an aquarium of brown sugar and pecans. After several trips back to the kitchen, I returned triumphant after covering up burned crust with homemade ice cream, thus the day was saved."

As time went by, Lucie Lea developed her cooking expertise and her reputation for being a gracious hostess. She collected recipes wherever she lived. Orange rum cake is a recipe her mother-in-law shared with her. Buttermilk, citrus zest, and walnuts combine into a cake that's a taste treat by itself. Add the syrup, and orange rum cake becomes a sweet-smelling dessert that everyone will love.

Cake

2 sticks (1 cup) butter, softened

1 cup sugar

grated zest of 2 large oranges and 1 lemon

2 eggs

2 1/2 cups all-purpose flour

2 teaspoons baking powder

1 teaspoon baking soda

1 cup buttermilk

1 cup walnuts, chopped

Syrup

juice of 2 oranges and 1 lemon

1 cup sugar

1/4 cup rum

PREHEAT OVEN to 350°. Grease and flour a 10-inch tube pan. Cream the butter and sugar until light. Add the fruit zest; add the eggs, one at a time, blending well after each addition. In another bowl, combine the flour, baking powder, and baking soda. Add dry ingredients to the butter and egg mixture in thirds, alternating with the buttermilk, blending until smooth. Fold in the nuts. Pour the batter into the prepared pan. Bake for 50 to 60 minutes or until a cake tester inserted into the center of the cake comes out clean.

To make the syrup, strain the fruit juices into a saucepan. Add the sugar and rum and cook over medium heat until the mixture comes to a boil; remove from heat.

Remove the cake from the oven and pour the syrup over it while it is still in the pan. If the cake does not absorb all the liquid, pour the remainder on later. Be sure to let the cake stand for a few hours before turning out and serving.

Serves 10 to 12

Corn Cake

MARY CHARLES PAWLIKOWSKI, Nash County

"The nuts give the appearance of cornbread," Mary Charles Pawlikowski said. "This is simple, easy, and delicious. You can put fruit or a dollop of homemade whipped cream on top. Slices fit nicely in lunch boxes too."

Mary Charles Pawlikowski

1 1/2 cups self-rising flour
1 cup brown sugar
1 cup white sugar
4 eggs, beaten
1 cup vegetable oil
1 teaspoon vanilla extract
2 cups very finely chopped nuts

PREHEAT OVEN to 350°. Grease a 9 × 13-inch baking pan. Combine the flour and sugars in a mixing bowl. Add the eggs, oil, and vanilla extract. Beat until well blended. Fold in the nuts until they are evenly distributed. Pour the batter into the prepared pan. Bake for 35 to 40 minutes or until a toothpick or cake tester inserted into the center of the cake comes out clean.

Serves 10 to 12

Pumpkin Cake and Icing

FRANCES ROBINSON, Buncombe County

"Out in the country where I was raised, people grew a lot of their own food," Frances Robinson told me. "We didn't have running water or electricity. We had a box over a spring where we kept things like butter and milk cold. During the Great Depression, people who walked by knew that if they found a spring, they could find something to eat."

"Mother would dry beans; she would pickle beans; she always did canning. We picked berries. If we had to live like that now, we'd starve to death. I'm grateful we don't have to live like that any more. My grandmother used to make sweet bread. She put her hands in the dough and used molasses to sweeten it." Frances often makes pumpkin cake. "You can use any kind of cake mix you like. This is one of the best ones I've ever eaten. I cook this when I have a special occasion. Chocolate is tremendously good, but you can use yellow or any other kind. Remember, don't stir it."

Cake
2 sticks (1 cup) butter
1 can (15 ounces) pumpkin
1 1/2 cups milk
1/2 cup sugar
1 teaspoon vanilla extract
1 tablespoon cinnamon
1 box (18 1/4 ounces) dry cake mix—
　　whichever brand and flavor you prefer
1/4 cup pecans, chopped

Icing
1 cup cream cheese, softened
1/2 cup sugar
chopped pecans

PREHEAT OVEN to 350°. Melt 1 stick of butter in a 9 × 13-inch cake pan in the preheating oven. Combine the pumpkin, milk, sugar, vanilla extract, and cinnamon. Pour the mixture over the melted butter in the cake pan. Sprinkle the dry cake mix evenly on top. Smooth and press it in with your hands. Do not stir. Sprinkle crushed pecans on top. Melt the other stick of butter and pour it evenly over the mixture in the pan. Remember not to stir. Bake for 1 hour or until a toothpick inserted into the center of the cake comes out clean. Let cake cool before you ice it.

To make the icing, whip the cream cheese and sugar together. Spread evenly over the cake. Sprinkle a few pecans on top.

Serves 12 to 15

Red Velvet Cake and Icing

SUE KORNEGAY, Wake County

Sassy and sweet are hallmarks of this southern favorite. Today red food coloring gives red velvet cake its trademark tint. Historically, however, it was the Dutch-process cocoa, buttermilk, and vinegar that reacted chemically to turn the cake a reddish brown. It's devilishly good with white filling.

Cake

1 1/2 cups shortening, or any combination of shortening and
   butter or margarine, softened
3 cups sugar
7 eggs
3 cups all-purpose flour
1/2 teaspoon baking powder
1/2 teaspoon salt
1 cup milk
1 ounce red food coloring
2 teaspoons vanilla extract

PREHEAT OVEN to 350°. Grease and flour a 9 × 13-inch baking pan. Cream the sugar and shortening until fluffy. Add the eggs, one at a time, beating well after each addition. Add the flour, baking powder, salt, and milk. When the batter is smooth, blend in the red food coloring and vanilla extract. Pour the batter into the prepared pan and bake for 40 minutes or until a toothpick inserted into the center of the cake comes out clean.

Icing

1 cup cream cheese, softened
2 cups 10x powdered sugar
1 teaspoon vanilla extract

BLEND the cream cheese and powdered sugar until smooth. Stir in the vanilla extract. Spread on cake.

Serves 10 to 12

Aunt Lottie's Lane Cake and Frosting

ELOISE MACINTOSH, Yancey County

Yancey County is a beautiful, mountainous place where Eloise MacIntosh grew up. Her mother made this elaborate cake at Thanksgiving. After everyone enjoyed it, her mother placed it in a large container, covered it with a towel soaked in whiskey, then with a lid, and stored it in an unheated room or springhouse where it would stay cold. This kept the cake from spoiling and allowed the flavors to mingle, so that it was even better at Christmas.

Cake

3 1/4 cups all-purpose flour   *2 cups sugar*
3 1/2 teaspoons baking powder   *1 teaspoon vanilla extract*
3/4 teaspoon salt   *1 cup milk*
2 sticks (1 cup) butter, softened   *8 egg whites*

Frosting

8 egg yolks
1 1/4 cups sugar
1 stick (1/2 cup) butter
1 cup pecans, chopped
1 cup raisins, chopped
1 cup flaked coconut
1 cup candied cherries
1 1/2 cups bourbon or rye whiskey

PREHEAT OVEN to 350°. Grease and flour four 8- or 9-inch round cake pans. Combine the flour, baking powder, and salt; set aside. Cream the butter; add the sugar gradually, then add the vanilla extract and mix well. Add the dry ingredients, in thirds, alternately with the milk. Beat until smooth. In a separate bowl, beat the egg whites until stiff but not dry and fold them into the batter. Pour the batter into the prepared pans. Bake about 15 minutes or until a toothpick inserted into the center of the cake comes out clean. Let stand for 5 minutes before removing from the pans; place on a rack to cool.

To make the frosting, beat the egg yolks slightly in a cold saucepan. Add sugar and butter. Heat the mixture slowly over low heat, stirring constantly. Be careful and patient, as the eggs must cook gradually. When the sugar dissolves and the mixture thickens, remove saucepan from the heat; add the pecans, raisins, coconut, and cherries. When the mixture is cool, add the whiskey.

To assemble the cake, place a single layer on a plate, then spread it with icing. Place the next layer on the first and spread it with icing; do the same with the remaining layers until all four layers are covered completely. Extra coconut, cherries, and pecans may be sprinkled on top as decoration.

Serves 10 to 12

Queen Elizabeth Cake and Icing

ALICE WARD ALLEN, Wake County

"This is utterly delicious," says a note my grandmother, Alice Ward Allen, wrote at the top of this recipe for Queen Elizabeth cake when she copied it down for my mother, Sarah Sawyer Allen, in the 1950s.

Cake	Icing
1 cup dates, pitted and chopped	*5 tablespoons sugar*
1 teaspoon baking soda	*5 tablespoons cream*
1 cup boiling water	*5 tablespoons butter*
1 cup sugar	*1 cup chopped nuts and/or*
1/2 stick (1/4 cup) butter, softened	*flaked coconut*
1 egg, beaten	
1 1/2 cups all-purpose flour	
1/4 teaspoon salt	
1 teaspoon vanilla extract	
1/2 cup nuts, coarsely chopped	

PREHEAT OVEN to 350°. Grease and flour an 8-inch-square baking pan. Combine the dates and baking soda in a small bowl. Pour the boiling water over them and set aside. In a separate bowl, combine the sugar, butter, egg, flour, and salt. Mix until well blended. Blend in the vanilla extract. Fold in the nuts and dates until evenly distributed in the batter. Pour the batter into the prepared pan. Bake for 20 to 25 minutes or until a toothpick inserted into the center of the cake comes out clean. Set aside to cool.

To make the icing, heat the sugar, cream, and butter in a saucepan. Bring to a slow boil and cook for 3 minutes, stirring constantly. Spread the warm icing on the cake. Sprinkle the nuts and/or coconut on top. Refrigerate any leftovers.

Serves 9 to 12

Rum Cake and Glaze

KATHERINE SAWYER WARD, Bertie County

If you have only a few minutes to prepare a dessert that will make you popular, try my cousin Katherine's rum cake. You can make it the day before you share it.

Cake
1/2 cup pecans, chopped
1 box (18 1/4 ounces) butter
    cake mix
1 package (4-serving size)
    vanilla pudding mix
1/2 cup water
1/2 cup or canola oil
4 eggs
1/2 cup rum

Glaze
1 stick (1/2 cup) butter
1 cup sugar
1/4 cup water
1/4 cup rum

PREHEAT OVEN to 325°. Grease and flour a 10-inch tube pan. Sprinkle the bottom of the pan with the pecans. In a large bowl, combine all the other cake ingredients. Beat for 2 minutes. Pour the batter into the prepared pan. Bake for 50 to 60 minutes or until a toothpick inserted into the center of the cake comes out clean. Remove the cake from the oven but do not remove from the pan. Poke holes evenly over the cake with an icepick or skewer so that when the glaze is poured over the cake, it will be absorbed throughout.

To make the glaze, combine the butter, sugar, water, and rum in a saucepan over medium heat. Boil for 3 minutes, stirring constantly. Pour the hot filling slowly over the cake. Let cake stand a few minutes before turning out.

Serves 10 to 12

Hermit Cake

KAY BAKER, Lenoir County

"My mother loves fruit cake, but my sister, Carol, and I don't," Kay Baker of Kinston told me. "My mother found this recipe that only uses dates and nuts; we all enjoy it. It's the only thing she wants me to give her at Christmas, but she insists that I make it in her old pan. The cake is better if you place a pan of water on a second shelf in the oven below the pan itself. The hot water keeps the cake moist while it bakes."

a little cornmeal
1 1/4 cups brown sugar
2 sticks (1 cup) butter, softened
3 large eggs
2 1/4 cups all-purpose flour, divided
1 teaspoon baking soda
3/4 pound chopped dates
1 cup shelled English walnuts, chopped
1 cup flaked coconut
1 tablespoon vanilla extract
juice of 1/2 lemon or 1/2 teaspoon lemon extract

PREHEAT OVEN to 250°. Grease a 10-inch tube pan and coat the interior with cornmeal. Blend the brown sugar and the butter until smooth. Continue blending as you add the eggs. In a separate bowl, combine 2 cups of flour and the baking soda. Add the flour mixture to the sugar mixture. Blend until smooth. Combine 1/4 cup flour with the dates, walnuts, and coconut and fold the coated fruit and nuts into the batter. Add the vanilla extract and lemon juice. Blend until smooth. Pour the batter into the prepared pan. Bake for 3 hours or until the cake pulls away from the pan and it springs back when touched in the middle. Cool for 30 minutes. Turn out, slice, and enjoy to the last morsel.

Serves 12 to 15

Miss Sadie's Pound Cake

BARBARA NEWBOLD FLETCHER, Pasquotank County

"Miss Sadie was my mother-in-law," Barbara Newbold Fletcher told me when I visited her in Elizabeth City. "I learned a lot from her. She gave me several recipes."

"My son and his wife have been married for 14 years. I taught my daughter-in-law how to make Miss Sadie's pound cake soon after they were married. It's been going through the family for right many years now. My daughter-in-law makes it for the Elizabeth City Fire Department. My son is a fireman, and they love to go through these. This is definitely like the old-timey days where they used to use a pound of this and a pound of that."

2 cups all-purpose flour
1 teaspoon salt
2 sticks (1 cup) margarine, softened
2 sticks (1 cup) butter, softened
2 cups sugar
10 eggs
1 1/2 teaspoons vanilla extract

PREHEAT OVEN to 275°. Grease and flour a 10-inch tube pan. Combine the salt and flour; set aside. Cream the margarine and butter together until fluffy. Add the sugar; blend well. Add the eggs one at a time, beating well after each addition. Add the flour mixture gradually, blending until the batter is smooth. Stir in the vanilla extract. Pour the batter into the prepared pan. Bake for 1 hour and 25 to 35 minutes or until a toothpick inserted into the center of the cake comes out clean.

Serves 10 to 12

Cold-Oven Pound Cake

JANET HAIRE MANUEL, Martin County

Janet Haire Manuel of Jamesville is interested in preserving history. Janet worked for many years at the Mordecai House, a historic site open to the public in Raleigh. Joel Lane built the original house in 1785 on property near the outskirts of Raleigh. It stands proudly today about a mile from downtown; the well-built house was home to five generations of Lane's descendents, including the Mordecai family. Cookbooks owned by the family remain on the shelves in the library. Janet and her relatives have preserved some of their own history by creating a family cookbook that includes cold-oven pound cake. You will need a tall tube pan to make this cake.

2 sticks (1 cup) butter, softened
2 cups sugar
6 eggs, well beaten
3 cups all-purpose flour

1 cup cream
1 1/2 teaspoons vanilla extract
1/2 teaspoon almond extract

DO NOT preheat oven for this cake. Grease and flour a 5-inch-high, 10-inch-diameter tube pan. In a large mixing bowl, cream the butter and sugar together until smooth. Add the eggs and blend well. Continue mixing while alternately adding the flour and cream. Add the vanilla and almond extracts. Pour the batter into the prepared pan and place the pan in a cold oven. Heat the oven to 325°. Bake for 1 hour and 15 minutes without opening the oven door. Check for doneness (a toothpick inserted into the center of the cake will come out clean), as it may need a few more minutes. Remove from the oven and cool for 10 minutes on a rack. Invert the cake onto a cake plate; let cool completely before slicing.

Serves 10 to 12

Brown Sugar Pound Cake and Frosting

MARIE BATCHELOR, Duplin County

"Season your food with love," said Marie Batchelor of Beaulaville. She does just that in this recipe for her family's favorite birthday cake.

Cake
1 cup shortening (Marie
    prefers Crisco)
1 stick (1/2 cup) margarine,
    softened
2 cups light brown sugar
5 eggs
3 cups all-purpose flour
1 teaspoon salt
2 teaspoons baking powder
1 cup evaporated milk
2 teaspoons maple flavoring
1/4 cup chopped walnuts (optional)

Frosting
1 stick (1/2 cup) margarine,
    softened
1 cup dark brown sugar
1/4 cup evaporated milk
1 teaspoon vanilla extract
3 cups 10X powdered sugar

PREHEAT OVEN to 300°. Grease and flour a 10-inch tube pan. Cream the shortening, margarine, and light brown sugar together. Add the eggs one at a time, mixing well after each addition. In another bowl, combine the flour, salt, and baking powder. Add the flour mixture to the wet ingredients, alternating with the milk, beginning and ending with the flour. Add the flavoring; blend well. Fold in the nuts, if desired. Pour the batter into the prepared pan. Bake for 1 hour and 30 minutes or until a toothpick inserted into the center of the cake comes out clean.

To make the frosting, combine the margarine and the dark brown sugar; stir for one minute. Add the milk slowly, blending until smooth. Stir in the vanilla extract. Continue beating as you add the powdered sugar. When smooth, spread onto cooled cake.

Serves 10 to 12

Cream Cheese Pound Cake

HATTIE ANNE HAGER COBB, Lincoln County

Hattie Anne Hager Cobb grew up on a farm in Lincoln County. She helped raise vegetables and also worked in cotton fields. "My mother was born in 1894," Hattie Anne told me when I visited her in Stanley. "I learned to cook by watching my mother. She had five girls and four boys. Cooking was part of growing up. Everyone on the farm worked. We started preparing Sunday dinner on Saturday. It was a big occasion. We often killed a chicken on Saturday, so we could get it ready to cook Sunday morning. I liked everything. We also had cake or pie. Mother used the dump method and hardly ever measured." Hattie Anne carries on the fine family dessert tradition by making cream cheese pound cake.

3 sticks (1 1/2 cups) margarine, softened
1 cup cream cheese, softened
3 cups sugar
dash salt
1 1/2 teaspoons vanilla extract
6 eggs
3 cups all-purpose flour, sifted

PREHEAT OVEN to 325°. Grease and flour a 5-inch-high, 10-inch-diameter tube pan. Cream the margarine, cream cheese, and sugar until light. Add the salt and vanilla extract; beat until smooth. Add the eggs one at a time, beating well after each addition. Stir in the flour; beat until smooth. Pour the batter into the prepared pan. Bake for 1 hour and 30 minutes or until a toothpick inserted into the center of the cake comes out clean.

Serves 10 to 12

Five-Flavor
Pound Cake and Glaze

· ·

IMOGENE TOMBERLIN, Yancey County

Levie Wilson describing his
family history at the reunion

Imogene Tomberlin lives in the Bald Creek section of
Yancey County where her home overlooks a lush, green
valley. Loucinda Wilson is buried nearby. Loucinda was
born a slave in 1843. She was emancipated after the Civil
War and later owned land that she contributed to the
county for a school to educate African American children.
Loucinda spent her life in Yancey County and died in the
early-twentieth-century flu pandemic. Today Imogene
maintains close ties with the Wilson family. Each fall
they gather at Imogene's home for a reunion that honors
Loucinda Wilson.

Jessie Coleman (left),
Charity Ray (middle), and
Dorothy Coone (right) at the
Wilson family reunion.

"Oh, people come from Ohio, Tennessee, and Maryland,
even Texas," Charity Ray, Imogene's friend and a Wilson
family member, told me. "We start with a decoration [of the
grave], then have some prayers and a big covered-dish dinner." I was fortunate to attend the event with Charity and
her sister, Dorothy Coone, in 2003. Alpine trees showed the
first blush of fall as we drove into the beautiful valley. The
Wilson family members were all dressed in bright golden
shirts. As they roamed the hills and meadows, they looked
like the swaying coreopsis blossoms that grew nearby.

"We are some of the bunch," Levie Wilson told me. "I was born in
1906." His sister, Hattie Smith, spoke up: "[I was born in] 1907." "I tell
you," Levie continued, "most of the people back in my days, they know'd
how to cook. They didn't measure the stuff with things like that, they just
took their hands, they measured but they measured with the hand and
they dipped so much out. We raised most of the stuff we used, chickens,
eggs, and things of that kind and we didn't have like they do now, you see?

We might have corn bread for breakfast as far as that goes. We eat what we raised, and we raised what we had to eat, you might say, and the only thing we bought mostly was coffee and sugar."

"We here just coming back to the old home place," Levie said, "homecoming, getting together. We been coming back here every year, some of the family. We moved over here on account of school. But some of the family most of the time, some of the family from Ohio, down here at Spruce Pine and Burnsville, they generally come. Grandmother [Loucinda Wilson, 1843–1917] was buried up in the white cemetery up there. Every year some of us goes up to the cemetery up here. I remember her very well, because she was a midwife." "A midwife for the black people." Hattie added. "She was brought up in slave times."

"Now we all lived pretty close together at that time," Levie said, referring to his childhood. "And we lived in houses that looked like, well, they looked like you couldn't stay in them in a way, ya see, but we never was sick nor nothing like that, but when the snow would blow, that old wooden shingles made of it, boards. I've made boards myself. They called it a floor. They made it and made the boards out of a certain wood and covered the house with it. They call it shingles now but they called it boards then. And they could nail them up on the house, and the water wouldn't run in but if the snow come on there and the wind blowed, it blowed it back into that house, maybe on to your bed. Sometime you'd get up when it come a'snowing and the wind blowed, your bed would be covered with snow the next morning.

"But we stayed safe and some of the houses we'd live in, the chickens would come in under the floor and you could see the chickens through under the floor. They'd come in and lay eggs on the bed! And most of the people at them times, it wasn't just only the colored people but the white too, some of them was poor too, ya see, and some had to live just like we did. They had a cat hole. Nearly everyone had a cat."

Imogene's tasty cake is a great dessert to take to any reunion.

Cake

1 cup shortening (Imogene prefers Crisco)

2 cups sugar

4 eggs

2 1/2 cups all-purpose flour

1/2 cup self-rising flour

1 cup milk

*1 teaspoon each vanilla, lemon, coconut, butter,
   and rum extracts*

Glaze

1/2 stick (1/4 cup) margarine, melted

2 cups 10x powdered sugar

1 to 2 tablespoons milk

*1/4 teaspoon each vanilla, lemon, coconut, butter,
   and rum extracts*

PREHEAT OVEN to 325°. Grease and flour a 10-inch tube pan. Cream
the shortening and sugar together. Add the eggs one at a time, beating
well after each addition. Combine the flours in a separate bowl, then
add them in thirds to the egg mixture, alternately with the milk. When
smooth, blend in the flavorings. Pour the batter into the prepared pan.
Bake for 1 hour or until a toothpick inserted into the center of the cake
comes out clean.

To make the glaze, combine the margarine and the powdered sugar
and blend until smooth. Add the milk, a little at a time, until the mixture reaches a spreading consistency. Add the 5 flavorings and mix well;
drizzle the glaze over the cake while it is still warm.

Serves 10 to 12

Lemon Pound Cake and Icing

Buena Walton

BUENA WALTON, Perquimans County

"My recipe is so simple," Buena Walton from Belvedere told me. "The secret to this is the glaze. Use fresh lemons. Spread it on the cake while it's still hot and it's so tasty. I've made it for many people who say that it's so light and it's so good."

Boxed cake mixes were introduced early in the twentieth century. They really became popular when Betty Crocker introduced mixes in 1947. Today the boxed cake mix is considered not just a stand-alone convenience food but also an ingredient, as in lemon pound cake.

Cake
1 box (18 1/4 ounces) white cake mix
1 box (4-serving size) lemon Jell-O
4 eggs
2/3 cup oil
2/3 cup water

Icing
juice of 1 lemon
4 cups 10x powdered sugar
water, as needed

PREHEAT OVEN to 325°. Grease and flour a 10-inch tube pan. Blend all the cake ingredients together; beat until the batter is smooth. Pour the batter into the prepared pan. Bake for 1 hour until a toothpick inserted into the center of the cake comes out clean.

To make the icing, mix the lemon juice with the sugar. Add enough water to make the icing a spreadable consistency.

Serves 10 to 12

Banana Pound Cake and Icing

CARRIE BLAIR, Davidson County

"This was passed down to me from a girl I used to work with at Old Dominion Freight Line," said Carrie Blair of Thomasville. "This is a really moist cake. You can make it and eat it right straight, and it isn't dry at all. Some people like icing and some people don't. I've had this recipe for at least twenty years. I make it quite a bit, and everyone likes it."

Cake

3 cups all-purpose flour (Carrie prefers White Lily brand)
1 teaspoon baking powder
pinch salt
1 stick (1/2 cup) butter, softened
1 cup shortening
2 3/4 cups sugar
5 eggs, beaten
3 tablespoons milk
1 teaspoon banana extract
1 teaspoon vanilla extract
3 ripe bananas, mashed

Icing

3 ounces cream cheese, softened
1/2 stick (1/4 cup) butter, softened
1 teaspoon banana extract
1 to 2 cups 10X powdered sugar
just enough milk to make icing smooth

PREHEAT OVEN to 325°. Grease and flour a 10-inch tube pan. Combine the flour, baking powder, and salt; set aside. In a separate bowl, cream the butter, shortening, and sugar. Add the eggs and milk; mix well. Add the flour mixture to the wet ingredients in thirds, beating well after each addition. Add the flavorings and bananas. Blend until smooth. Pour the batter into the prepared pan. Bake for 1 hour and 15 minutes or until a toothpick inserted into the center of the cake comes out clean.

To make the icing, beat the cream cheese and butter together. Add the flavoring and 1 1/2 cups powdered sugar. Add just enough milk to make the icing a spreadable consistency. If you start spreading the icing and find it too soft, add a little more powdered sugar.

Serves 10 to 12

Black Walnut Pound Cake

CARRIE CATHERINE BYRD, Swain County

Carrie Catherine Byrd was born in Bryson City. "This lady, Anne Holdsclaw, got me started on pound cakes," she told me. "She bought me a tube pan. She taught me how to mix it up, the first ingredients for a long time until they were creamy. She made the best pound cake I ever tasted. I met her in a boardinghouse. She always treated me like one of her kids. I more or less added stuff to another recipe to get this one."

3 cups all-purpose flour
1/2 teaspoon baking powder
1 cup black walnut pieces
3 cups sugar
2 sticks (1 cup) butter or margarine, softened
1/2 cup shortening (Carrie prefers Crisco)
4 eggs
1/4 cup milk
1 cup sour cream

PREHEAT OVEN to 325°. Grease and flour a 5-inch-high, 10-inch-diameter tube pan. Combine the flour and baking powder. Mix the nuts with the flour mixture until nuts are well covered. In a separate bowl, mix sugar, butter or margarine, and shortening together until creamy. Add the dry ingredients in thirds, alternately with the milk, eggs, and sour cream. Pour the batter into the prepared pan. Bake for 1 hour and 15 to 30 minutes or until a toothpick inserted into the center of the cake comes out clean.

Serves 10 to 12

Sybil's Pineapple Pound Cake

SYBIL THOMAS, Greene County

Sybil Thomas was born in late 1918 near Snow Hill. "I was born in a real old unpainted house, up a long lane with wild plum bushes on either side," she told me. "We always looked forward to eating plums in the spring. My Daddy built a kitchen at the end of the porch to replace the old one, which was part of a great long room. Mama and Daddy made two bedrooms from that old room by hanging a curtain across the middle of it."

"We had a big old wood stove to cook on. It had a warming closet for food and a large reservoir section to heat water. We thought we were hot stuff, because we had a Majestic Range. It was so warm in that kitchen, that's where we sat in winter, because it was a lot warmer than the front of the house, even though we had room in the front. We had a living room, but we didn't use it in the wintertime very much. It was too cold for us. We had a fireplace there. I remember the next-door neighbors; a lot of them were kin people. They would come to our house and Mama and Daddy would play cards at the kitchen table. It was tough. I have happy memories, because we made it that way."

This cake is one of the ways Sybil makes happy memories today. I know, because she's made it for me on my birthday.

2 cups sugar

1 teaspoon cinnamon

1/2 teaspoon nutmeg

4 eggs, separated

1 cup canola oil

2 1/2 cups self-rising flour

1/4 cup cold water

8 ounces crushed pineapple, undrained

1 cup pecans, chopped and toasted

PREHEAT OVEN to 325°. Grease a 10-inch tube pan. In a small bowl, combine the sugar, cinnamon, and nutmeg. Set aside. Beat the egg whites until stiff. Continue beating as you add 1/4 cup of the sugar mixture. Set aside. Combine the rest of the sugar mixture with the egg yolks and oil. Add the flour. Continue beating as you pour in the water and pineapple. When batter is smooth, add the nuts. Fold in the beaten egg whites. Pour the batter into the prepared pan. Bake for 1 hour and 25 minutes or until a toothpick inserted into the center of the cake comes out clean. Cool the cake in the pan for 20 minutes before turning it out.

Serves 10 to 12

Southern Pound Cake

MARGUERITE HUGHEY, Buncombe County

Nancy Stancil gave this recipe to Marguerite in 1957. You may substitute orange juice for the bourbon.

2 sticks (1 cup) butter, softened
3 cups sugar
8 large eggs or 9 medium eggs,
*   separated*
3 cups self-rising flour

2 teaspoons vanilla extract
2 teaspoons almond extract
2 jiggers (3 ounces) bourbon
1 cup pecans, chopped

PREHEAT OVEN to 300°. Grease and flour a 5-inch-high, 10-inch-diameter tube pan. Sprinkle the bottom of the pan with 1/2 cup pecans. Cream the butter and sugar. Add the egg yolks and beat well. Add the flour, followed by flavorings and bourbon. In a separate bowl, beat the egg whites until stiff. Fold them into the batter until well incorporated. Pour the batter into the prepared pan. Sprinkle remaining pecans over the batter. Bake for 1 hour and 30 minutes or until a toothpick inserted into the center of the cake comes out clean.

Serves 10 to 12

Big Mama's Apple Cake

TOM BROWN, Forsyth County

Tom Brown

My husband, Jerry, and I met Tom Brown in September of 2003 at the annual corn husking held at Horne Creek Living Historical Farm. The farm is located in rural Stokes County near the Virginia border and is a bustling living history center. Outdoor cooking fires popped beneath large, black iron pots filled with chicken stew and apple butter. City children laughed as they learned to push corn cobs through an old fashioned husker, mules briskly pulled wooden plows through a garden patch, and a shape note choir sang old hymns.

"My Hobby Finding 'Lost' Apple Varieties" read a sign over rows of colorful apples spread out neatly on poster paper. Some were identified; others had yet to reveal their origins. Tom Brown, a resident of Forsythe County, stood by them, ready to pick passersby's brains for their personal knowledge of heritage apples. Finding lost apple varieties is Tom's passion. This is not a paid pursuit; in fact, he hasn't earned a dime from his discoveries. He held us spellbound with his stories of striding down dusty roads, over hill and dale, to search out the old strains our ancestors used to make tangy pies, applesauce, vinegar, and cakes, like the one below. Once an apple is identified, Tom restores the tree to production and tries to interest local nurseries in distributing it to the public. Currently, he's found over 500 varieties and expressed his desire to continue looking until he's found 755, "to equal the number of home runs Hank Aaron hit!" said Tom. He also uses his homegrown apples to make Big Mama's apple cake. Big Mama is Tom's mother-in-law.

3 cups tart apples

1 1/4 cups oil

2 cups sugar

3 eggs

2 1/2 cups all-purpose flour

1 teaspoon baking soda

2 teaspoons baking powder

1 teaspoon salt

1 teaspoon cinnamon

1 teaspoon allspice

1 teaspoon vanilla extract

1 cup walnuts or pecans, chopped

PREHEAT OVEN to 350°. Grease and flour a 10-inch tube pan. Peel and core the apples and chop into small pieces; set aside. Combine the oil, sugar, and eggs in a large mixing bowl and beat well. In another bowl, combine the flour, baking soda, baking powder, salt, and spices. Add the flour mixture to the creamed mix; add the vanilla extract. Fold in the apples and nuts and pour the batter into the prepared pan. Bake for 1 hour or until a toothpick inserted into the center of the cake comes out clean.

Serves 10 to 12

Dried-Apple Stack Cake

. . . .

MISS CHARITY RAY, Madison County

When I headed to western North Carolina, I heard about a famous local dessert, apple stack cake. After months of searching, a friend gave me an address for Charity Ray, who resides in the lovely alpine town of Mars Hill with her sister, Dorothy Coone. You can see the Blue Ridge Parkway from their kitchen window. "We had a fruit orchard in the backyard when we were young, pear trees, apple trees, peach trees," Charity told me. "We dried our apples outside in the sun. My mother used a piece of tin with a clean cloth on it and spread the apples over it; they're better when they're dried outside," she continued. "You peel them, then slice them thin, and put them on the screen in the sun in July or August," Dorothy added. "It only takes a few days. Bring them in at night so that the dew and rain don't get them wet."

"Apple stack cake was the only thing my mother would give us to eat on Christmas Eve, because we were so excited," Charity remembered. "'Mama, can we have a piece of (we called it) fruit cake?'" she and Dorothy asked each year. They went right to sleep after consuming the sweet, traditional treat. "Mom always made her apple stack cake like biscuit dough," says Charity. "We never measured a thing. This is for the modern cook." Now you can make it too.

Apple Filling

1 pound dried apples
1 teaspoon cinnamon
1 cup sugar
1/2 teaspoon salt

THIS MIXTURE will make a juicy applesauce-type filling. Begin the filling the night before you plan to make the cakes. Soak the dried apples overnight in enough water to cover. The next day, cook them on low heat until tender. Remove the pan from the heat and mash the apples until they are smooth. Add the cinnamon, sugar, and salt. Return the pan to the heat and bring the mixture to a boil, being careful not to scorch. When the sugar is dissolved and the mixture is thick, remove the applesauce from the heat and cool.

Cakes

4 to 5 cups self-rising flour	*1/2 cup sugar*
1 teaspoon baking soda	*1 cup molasses*
2 teaspoons ginger	*2 eggs*
1 teaspoon cinnamon	*1/2 cup buttermilk*
cloves, to taste	*1 tablespoon vanilla extract*
1/2 cup shortening	

PREHEAT OVEN to 350°. Lightly grease eight 8- or 9-inch round cake pans. Combine the flour, baking soda, ginger, cinnamon, and cloves; set aside. Cream the shortening and sugar together until the mixture is light and fluffy. Blend in the molasses. Add the eggs, beating well. Add the dry ingredients to the creamed mixture in thirds, alternating with buttermilk and beating well after each addition. Add the vanilla extract last. The dough will be very stiff and have the consistency of corn bread batter. Place the dough on a well-floured surface, working in enough flour to make it easy to handle. Divide the dough into eight balls. Roll the balls out to about 6 inches in diameter and press one each into the prepared cake pans. Bake the cakes for 12 to 15 minutes or until lightly browned. Remove cakes from the oven and cool.

Putting It All Together

Put a cake on a plate and spread some apple filling on top. Place the next layer on the first and spread it with filling. Repeat with remaining layers, building them into a stack. Spread the remaining filling on the sides to help keep the cake moist. Cover and refrigerate. Letting it age makes it even better; stack cakes made in November or early December can be served at Christmas.

Serves 10 to 12

Apple Crumb Cake

. . . .

LUCIE LEA ROBSON, Mecklenburg County

"My sons, Charlie and Patrick, and I spent a great deal of time in the Blue Ridge Mountains, where we had a house surrounded by apple trees," Lucie Lea Robson of Mecklenburg County told me. "One of the boys would climb the tree and shake the branches while the other one gathered the apples. We also had an old apple picker. It was a tool that looked a little like a rake with a basket on the end. You would reach around limbs with it to get those apples that you couldn't shake down. We enjoyed many apple desserts like this one."

6 to 7 apples, peeled, cored, and sliced	*1 1/2 sticks (3/4 cup) butter, divided*
1/3 cup water	*1 egg yolk*
1 cup sugar, divided	*2 cups self-rising flour*

PREHEAT OVEN to 350°. Cook the apples, water, and 1/4 cup sugar until the apples are soft. Remove from heat and set aside to cool. In a separate bowl, blend 3/4 cup sugar, 1/2 cup butter, and the egg. Gradually add the flour and mix well. The dough will be crumbly. Reserve 1 cup of the dough; press the remaining dough into a greased 9-inch springform pan to make a crust. Pour the cooked apples over the crust. Sprinkle the reserved cup of mixture over the apples. Dot the top with the remaining butter. Bake until golden brown, about 30 minutes.

Serves 10 to 12

Apple Nut Cake and Icing

SAM KORNEGAY, Duplin County

Sam Kornegay, like many natives of Duplin County, can take a twig and grow a tree. He raises a large garden every year, puts up pickles, picks out nuts, and, if you're a friend of his, makes this moist, delicious cake for your birthday.

Cake
1 cup cooking oil
1 stick (1/2 cup) margarine
3 eggs
2 cups sugar
3 cups all-purpose flour
2 teaspoons baking soda
2 teaspoons vanilla extract
3 cups peeled and diced apples,
   fresh or frozen
1 cup either pecans or black
   walnuts, or a combination
   of both (Sam says the cake
   is better if black walnuts are
   included.)

Icing
1 stick (1/2 cup) butter or
   margarine, melted
1/4 cup evaporated milk
1 cup brown sugar

PREHEAT OVEN to 375°. Grease and flour a 10-inch tube pan. Combine the first 6 ingredients and blend well. Add the vanilla extract, apples, and nuts and blend well. Pour the batter into the prepared pan. Bake for 45 minutes or until a cake tester inserted into the center of the cake comes out clean. Remove the cake from the pan to cool.

To make the icing, combine the butter or margarine, evaporated milk, and brown sugar, and blend until smooth. Drizzle the icing over the cake.

Serves 10 to 12

Applesauce Cake

. . . .

KATHERINE SAWYER WARD, Bertie County

The Cashie River runs through Windsor, where my cousin Katherine Sawyer Ward lives in the Sawyer family home. Katherine, like many North Carolinians, has a personal collection of recipes gleaned from family and friends. Her former neighbor Della Gillam shared this recipe with her many, many years ago.

1 stick (1/2 cup) butter, softened
2 cups sugar
3 eggs, beaten
1/2 teaspoon baking soda
2 cups applesauce
2 1/2 cups self-rising flour
1 teaspoon cinnamon
1/2 teaspoon nutmeg
1 cup pecans, chopped
1 cup raisins

PREHEAT OVEN to 325°. Grease and flour a 10-inch tube pan. Cream the butter and sugar together in a large mixing bowl. Add the eggs and blend well. In a separate bowl, combine the baking soda and applesauce and set aside. The mixture will bubble. In another bowl, combine the flour, cinnamon, and nutmeg. Add the dry ingredients to the butter mixture in thirds, mixing well after each addition. Blend in the applesauce mixture. Add the pecans and raisins and mix thoroughly. Pour the batter into the prepared pan. Bake for 1 hour. Good served with whipped or ice cream.

Serves 10 to 12

Blueberry Cake and Icing

MRS. ALMA ROUNTREE, Camden County

This recipe calls for canned pie filling, but you can make your own. To do so, combine about 2 1/2 cups of fresh blueberries with 2/3 cup sugar and 1/4 cup cornstarch and heat until the sugar and cornstarch dissolve. This recipe is divine. Blueberry cake is a tantalizing dessert, or it's a great dish for brunch.

Cake
1 box (18 1/4 ounces) yellow cake mix
1 stick (1/2 cup) butter, softened
4 eggs
2/3 cup milk
1 teaspoon vanilla extract

Filling for Cake Layers
1 can (21 ounces) blueberry pie filling

Icing
1 1/2 cups cream cheese, softened
1 1/2 cups sugar
1 cup whipped cream

PREHEAT OVEN to 350°. Grease and flour five 8- or 9-inch round cake pans. Combine the cake mix, butter, eggs, milk, and vanilla extract and blend well. Pour the batter into the prepared pans. Bake for 10 minutes or until a toothpick inserted into the center of the cake comes out clean. Cool for 20 to 30 minutes.

To make the icing, combine the cream cheese, sugar, and whipped cream and beat until smooth.

To assemble the cake, place one layer on a cake plate. Spread with 1/5 of the icing and top that with 1/5 of the pie filling. Place the next cake layer on top, and spread with icing and pie filling. Continue until all layers are iced and filled.

For variety, use other pie fillings.

Serves 10 to 12

Prune Cake and Glaze

LOUISE MCFALLS, McDowell County

Louise Byrd McFalls is from Tom's Creek and remembers when local grocery stores in Marion displayed their wares in baskets on the sidewalk. This recipe is so old she can't remember where she got it, but she always made it for her children, Judy, Cheryl, Nancy, Jerry, and Mike. "They won't let me take it anywhere," she told me. "Instead they save it for themselves!" Louise is a great-grandmother now; her children still love it.

Cake
1 cup buttermilk
1 cup cooking oil
1 1/2 cups sugar
3 eggs
2 cups self-rising flour
1 teaspoon allspice
1 teaspoon nutmeg
1 teaspoon cinnamon
1 teaspoon vanilla extract
1 cup cooked prunes
1 cup nuts, chopped (Louise uses pecans)

PREHEAT OVEN to 350°. Grease a 10-inch tube pan. Mix together the buttermilk, cooking oil, and sugar. Add the eggs one at a time, beating well after each addition. In a separate bowl, combine the flour, allspice, nutmeg, and cinnamon. Add this to the liquid mixture and blend well. Add the vanilla extract, cooked prunes, and nuts, stirring until they are well incorporated. Pour the batter into the prepared pan. Bake for 1 hour or until brown.

Glaze
1 cup sugar
1 tablespoon margarine
1/4 cup buttermilk
1 teaspoon light corn syrup
1/2 teaspoon baking soda

COMBINE all the ingredients in a saucepan. Bring the mixture slowly to a boil. Reduce the heat and cook the mixture until it turns a golden brown. Drizzle the glaze over the warm cake.

Serves 10 to 12

Cherokee Persimmon Cake

BETTY OXENDINE MANGUM, Robeson County

Betty Oxendine Mangum is originally from Robeson County but makes her home in Wake County now, where she has been a teacher and a Wake County commissioner. Betty has two distinct cooking styles, one traditional and the other gourmet. This is just one of the Native American recipes she shared with her students while she was a
Betty Mangum
teacher. If you are going to gather your own persimmons, be sure they are fully ripe (wait until the tree has dropped most of its leaves and the fruit is almost soft), and you'll be rewarded with a rich, fresh taste treat that makes a beautiful orange-colored cake.

1 cup persimmon pulp	1 cup all-purpose flour
1/2 cup sugar	1 teaspoon baking powder
1 egg	1/2 teaspoon baking soda
1 tablespoon butter, softened	

PREHEAT OVEN to 350°. Grease and flour an 8-inch-square baking pan. Combine all the ingredients. Mix well and pour the batter into the prepared pan. Bake for 25 to 30 minutes or until a toothpick or cake tester inserted into the center of the cake comes out clean.

Serves 4

Upside-Down Cake

MARTHA BARNES, Pitt County

Upside-down cake is a colorful crowd pleaser that can be made the day before serving. If you've never made an upside-down cake before, and you're concerned about how to flip it over, you might try practicing with an empty pan before you actually cook the cake. While the cake pan is right-side up, place a serving dish on top of it and then flip the pan over onto the dish. My mother used maraschino cherries with the pineapple slices to make the cake more festive during the winter holidays.

1 cup pineapple chunks or slices	2 eggs
1 stick (1/2 cup) butter, melted	1 cup all-purpose flour
1 cup brown sugar	1 teaspoon baking powder
1 cup nuts, chopped	1/2 teaspoon salt
1/2 cup white sugar	

PREHEAT OVEN to 350°. If you're using canned pineapple, drain it, reserving the juice. (If you're using fresh pineapple, cut it into a bowl so you can reserve the juice.) Set aside. Combine the butter and the brown sugar, mixing well. Pour the sugar mixture into the bottom of an 8-inch-square cake pan. Arrange the pineapple chunks or slices over the sugar mixture and sprinkle with the nuts. In a mixing bowl, combine the white sugar, eggs, flour, baking powder, salt, and reserved pineapple juice and beat until smooth. Pour the batter evenly over the pineapple. Bake for 25 minutes or until a toothpick inserted into the center of the cake comes out clean. Let the cake cool 10 minutes in the pan before turning it out onto a plate. Serve with sweetened whipped cream or nondairy whipped topping.

Serves 9 to 12

Icebox Fruitcake

MILDRED ROSSER COTTON, Lee County

"I grew up in the country," Mildred Rosser Cotton of Sanford told me. "I learned to cook when I was a girl on a farm. My mother was sick for a long time, so my two sisters and I did the most of the cooking. We always had greens, turnip greens, collards, or cabbage, whatever was in season. We raised almost everything we ate. We had our own meat. The only things my father had to buy were coffee, flour, and sugar."

"I've been making this icebox fruitcake for about thirty years for my family and friends," she continued. "You can make it in a tube pan or you can make it in small loaf pans, because I give them as individual gifts. I have five grandchildren, and I give each one a cake. It takes a big pan, because it's a lot to mix." You'll need rubber gloves for mixing the dough.

1 package (48 ounces) Ritz crackers

1 cup flaked coconut (Mildred prefers Baker's Angel Flake brand)

2 cups candied, diced cherries

2 cups candied, diced pineapple

4 cups pecans, chopped

2 cups Brazil nuts, chopped

2 cups English walnuts, chopped

*2 cans (14 ounces each) sweetened condensed milk
    (Mildred prefers Eagle brand)*

1 package (10 ounces) miniature marshmallows

PLACE THE CRACKERS in a plastic bag and crush them with a rolling pin until they are fine crumbs. Combine the cracker crumbs with the coconut, cherries, pineapple, and nuts and mix well. On top of the stove or in a microwave oven, combine the marshmallows and the sweetened condensed milk. Heat slowly, stirring occasionally, until the marshmallows are melted and completely mixed with milk. Pour the mixture over the cracker crumb mixture. Work the dough with your hands until it is well blended. Pack 5 ungreased 9 × 5-inch Pyrex or metal loaf pans and cover them with plastic wrap. Refrigerate the fruitcakes over night.

To remove the cakes from the pans, place a few inches of hot water in the sink and set the pans in it for a few minutes, then turn them out.

Each loaf serves 8 to 10

7-Up Cake

ESTELLE TURNER HURDLE, Perquimans County

Estelle Hurdle makes this cake so often that she has the recipe memorized. She wrote it down on a napkin for me the day I met her. 7-Up adds a tart flavor and lightness that are a welcome surprise in a cake. The cake calls for only a cup of 7-Up; you might enjoy the rest of the bubbly drink while you're making this easy and delicious dessert. Or you can save it to make an ice cream float to enjoy with your first slice of the warm cake.

3 cups all-purpose flour	*1 cup 7-Up soft drink (the diet*
1 1/2 cups (3 sticks) butter,	*variety will not work)*
softened	*4 eggs*
3 cups sugar	*3 teaspoons lemon flavoring*

PREHEAT OVEN to 350°. Grease and flour a 10-inch tube pan. Mix all the ingredients well. Pour the batter into the prepared pan. Bake for 1 hour.

Serves 10 to 12

$100 Cake and Icing

WANDA BROOKS, Stanly County

Long before cable television and the Home and Garden Television network were conceived, Betty Feezor demonstrated recipes and other household projects on a television show that was broadcast from 1952 until 1977 by WBTV in Charlotte. I talked with many cooks living in the North Carolina Piedmont who considered Betty a friend. Wanda Brooks's younger sister, Linda, was seven or eight years old when she saw Betty Feezor make $100 cake on her television show. "I still have the original copy in her handwriting," Wanda told me. "As I remember Mrs. Feezor's story, a lady had lunch at the Waldorf-Astoria Hotel in New York City and was so impressed with the chocolate cake she had for dessert that she asked for the recipe. The recipe was brought to her, but when she received her check for the meal, $100 had been added for the cost of the recipe. As the story goes, the lady decided that since she had paid that much for the recipe, she would share it." And, here it is.

Cake

1 stick (1/2 cup) butter, softened
2 cups sugar
2 eggs
2 cups all-purpose flour
2 teaspoons baking powder
1 teaspoon salt
1/2 cup cocoa mixed with
    1/4 cup warm water
1 1/2 cups milk
2 teaspoons vanilla extract
1 cup chopped nuts (optional)

Icing

1 stick (1/2 cup) butter, softened
1/4 cup cocoa
1 teaspoon vanilla extract
2 cups 10X powdered sugar
1 cup chopped nuts (optional)

PREHEAT OVEN to 375°. Grease and flour three 8- or 9-inch round cake pans. Mix all the cake ingredients, except the nuts, together into a smooth batter. Add the nuts if desired. Pour the batter into the prepared pans. Bake for 25 to 30 minutes.

To make the icing, combine all the ingredients and mix until well blended. Spread on cake layers.

Serves 10 to 12

Pies, Cobblers, Dumplings, and a Sonker

Chest Pie

Buttermilk Pie

Grandma's Pie

Cracker Pie

Vinegar Pie

Lemon Chess Pie

Ole-Timey Egg Custard Pie

Brown Sugar Pie

Miss Peach's Sweet Potato Pie

Fried Sweet Potato Pies

Granny's Green Tomato Pie

Jamie's Magic Pumpkin Pie

Apple Pie

Deep-Dish Apple Pie

Sour Cream Apple Pie

Dried-Apple Pie

Easy Apple Dumplings

Fried Apple Pies

Apple Crisp

Brown Betty

Blueberry Pie

Blueberry Dessert

Berma's Cherry Pie

Quick Cobbler

Blackberry Cobbler

Scuppernong Grape Pie

Open-Face Peach Pie

Peach and Sour Cream Pie

Pear Pie

Lemon Custard Pie

Lemon Meringue Pie

Lemon Chiffon Pie

Lemon Icebox Pie

Affinity (Banana Cream) Pie

Strawberry Pizza Pie

Pineapple Pie

Pineapple Coconut Pie

Coconut Pie

Impossible Coconut Pie

Coconut Butterscotch Pie

German Chocolate Pie

Mama's Christmas Pie

Betsy's Pecan Pie

Pecan Raisin Pie

Peanut Chess Pie

Peanut Butter Pie

Cousin Elizabeth's
   Chocolate Pie

Chocolate Chess Pie

Chocolate Amaretto Pie

Blender Chocolate Pie

Fudge Pie

Grandma's Quick Chocolate
   Pie

Refrigerator Pie

Sour Cream Pie

Grandma Davis's Blueberry
   Biscuits

Blackberry Dumplings

Lazy-Day Sonker

ERHAPS THE DELICIOUS SUCCESS of pouring a filling inside a simple pastry makes the humble pie such a beloved dessert. Or maybe it's the pleasure of selecting a filling from a myriad of possibilities—nuts, chocolate, eggs, and fruit. As they bake, these large pastries emit tantalizing aromas that appeal to everyone.

Pies are economical. They are also surprisingly easy to make and pack for visits, sweetly satisfying, and enjoyed by all. My cousin Katherine Ward from Bertie County told me that during the 1950s her mother turned out a piecrust, baked it, and filled it with homemade applesauce, still warm, to create a delectable dessert that she served warm with whipped cream. Pies were so popular in our past that a piece of furniture, the pie safe, was built to shelter them. A pie safe is a wooden cooling chest that usually has two doors covered with a sheet of tin or other metal that has been pricked with holes to let air—but not insects—pass in and out. Pies that were made to fill up the pie safe are called "chest pies." One hundred and four–year-old Nolie Zimmerman of Rowan County contributed her recipe for chest pie in this collection.

Lula Owl, an octogenarian who grew up on the Cherokee Reservation in western North Carolina, tells the story of Sunday dinner at her parents' home. During her youth, pies were not just for dessert; they were also for sustenance. "On Sunday after church we'd go home and the porch would be full of people, and they stayed for lunch," Mrs. Owl recounts. "And I don't know how my parents fed all of them. They never left till after lunch. Well they just came. You weren't invited, they just came. They always a'visited." Lula describes the apple pies her parents made to feed such crowds of visitors. "[My parents] made a long time ago a lot of stack pies with apples. We dried a lot of apples. We had our own apples back then. Today nobody has their own apples. You dried them. You put them out on a clean sheet, a white cloth on a little stand outside and dry them and you take them in every night and take them back out every morning and then you sacked them up and then you cooked them in the winter time and made like wheat bread, biscuit bread. You put a layer of biscuit bread and then a layer of apples, cooked apples on there and we called it stack pie."

Lula Owl

Lula's method of cooking without the use of measurements is called the "dump" or "by eye" method: the cook knows how much of an ingredient to dump into the bowl or simply looks at the ingredients to see how much to include. These cooks have prepared foods for so long that they don't need to measure in cups and teaspoons. Eula Mae Kilby of Jackson County, a busy grandmother, prepares pie dough and stews apples without measuring anything. Her hot, mouthwatering fried apple pies are so popular she makes them by the dozens.

Providing food for a family in need is a way many folks show support and affection, and creating a homemade pie is one way to do this. My aunt Julia Maxwell Allen of New Bern contributed her lemon chess pie recipe to this collection. She often made it for friends and neighbors. New Hanover County's Harriet Guyton shares her cousin Elizabeth's chocolate pie recipe. Elizabeth had a fresh pie waiting whenever family visited, no matter what.

My own family specializes in classic American pies: my cousin makes pecan, my brother makes luscious, thick blueberry, and I make peach and sour cream. Though each of these has a unique texture and flavor, all are made from locally grown ingredients.

"As easy as pie" has never been more true than in this age of accessible ingredients. For a quick solution to what's for dessert, try these recipes and then experiment with your own fillings. And read on to find out about that sonker.

Tips for Successful Pie Making

* Piecrusts can be purchased but can be easily made. See the recipes at the end of this section.

* Most of the recipes in this chapter require a standard, 9-inch pie plate, which will be about 1 inch deep. Some require a deep-dish, 9-inch pie plate, which is typically over 1 1/2 inches deep.

* Jane Lasley of Iredell County has these tips on making piecrusts: Handle pie pastry like it's a piece of glass. Begin by mixing the shortening into the flour with your fingertips until the dough resembles course

meal. Sprinkle the dough with ice-cold water, mixing it, a little at a time, into the flour and shortening with a fork until the dough is in small pieces the size of rice. When you can gather the dough into your hands and it holds together well, it's ready to roll out. Roll out crust on a pastry cloth that comes right out of the freezer and is sprinkled with flour. Invest in a marble rolling pin and keep it in the freezer when not in use; the weight of the rolling pin pushes down the dough, and chilling it prevents the dough from sticking. Make several piecrusts at a time and double-bag and freeze them. They'll keep in the freezer for as long as a month.

    * Some of the recipes below call for a graham cracker crust, but you can use other types of cookies for the crust if you don't have graham crackers.

    * When baking pies, it's a good idea to bake them on a cookie sheet so that any spillover will not fall into the bottom of your oven.

    * To improve your meringue, Donna Saad, originally from Vance County, recommends chilling your mixer beaters in the freezer before whipping eggs.

Basic Piecrust

This recipe is from Ida Mae Blount, a native of Kinston, Lenoir County.

2 cups all-purpose flour
1 teaspoon salt
2/3 cup shortening
5 to 6 tablespoons cold water

IF A RECIPE calls for a baked crust, preheat oven to 400°. Sift the flour with salt; cut in the shortening with a pastry blender until the mixture resembles fine meal. Sprinkle the water over the dough, a tablespoon at a time, mixing lightly with a fork until all of the flour is moistened. Gather the dough with your hands into a ball, and then divide the dough in half. Roll out each half onto a floured board until it is 1/8 inch thick. Fit the pastry loosely into a pie plate. Prick the bottom and sides with fork; trim and flute the edges with a fork. Bake for 10 to 12 minutes or until golden brown. Makes crusts to fit two 9-inch pie plates or 1 double crust.

Cream Cheese Piecrust

3 ounces cream cheese, softened
1 stick (1/2 cup) butter or margarine, softened
1 1/3 cups all-purpose flour

IF A RECIPE calls for a baked crust, preheat oven to 425°. Combine the cream cheese and butter until smooth. Add the flour and mix until the dough is smooth. Press the dough into the bottom of a 9-inch pie pan. Prick the dough three or four times with a fork. Bake for 10 to 12 minutes or until golden brown.

Graham Cracker Piecrust

2 cups graham cracker crumbs
1/4 cup sugar
1 teaspoon cinnamon (optional)
1/3 cup butter, softened

PREHEAT OVEN to 350°. Combine the graham cracker crumbs, sugar, and cinnamon, if desired. Use a fork to blend in the butter. When well combined, press the mixture into the bottom and up the sides of a 9-inch pie plate. Bake for 10 to 12 minutes.

Chest Pie

NOLIE RIDENHOUR ZIMMERMAN, Rowan County

Nolie Ridenhour Zimmerman was born in rural Rowan County on October 6, 1899, and lived until 2004. She heard this recipe while waiting to use the phone on a party line sometime in the 1920s. Nolie was 104 years old when she told me how she obtained the directions for chest pie.

"Chest pie," she told me, "now that's a good pie. I caught that [recipe] on the telephone," she laughed. "But that was when we first moved to the country when we had them old telephones [that] was on the wall, you know? I picked up the receiver to see if anybody was talking and not ringing. You had to ring a bell. Turn that handle, you know, and to get Salisbury [operator] to answer, but we had about ten on the line, and you didn't know they was talking or not unless you picked the receiver up, and if wasn't nobody on there, you could use it. If there was, you could sit there, and listen like I did; so one Saturday morning I was going to call somebody for something, and I picked up the telephone and heard Mrs. Limley, [who] lived down the road down here talking with her mother over to Salisbury, and she said, 'I want to know how to bake a chest pie.' Well then I did want to hear it; so she told that recipe. I had made chest pies, but not like that, and not good like that 'cause I didn't know how to make chest pies. I went and made me some crusties while it was fresh on my mind, and I baked me a chest pie. That was so good! I didn't mean to eavesdrop."

It's a good pie no matter how she got it.

2 unbaked 9-inch piecrusts
3 eggs
1 stick (1/2 cup) butter, softened
1 cup white sugar
1 cup brown sugar
3 1/2 tablespoons cream or milk
1 teaspoon vanilla extract
pecans (optional)

PREHEAT OVEN to 350°. Combine the filling ingredients and blend well. Divide the mixture evenly between the prepared crusts. Bake for 10 minutes. Turn the oven down to 325° and bake for 20 to 25 minutes more, or until done.

Makes 2 pies, 6 to 8 servings each

Buttermilk Pie
. . . .

MILDRED ROSSER COTTON, Lee County

This is a great way to enjoy the contrasting tastes of buttermilk and sugar. Buttermilk pie takes less than 30 minutes to prepare.

1 unbaked deep-dish, 9-inch piecrust
2 eggs
1 1/4 cup sugar
1/2 cup all-purpose flour
1/2 stick (1/4 cup) butter
1 cup buttermilk

PREHEAT OVEN to 350°. Combine the filling ingredients and mix well. Pour the mixture into the prepared piecrust. Bake for about 1 hour or until the filling is firm.

Serves 6 to 8

Grandma's Pie

LU ANN THOMPSON, Granville County

"Grandma's pie was from my maternal grandmother," said Lu Ann Thompson of Franklinton. "She was quite a lady, born in 1900, in that she caught the train to Temple University upon her graduation from high school, and went to take a business course in Philadelphia. So she was quite an extraordinary woman. The recipe was given to me as a wedding gift. When she gave me several pie recipes, she prefaced them by giving me a quote that said, 'Love is eternal. Let's keep it that way.' When she married my grandfather, she was a homemaker. She didn't like a lot of housekeeping, but she liked to go fishing every day with her collie dog."

"She loved to cook. When she made pies, she might make ten. It was quite a day's ordeal in that she would make the crusts. After she would bake them, she would put them on cooling racks, and they would stack up four, five, six high. There was always pie on the stove for anyone to eat, because it was a home that people were in and out of a lot—neighbors, family, whatever, right in this neighborhood of Pocomoke, which was named after an Indian reservation that was near here."

1 unbaked 9-inch piecrust

2 eggs

3/4 cup dark molasses (Lu Ann prefers Grandma's brand)

1 cup sugar

1/2 stick (1/4 cup) butter, melted

PREHEAT OVEN to 350°. Whip the eggs. Add the molasses, sugar, and melted butter and mix well. Pour the filling into the prepared piecrust. Bake for 25 to 30 minutes or until the filling is set and the crust is golden brown.

Serves 6 to 8

Cracker Pie

SARAH SAWYER ALLEN, Lenoir County

You may not believe that you can make a pie just from crackers, but you can. I've also seen this one called mock apple pie. Historic recipes show pies like this were made during the Civil War from hardtack, a cracker widely used by the military, when even apples were in short supply. My mother, Sarah Sawyer Allen, of Kinston, left a handwritten note indicating that her copy of the recipe came from a friend, Linda Stephenson, who suggests that you make it the day before serving if you can.

1 cup sugar
3 egg whites
1 teaspoon baking powder
1 teaspoon vanilla extract
1 cup Ritz-type crackers, crushed
3/4 cup chopped pecans

PREHEAT OVEN to 350°. Grease a pie plate. In a mixing bowl, beat the egg whites until stiff. Gradually blend in the sugar. Add the baking powder and vanilla extract and continue beating until well blended. Fold in the crackers and chopped pecans. Pour the mixture into the prepared pie plate. Bake for 30 minutes. Cool and top with whipped cream.

Serves 6

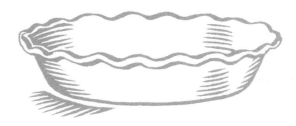

Vinegar Pie

MISS CHARITY RAY, Madison County

Miss Charity's mother gave her this recipe. I've always marveled at how practical some dishes are. Like a chess pie, a tasty vinegar pie makes a good dessert even when your pantry is low on ingredients.

1 unbaked 9-inch piecrust
1 stick (1/2 cup) butter, melted and cooled
3 eggs
1 1/2 cups sugar
1 1/2 tablespoons white vinegar
1 teaspoon vanilla extract

PREHEAT OVEN to 325°. Combine the filling ingredients and blend well. Pour the filling into the prepared piecrust. Bake for 10 minutes at 325°, then increase the oven temperature to 350° and bake for 35 minutes more.

Serves 6 to 8

Lemon Chess Pie

JULIA MAXWELL ALLEN, Craven County

Some say that chess pies used to contain cheese. Others say that chess pie was originally "jest" ("just") pie made from ingredients typically found in the larder like eggs, sugar, butter, and flavoring. Perhaps a lattice crust was placed on top and the pie became known as "chess" pie because of its resemblance to a chessboard. Tradition holds that you only have to stir the ingredients six times and they're ready to pour into the crust. My aunt Julia Maxwell Allen, who contributed this recipe, was from New Bern.

1 unbaked 9-inch piecrust

2 eggs

1 tablespoon all-purpose flour

1 cup sugar

juice of one lemon or 1/4 cup lemon juice

1 tablespoon grated lemon zest

1/2 stick (1/4 cup) butter, melted

PREHEAT OVEN to 350°. Beat the eggs slightly. Add the rest of the filling ingredients, then blend until smooth. Pour the filling into the prepared piecrust. Bake for 5 minutes at 350°, then increase the oven temperature to 425° and bake for 5 minutes more. Finally, reduce the heat to 300° and bake for 30 minutes more. Be sure the filling is set and that it is brown on top.

Serves 6 to 8

Ole-Timey Egg Custard Pie

RILEY BURTON, Rowan County

"I grew up in the country on a farm," Riley Burton told me. "[During the Depression] a lot of people didn't have food to eat, but we had everything. We were very fortunate. My father raised his grain. He took his wheat to the mill and had it ground. We had our flour. We raised corn. He took it to the mill. We had our cornmeal. We had milk, homemade butter, good, ole country cream. We had chickens. We had our eggs. He raised hogs; so we had all kinds of good hog meat, and they used homemade lard back then that they got from the hogs. We had beef. We raised Irish potatoes; we raised sweet potatoes, green beans, sugar peas, butter beans. He had peach trees, apple trees. We dried apples; we dried peaches. We had peaches canned, apples to can."

Riley learned to make old-timey egg custard pie from her mother.

1 unbaked 9-inch piecrust

2 1/2 cups milk

1 tablespoon butter

1/4 tablespoon salt

1 cup sugar

1 tablespoon vanilla extract

4 eggs

PREHEAT OVEN to 450°. Heat the milk in a saucepan almost to boiling; add the butter and stir until it melts. Remove from heat. Combine the salt, sugar, vanilla extract, and eggs. Pour the milk mixture over the egg mixture and blend well. Pour the filling into the prepared piecrust. Bake for 5 minutes at 450°. Reduce the oven temperature to 425° and bake for 10 more minutes or until the filling is set.

Serves 6 to 8

Brown Sugar Pie

MARY CHARLES PAWLIKOWSKI, Nash County

"This was one of Grandmama's [Kate Capehart Bell] recipes, but I believe the handwriting to be that of her dear friend Louise Sandridge of Windsor," Mary Charles Pawlikowski explained. "I'm sure Grandmama tried the pie and asked Louise for the recipe. It tastes somewhat like a pecan pie and was probably carried to many after-church lunches and covered dish suppers."

1 unbaked 9-inch piecrust

2 eggs

1 cup brown sugar

3 tablespoons butter, melted

1 teaspoon vanilla extract

1 cup pecans

PREHEAT OVEN to 350°. Beat the eggs well. Blend in the brown sugar, butter, and vanilla extract until the filling is smooth. Fold in the pecans. Pour the filling into the prepared piecrust. Bake for 35 minutes or until the filling is golden brown and set.

Serves 6 to 8

Miss Peach's Sweet Potato Pie

ESSIE GILLIARD, Mecklenburg County

When I visited her in the summer of 2001, Essie Gilliard told me that she got up at 4 A.M. every morning. I met her in her bustling store in Charlotte. She told me that everyone calls her Mom. "This started off like a hobby," she said. "We got this restaurant in 1986. It used to be called Villa Heights Grocery and Grill. We were just going to sell home-cooked food. It was like a convenience store in the front and home-cooked food in the back."

"Then I decided I wanted to do this. I had never baked before. I used to make cobblers. I think I use it as an outlet, because I do a lot of stuff—I get real stressed out. When I'm baking, I just enjoy it. I get into it, and I don't have a problem. When we had family gatherings, I wanted to make a sweet potato pie." "Always use your fresh potatoes," Miss Peach, Mom's 101-year-old mother-in-law told her. "She's a wise lady," Mom continued. "Her mind is clear as a bell." Here is the result of that collaboration. You might want to make more than one, because you probably won't have a morsel left when you serve it.

Crust

1 cup all-purpose flour
1/2 teaspoon salt
3 tablespoons shortening
ice water

Filling

4 sweet potatoes, peeled and cut
    into small chunks (select orange
    sweet potatoes with smooth
    skins and no spots)
5 eggs
2 1/2 cups sugar
1/4 cup vanilla extract
2 sticks (1 cup) butter, softened
2 teaspoons nutmeg
5 ounces evaporated milk

PREHEAT OVEN to 325°. To make the piecrust, combine the flour and salt, and cut in the shortening until the mixture resembles coarse meal. Add the ice water, a little bit at a time, until the pastry is smooth. Roll out and line a 9-inch pie dish.

For the filling, in a saucepan, combine the sweet potatoes and just enough water to cover them. Boil the potatoes until they're soft. Remove from heat and mash them together in a bowl with the eggs and sugar. When they are well blended, stir in the vanilla extract, butter, and nutmeg. Add the evaporated milk and beat until smooth. Pour the filling into the prepared crust. Bake for 1 hour or until the crust is golden brown.

Serves 6 to 8

Fried Sweet Potato Pies

GLADYS UMFLET JENNINGS, Pasquotank County

Where I come from, we called fried turnovers like the ones Gladys Umflet Jennings makes "jacks." Gladys fills hers with sweet potatoes: "I just do my sweet potato; I do my sugar; and I do vanilla flavoring, and I stir it up and taste of it and, if it tastes right, that's it," says Gladys Umflet Jennings, who lives in the Weeksville area. "Mother made sweet potato jacks; she used to make her own dough, but over the years I have learned to use biscuit dough. I just roll them out. I use an iron frying pan." And she makes a marvelous fried sweet potato pie.

Pastry
*Homemade biscuit dough or a
    tube of refrigerated buttermilk
    biscuits*

Filling
*1 large sweet potato, Beauregard
    variety preferred*
1/2 to 1 cup sugar, or to taste
*1 teaspoon vanilla extract,
    or to taste*
1 egg
vegetable oil for frying

TO MAKE the filling, cook the sweet potato until tender. Peel it and mash it well in a large mixing bowl. Add the sugar and vanilla extract. Beat in the egg.

To prepare the pies, roll out the biscuit dough on a floured surface to about 1/4 to 3/8 inch thick, as you would for a pie. Cut the dough into 8 circles about 3 1/2 to 4 inches in diameter. Spoon an equal amount of filling onto the dough circles. Fold each circle in half and seal the edges with a fork. Heat an inch of oil in an iron frying pan over medium heat. Fry the pies in the oil until they are golden brown on both sides. Remove with a slotted spoon; drain on paper towels.

Makes 8 pies

Granny's Green Tomato Pie

KATHERINE SAWYER WARD, Bertie County
MARY CHARLES PAWLIKOWSKI, Nash County

"Granny was my great-grandmother, Kate Capehart Bell, born in 1877," Mary Charles Pawlikowski explained. "Kate gave it to my mother, Katherine Sawyer Ward, who gave it to me."

This is a special pie in several ways, first because you can have it only when tomatoes are in season. Second, the bright green tomatoes and yellow lemons make a beautiful combination of layers. Perhaps best of all, Granny's green tomato pie has a unique, fresh flavor. I think it's just the right finish to a summer meal.

piecrusts for a double-crusted, 9-inch pie	*3/4 cup all-purpose flour*
4 large fresh green tomatoes, sliced thinly	*3/4 cup sugar*
	1 lemon, sliced very thinly
	1/2 stick (1/4 cup) butter

PREHEAT OVEN to 350°. Line a pie plate with one crust. Rinse the tomato slices well with water and then drain them. Combine the flour and sugar in a shallow mixing bowl. Press each side of the tomato slices into the flour and sugar until they are well covered. Line the bottom of the piecrust with the coated tomato slices. Next, place the lemon slices on top of the tomatoes, then dot well with butter. Continue layering until all the tomatoes and lemon slices are used. Sprinkle the remaining flour and sugar evenly over the tomatoes and lemons. Dot with remaining butter. Cover with the top crust and crimp the edges to seal. Cut slits in the crust to allow steam to escape during baking. Bake for 45 minutes or until brown.

Serves 6 to 8

Jamie's Magic Pumpkin Pie

CAROLYN GOFF, Harnett County

"My first remembrance of cooking was when I was five years old standing on a stool," Carolyn Goff told me. "Mama tried to teach me to make biscuits. My daddy said that if you opened up the oven, my mama's biscuits would just fly out they were so light, but I wasn't cut out for it. I could make cookies, mostly drop cookies, and I peeled potatoes. Mostly I cooked sweets. I cooked cakes when I was in the sixth grade. James Edward [her future husband] was in the sixth grade, and I had two more boyfriends in the sixth grade. James Edward and I were sort of sweethearts, but if I got mad with one, I had an extra. I was like an old Hudson car; I had an extra [tire]. One of my boyfriends would bring the sugar, one would bring the eggs, and one would bring the flour, and then I'd furnish the milk. When I got home, I'd make the cake, and the next day I'd take the cake to school, and they'd eat it. Pretty soon everybody wanted me to make cakes.

"I was working while James Edward was going to college. I was getting kind of skinny and had lost my appetite. Some of the women I worked with in a shipping department of a factory would bring something in [to eat] all the time. A woman I knew, Miss Ollie Rankin, brought a pie one day. I'd known her ever since I was a baby. She told me she wanted me to eat some of her pie, that it was like magic. She said it would do me some good. I tasted that pie and I said, 'Miss Ollie, what is that?' She said, 'I told you, it's magic. Do you want another piece?' I said 'Yes, M'am, I do.' She said, 'Well I tell you what, Carolyn, you can eat the whole thing if you want it.' And I felt like it, and I got my appetite back. I think the reason some people don't like pumpkin pie is the crust. I use a crumb crust."

1 9-inch graham cracker (or other cookie) crust
1 3/4 cups pumpkin (canned or fresh cooked)
1 cup sugar, divided
1/2 teaspoon each cinnamon, ginger, cloves
2 eggs, separated
1 ounce unflavored gelatin
1/4 cup water

COMBINE the pumpkin, 1/2 cup sugar, cinnamon, ginger, cloves, and egg yolks. Mix until smooth, then pour into a saucepan. Stir the mixture constantly over medium heat for 8 to 10 minutes or until the mixture thickens slightly. Remove from heat and refrigerate until cold. Preheat oven to 350°. Dissolve the gelatin in water. Beat the egg whites until stiff. Blend in 1/2 cup sugar. Fold the gelatin and the cold pumpkin mixture into the egg whites. Pour the the filling into the prepared crust. Bake for 15 minutes. Refrigerate any leftovers.

Serves 6 to 8

Apple Pie

TOM BROWN, Forsyth County

Tom Brown's hobby is looking for lost heritage apple varieties and restoring them so that future generations will also be able to enjoy them. "My wife and I both love farmers markets," he told me when I visited him at his home near Clemmons, "and so we would frequently go to the farmers market in Winston-Salem at the Dixie Classic Fairgrounds. And there was a man there who sells the old trees, but during the summer and early fall he comes there with some of the apples and sells the apples. And I was fascinated by all the names and textures and colors and tastes. We have found some amazing apples. Like we went to this elderly man's home named Langford Jordan, and he had a seedling there that he had found years ago. We were just amazed at the wonderful taste of the apple. I don't particularly really like Winesap apples, but there was one near Robbinsville, North Carolina, that's in the tip of the state near Fontana Dam. Probably called the Yellow Winesap, because it's yellow inside and that had the most delicious flavor of any apple I've ever tasted, but that just compares the old original Winesap to the modern ones that are picked early and there's a tremendous difference. And some of the apples are really, really tart."

You can experiment with various types of apples when you make this pie.

piecrusts for a double-crusted, 9-inch pie
8 apples, preferably a combination of tart, such as Granny Smith,
*   and sweet, such as Red Delicious or Gala*
1 tablespoon all-purpose flour
3/4 cup sugar
1 teaspoon cinnamon
1 stick (1/2 cup) butter
a small amount of milk, skim if you have it

PREHEAT OVEN to 350°. Line a ceramic or glass pie dish with the bottom piecrust. You may peel the apples if you prefer, then slice them thinly and evenly into the piecrust. Combine the flour, sugar, and cinnamon and sprinkle the mixture over the apple slices. Dot the top well with butter. Cover with the top crust and crimp the edges to seal. Brush the crust with milk, removing any milk puddles with a paper towel. Make slits in the center of the top crust to allow steam to escape during baking. Bake for approximately 1 hour, or until the liquid bubbles up through the crust slits.

Serves 6 to 8

Deep-Dish Apple Pie

SUSAN CARSON, Brunswick County

I sat in the dining room of Susan Carson's home on Atlantic Avenue in Southport one winter day. Known to her friends as Miss Susie, she sat among stacks of old books and several lounging cats. "I loved school," she told me. "I walked three blocks to school down there where the post office is today. I started in 1926. My daughter was born in 1948. Her first-grade teacher was the same as my first-grade teacher. I just had the best of growing up years. I can't think of anything I would have changed. We didn't know what a Depression was. I graduated from high school in 1937. In 1940 I got a job in a law office."

Miss Susie showed me a handwritten recipe for deep-dish apple pie. "If the apples are too sweet, add a tablespoon of lemon juice," she said. "If it's juiciness they need, add a tablespoonful or so of water before putting crumb mixture on top."

5 to 6 medium to large apples
1 1/2 cups brown sugar, divided
cinnamon, to taste

1 cup all-purpose flour
2 sticks (1 cup) butter
a little lemon juice, if needed
water, if needed

PREHEAT OVEN to 350°. Peel, core, and slice the apples. If the apples aren't tart, add a tablespoon of lemon juice to the them; or if they're dry, add a tablespoon of water. In a small bowl, combine 1/2 cup brown sugar and the cinnamon. In a 2-quart baking dish, arrange 1/3 to 1/2 of the apples in one layer. Sprinkle some of the sugar mixture over the layer. Arrange more apples over this layer and sprinkle with the sugar mixture. Repeat with the remaining apples and sugar. Mix the remaining cup of brown sugar with the flour. Work in the butter with your fingertips to make a crumbly mixture. Sprinkle this over the apples. Bake for 1 hour. You can serve it with heavy cream, whipped cream, or ice cream on top.

Serves 6 to 8

Sour Cream Apple Pie

. . . .

MARGUERITE HUGHEY, Buncombe County

The apple is America's favorite fruit, and North Carolina ranks seventh in producing it. Cold weather in the mountain counties of Henderson, Cleveland, Haywood, and Wilkes provides excellent growing conditions for the huge crop North Carolinians consume each year. You can usually find Rome, Gala, and Red and Golden Delicious at roadside stands and farmers markets each fall, but try not to eat them all on the way home so you can make this satisfying pie.

1 unbaked 9-inch piecrust

Filling
1/4 cup all-purpose flour
pinch salt
3/4 cup sugar
1 egg
1 cup sour cream
1/2 teaspoon vanilla extract
2 cups peeled and cored apples,
  very finely chopped

Topping
1/3 cup sugar
1 teaspoon cinnamon
1/3 cup all-purpose flour
1/2 stick (1/4 cup) butter, softened

PREHEAT OVEN to 400°. Combine the flour, salt, and sugar. Add the egg, sour cream, and vanilla extract. Beat until smooth. Add the apples and mix well. Pour the filling into the prepared piecrust. Bake for 15 minutes. Reduce the oven temperature to 350° and bake for 30 minutes. Remove the pie from the oven and return the oven temperature to 400°.

To prepare the topping, combine the sugar, cinnamon, flour, and butter in a small bowl and mix thoroughly. Spread the topping evenly over the pie. Return the pie to the oven and bake for 10 minutes. Cool and enjoy. Refrigerate any leftovers.

Serves 6 to 8

Dried-Apple Pie

Ruby Evans Edwards with a quilt she made. Photograph by Dr. Anne Phillips.

RUBY EVANS EDWARDS, Alleghany County

"I grew up on a farm, and we had chickens and cows and pigs," said Ruby Evans Edwards of Sparta. "We walked to school two and a half miles there and back. We went over creeks and foot logs and a hill. Some neighbor kids would go with us, and we'd meet some other kids, and we'd all go together. We took a little lard bucket. I guess it held about a half gallon. We'd take biscuit and jelly and, if we had some, pie or cake. We couldn't take any milk, because we didn't have any way to take it. It was just a one-room school; just one teacher taught all seven grades. Then when you got to eighth grade, you'd go to high school. At Christmas we expected the teacher to treat us and if he didn't, [we]'d lock him out of the school for awhile."

"We used to fix this, because everybody used to dry apples," Ruby continued. "We dried the old-timey apples, and they dried real well, four or five gallons of them and then we'd make these dried-apple pies. We put whipped cream on it when we used to have it. They liked them [dried apples] just to eat; just to cook a bowl full of them and sweeten it and add a little butter to it, and just eat it, usually had 'em of a noon. We used to have work hands, and they'd come in at dinner; so we'd fix that for dinner."

1 unbaked 9-inch piecrust
2 cups dried apples
1/2 cup sugar
1 teaspoon cinnamon

dash salt
1/2 cup cream or evaporated milk, refrigerated overnight (optional)

PREHEAT OVEN to 350°. Cover the dried apples with water in a 2-quart saucepan and simmer over medium heat until the apples are tender (as soon as they can be pierced easily with a fork). Drain the cooked apples and place them in a large mixing bowl. In a separate bowl, combine the sugar, cinnamon, and salt and stir the mixture into the cooked apples.

Pour the filling into the prepared piecrust. Bake for 30 minutes or until the crust is brown. Serve plain or with whipped cream or evaporated milk.

For a crustless dessert, cook the apples until they are tender. Remove from heat. Add butter and sugar, to taste. Serve.

Serves 6

Easy Apple Dumplings

JACOB ADAM KARRIKER, Stanly County

"I started having an interest in cooking when I was in ninth grade," Jacob Adam Karriker told me at North Stanly High School in New London where he was a student. "I watched the food channel and started trying to cook things and decided I liked it. I like to cook something that looks like it might be difficult for my friends, and they'll see it's not really that hard."

Jacob Adam Karriker

"This is real easy. I've taken two cooking classes. We had to do presentations and cook for the teachers. I cooked this; it's a lot of fun."

4 Granny Smith apples, peeled and cut into 8 wedges each
biscuit dough for 8 to 10 biscuits, or a tube of prepared biscuits
1 cup water
1 cup sugar
1 stick (1/2 cup) butter

PREHEAT OVEN to 350°. Wrap each apple wedge in a piece of biscuit dough. Arrange the dumplings in single layer in a 9 × 13-inch baking pan. Combine the water and sugar in a saucepan. Stir in the butter and heat to boiling. Pour the mixture over the apples. Bake for 30 minutes or until apples are soft. Delicious served warm with ice cream.

Serves 6 to 8

Fried Apple Pies

EULA MAE CONNER KILBY, Jackson County

"There were twelve of us," Eula Mae Conner Kilby told me at her home in Glenville. "We didn't have glass in our home; we had a wooden covering [over the windows] and a latch on our front door with a block of wood to turn to keep people out. We had oil lamps. We went to bed when it got dark. My mother died when I was eight years old. I just learned to cook on my own. I'd just watch other people, and I'd remember, and I'd go back and try it myself—you've got to want to get there. I've got recipes in my head that I just use. I used to make chocolate gravy and have it with hot biscuits and that'd be breakfast."

"I left home in 1957, and we never had a refrigerator," Eula Mae continued. "We were still cooking on an old wood stove, no washing machine neither. We still scrubbed our clothes out on the board. I don't see how the kids could do it today."

"We raise our apples: Grimes Golden, Golden Delicious, and another dark red apple. You can taste the apples, that's the best part of fried pies is the apples. My son was in the band, and one time I made a hundred [fried apple pies] in one day. You can make the dough ahead, shortening, flour, and a little water. You can roll it out better if you don't use milk. You can store them in a plastic container in the refrigerator, take them out when you're ready, and put them in the microwave to warm them. I serve them hot with ice cream."

Fried apple pies are as popular in the North Carolina mountains as beans and corn cooked together. Eula Mae doesn't need to measure ingredients. I've adapted her recipe using standard measurements. There's nothing like enjoying hot, pocket-sized pies right from Eula Mae's frying pan, but I hope these are the next best thing.

4 large fresh apples, peeled and cored
a little water
1/2 to 3/4 cups sugar, or to taste
1/2 teaspoon apple pie spice
1/2 teaspoon cinnamon
1 teaspoon vanilla extract
biscuit dough for 8 biscuits or a tube of refrigerator biscuits
vegetable oil for frying

CUT the apples into small chunks and put them in a saucepan with just enough water to cover them. Bring them to a boil, then turn the heat down to medium. Add sugar to taste (you may need to taste the apples at this point—they should retain some tartness). Add the apple pie spice and cinnamon and cook for 20 minutes. Remove the saucepan from the heat and stir in the vanilla extract.

Divide the biscuit dough into 8 equal pieces. Form each piece into a ball, flatten it, and roll it out on a floured surface into a circle about 5 inches in diameter. Place two tablespoons of the apple mixture into the middle of the circles, then fold the dough over the filling. Seal the edges together using a fork. Heat the oil in a frying pan over medium heat. Drop the pies into the hot oil; fry them until they're brown on one side, then turn them over and cook until they're brown on the other side. Remove the pies from the oil and drain them on paper towels. Cool before serving.

Makes 8

Apple Crisp

MARGUERITE HUGHEY, Buncombe County

You can have apple crisp in the oven in just minutes. Serve it plain or top it with ice cream or whipped cream. You can also melt a slice of American cheese over the top for a heartier version. "Pile up the apples," says a note at the top of the handwritten recipe that Marguerite Hughey shares here. "They sink when cooked."

Filling
4 cups peeled and chopped or sliced apples
1/4 cup water (a little more if apples are dry)
1 teaspoon cinnamon
1/2 teaspoon salt
a little lemon juice

Topping
1 cup all-purpose flour
1 1/2 cups sugar
1 stick (1/2 cup) butter

PREHEAT OVEN to 350°. Place the apples and water in a 9-inch pie dish. Sprinkle with cinnamon, salt, and lemon juice.

For the topping, in a small mixing bowl, combine the flour and sugar. Using a pastry blender, cut in the butter until the mixture resembles coarse meal. Sprinkle the crumbs over the apples. Bake uncovered for about 40 minutes.

Serves 6 to 8

Brown Betty

MARTHA BARNES, Pitt County

Brown Betty is an old standby; I can make it up at the last minute for dessert or serve it for brunch. You can add raisins and chopped nuts for variety.

2 cups unseasoned breadcrumbs
4 medium apples, peeled, cored, and thinly sliced
1 cup sugar
1 stick (1/2 cup) butter
1 teaspoon cinnamon
1/2 cup water

PREHEAT OVEN to 350°. Grease an 8-inch-square baking dish or pan. Cover the bottom of the pan or baking dish with half of the breadcrumbs. Arrange the apples in layers over the crumbs. Sprinkle with the sugar, bits of butter, and cinnamon. Cover with the rest of the breadcrumbs. Add the water. Bake for 35 to 40 minutes or until mixture bubbles and is crisp on top. Serve warm with lemon sauce (recipe in the Icings, Fillings, and Sweet Sauces chapter), whipped cream, or a scoop of vanilla ice cream.

Serves 6

Blueberry Pie

WILL ALLEN, Wake County

The blueberry is an American native. Its indigo skin encloses a tasty record of its origins in fields, deep woods, or cool lakeshores. Its flavor and texture include hot summer sunshine and honey left weeks earlier by pollinating bees. "The [pie] filling will hold together after it cools," says my brother, Will Allen, now of Raleigh. If served warm and topped with vanilla ice cream, a slice of this pie jiggles slightly, almost like it's chuckling.

piecrusts for a double-crusted, 9-inch pie
4 cups fresh blueberries
1 1/4 cups sugar
1/2 cup all-purpose flour or 1/4 cup all-purpose flour
*   plus 1/4 cup cornstarch*
1/2 rounded teaspoon cinnamon
healthy dash salt
1 teaspoon finely grated lime or lemon zest
1/4 cup lime or lemon juice
1/2 stick (1/4 cup) butter

PREHEAT OVEN to 350°. Line a pie plate with one unbaked crust. Wash and drain the blueberries; set aside. In a large mixing bowl, combine the sugar, flour, cinnamon, salt, and grated zest. Add the blueberries and mix until the blueberries are well coated with the dry ingredients. Pour the blueberries into the prepared pie plate, mounding them up in the center. Drizzle the lime or lemon juice evenly over the filling. Dot the top of the filling with butter. Add the top crust and crimp the edges to seal. Slit the top in several places to allow steam to escape. Place the pie on a cookie sheet, as the filling is juicy and may run. Bake for 45 minutes. Cool on a wire rack.

Serves 6 to 8

Blueberry Dessert

EULA MAE CONNER KILBY, Jackson County

I met Eula Mae Conner Kilby on a late summer day at her home near Cullowee. Great-grandchildren surrounded her. Eula Mae's husband raises corn, okra, tomatoes, apples, and blueberries. "We've been married for forty-three years," Eula Mae told me. "He has about 100 blueberry bushes down there. I'm going to give you a bag [of blueberries] to take home with you. I have a croissant blueberry dessert. I cook my blueberries and thicken them. That's what we eat in the summertime when we have fresh blueberries all the time."

1 quart blueberries
1 cup water
1/4 cup cornstarch
1 cup sugar
1 cup cream cheese, softened
1 cup 10X powdered sugar
8 store-bought croissants cut in half lengthwise
1 stick (1/2 cup) butter, melted

WASH the blueberries thoroughly, then place them in a saucepan with the water. Bring to a boil. Reduce to medium heat. Add the cornstarch and sugar. Stir until thickened. Remove from heat.

Preheat oven to 350°. Combine the cream cheese and powdered sugar. Blend until smooth. Spread eight of the croissant halves with the cream cheese and sugar mixture. Place the bottom halves of the croissants in a 9 × 13-inch metal or ovenproof glass baking pan. Pour the blueberry mixture over the croissants. Place the top croissant halves on top of the blueberries. Pour the melted butter over all. Bake for 30 to 45 minutes or until the mixture is bubbling and the croissants are lightly browned.

Serves 8

Berma's Cherry Pie

REBECCA KINNAMON NEFF, Forsyth County

"When I was growing up in the 1940s and '50s," Rebecca, now of Raleigh, told me of her childhood in Forsyth County, "our family did a lot of visiting with friends and relatives, especially on Sunday afternoons. These visits often included sharing food, sometimes entire meals. I especially enjoyed visiting my uncle Joe and aunt Edith Kinnamon and my uncle Sam and aunt Berma Kinnamon. Both aunts were good cooks, and I always looked forward to being served some special treat. My uncles, like my father, were great storytellers. On one occasion, Uncle Sam entertained us with a story about Aunt Berma's cream cheese cherry pie. It was a beautiful pie, but after a couple of bites, they agreed that something was not quite right. The pie had an 'off-taste' usually associated with milk from cows that had been grazing on wild onions and familiar to anyone who grew up drinking fresh farm milk. 'But how did that taste get into the pie?' they wondered. It turns out that instead of using plain cream cheese, Aunt Berma had mistakenly used cream cheese with chives! Aunt Berma may have given up on that recipe, because some years later I found this one for Berma's cherry pie among my father's collection of recipes, in his handwriting. It makes a dessert more like a cobbler than a typical pie, and it has no cream cheese."

> 1 1/2 cups sugar, divided
> 1 cup milk
> 1 cup self-rising flour
> 1/4 stick (2 tablespoons) margarine, softened
> 1 teaspoon vanilla extract
> pinch of nutmeg
> 1 quart fresh cherries, pitted, or 3 cans (14.5 ounces each)
>   cherries, drained
> 1 teaspoon lemon juice

PREHEAT OVEN to 400°. Blend together 1 cup of sugar, the milk, flour, margarine, vanilla extract, and nutmeg. Set aside. Mix the fruit with the remaining 1/2 cup of sugar and lemon juice, then pour the mixture into a deep-dish, 9-inch pie plate. Pour the batter over the fruit and bake for 10 minutes. Reduce the heat to 350° and bake another 25 to 30 minutes or until the top is nicely brown.

Serves 6 to 8

Quick Cobbler

WANDA BROOKS, Stanly County

Wanda Brooks is a practical cook who knows how to get things done. This basic recipe can be whipped up in a matter of minutes when you have fresh fruit available. You can make it with blueberries, apples, blackberries, or fresh peaches.

1 stick (1/2 cup) butter
2 cups of drained canned or fresh peaches or other fruit
1 cup self-rising flour
1 cup sugar
1/4 cup shortening
3/4 cup milk

PREHEAT OVEN to 350°. Melt the butter in a 1-quart baking dish. Pour the fruit into the dish over the butter. Combine the flour and sugar in a mixing bowl. Cut in the shortening; add the milk slowly, mixing with a fork. Drop the batter over the fruit by spoonful. Bake for 30 minutes.

Serves 6

Blackberry Cobbler

MARY DEAL, Rowan County

"I was born near a community called Mill Bridge on May 19, 1912," Mary Deal told me when I met her at the Lutheran Home at Trinity Oaks in Salisbury. She was bright eyed and carried an antique cookbook. Mary told me that she had owned it since 1936. It was crammed with recipes, recorded in her own handwriting, written on scraps of paper. She pulled out one for blackberry cobbler. "I got this recipe from my mother, Mary Esther Basinger," she continued. "You can use it with peaches or blueberries or any fruit."

1 cup all-purpose flour
1 cup sugar
1 egg
4 cups fresh blackberries (sweetened with sugar to taste)
1 stick (1/2 cup) butter, melted

PREHEAT OVEN to 375°. Combine the flour, sugar, and egg to make a crumb mixture. Set aside. Place the blackberries in a 1-quart baking dish. Sprinkle the crumb mixture over the blackberries. Pour the melted butter over the crumbs. Bake for 30 minutes.

Serves 4 to 6

Scuppernong Grape Pie

AMMIE BEST, Duplin County

The scuppernong grape is a famous North Carolina native. After his first expedition to Manteo Island in Dare County in 1584 Sir Walter Raleigh recounted the beauty of grapes that grew right down to the incoming tides on the coast. Other early explorers wrote that the land "was so full of grapes that the very beating and surge of the sea overflowed them. In all the world, a similar abundance was not to be found." Scuppernongs are beautiful, luscious globes that turn golden in late summer. The grapes have tough, sour skins, but the dense, sweet, and musky centers make succulent pies. This recipe came from my mother-in-law, Ammie Best of Warsaw. She had scuppernong grape vines in her backyard. It's a special favorite in the early fall.

1 unbaked 9-inch piecrust

Filling
1 pint scuppernong grapes (plus a
few more to munch on
while you prepare the pie)
1 cup sugar
2 egg yolks
3 tablespoons milk

Meringue
2 egg whites
1/2 cup sugar

PREHEAT OVEN to 350°. Cut the grapes in half and remove the seeds. Combine the sugar, egg yolks, and milk. Blend until smooth. Add the grape halves and mix until well incorporated. Pour the mixture into the prepared piecrust. Bake for 30 minutes.

To prepare the meringue, beat the egg whites until they form soft peaks. Continue beating as you add the sugar. Spread the meringue over the pie. Return the pie to the oven and bake for 10 minutes or until the meringue is golden brown.

Serves 6 to 8

Open-Face Peach Pie

BARBARA MICHOS, Wake County

Barbara Michos lives in her childhood home a block from North Carolina State University. She learned to cook from her mother, who attended a culinary school at the old Ambassador Theater on Fayetteville Street in Raleigh. Barbara's father raised a victory garden during World War II; the plot is still available to neighbors and friends who enjoy growing their own tomatoes, corn, and cucumbers.

Barbara is active in her local church, which raises money by auctioning off home-cooked meals in members' homes. "We have had airplane rides, trips to potteries with picnic lunches," she told me, "evenings of coffee and desserts, pool parties, breakfast served in bed, just about anything you can think of." The cooking must be exceptionally good; she estimated that it has raised more than $500,000 over the last twenty-five years. This pie is one of the reasons why.

1 unbaked 9-inch piecrust
1/3 to 1 cup of sugar (depending on how tart the peaches are)
1 1/2 tablespoons cornstarch
1 teaspoon cinnamon
5 to 6 fresh peaches, peeled (Barbara recommends Sand Hill peaches, in season)

1 1/4 cups milk or cream
1 egg
1 teaspoon almond extract
1/2 teaspoon vanilla extract
a little freshly grated nutmeg
1/2 cup shaved almonds (optional)

PREHEAT OVEN to 450°. Sprinkle a little of the sugar over the prepared piecrust. Combine the remaining sugar, cornstarch, and cinnamon in a bowl or plastic bag. Set aside. Peel the peaches, cut them in half, and remove the stones. Drop the peach halves, a few at a time, into the sugar mixture and dredge. Place them cut side up in the baking dish. Reserve the remaining sugar mixture.

Whip the egg with a fork; set it aside. In a saucepan, heat the milk or cream over medium-low heat until hot but not boiling. Pour a little of the hot milk into the egg and stir. Pour the egg mixture back into the hot milk; add the remaining sugar mixture and stir until the mixture becomes smooth. Add the almond and vanilla extracts, then pour the liquid over the peaches. Sprinkle the top with nutmeg and almonds. Bake for 10 minutes. Reduce the heat to 350° and continue baking for another 30 to 35 minutes. This pie is best served warm.

Serves 6 to 8

Peach and Sour Cream Pie

FOY ALLEN EDELMAN, Lenoir County

When it's golden, blushing, and juicy, I don't think there's any better food in the universe than a fresh, ripe peach. After I've satisfied my initial appetite in the early summer and dried the juice stains from my chin, I start to match them up with other ingredients, like spices and sour cream in this recipe for peach pie.

1 unbaked 9-inch piecrust
6 fresh peaches
3/4 cup sugar, divided
1/4 cup flour
1/2 teaspoon cinnamon

1 cup sour cream
1/4 cup sugar
1/2 teaspoon cinnamon

PREHEAT OVEN to 400°. Peel the peaches, cut them in half, and remove the stones. Place 11 of the peach halves in the piecrust, cut side down. Eat the remaining peach half. Mix 1/2 cup of the sugar, flour, and cinnamon together in small bowl. Sprinkle the mixture over the peaches. Swirl dollops of the sour cream evenly over the peaches. Sprinkle the remaining 1/4 cup sugar and the cinnamon over all. Bake for 10 minutes. Reduce heat to 350°. Bake for 30 minutes more, remove from oven, cool (if you can wait!), and cut yourself a slice. Refrigerate any leftovers.

Serves 6 to 8

Pear Pie

LYNN PIERCE, Warren County

Lynn Pierce comes from a large family of enthusiastic cooks. We sat at the dining room table in her home in Vaughn. It was covered with family cookbooks. Lynn picked up a book titled *Livers and Gizzards and Other Good Stuff.* "This is a cookbook that we did to help defray the costs of my second daughter's prescriptions," she told me. "Sallie had to have a liver transplant in 1999. At the time, her insurance company was not willing to help with her medicines. We sent out a letter on the internet, and in sixty days we had over 1,000 recipe responses. We came up with a total of 432 pages."

"My mother and mother-in-law were both excellent cooks," Lynn continued as she poured over their recipes in a loose-leaf notebook. "My mother-in-law was very generous in sharing her recipes. We have several that we continue to use in our family and pass them down from one generation to the next. My mother, Ruth Mincher, wrote a newspaper column called 'Worth Mentioning' and she would run her favorite recipes." Lynn began reading one of her mother's relish recipes with me. Suddenly she got very quiet. At the bottom of the page was a handwritten note that read, "Honey, Please don't give this recipe to any body—Love you, Mother."

Pear pie is one of Mrs. Mincher's recipes that Lynn wants to share.

piecrusts for a double-crusted, 9-inch pie
4 large ripe pears, peeled, cored, and thinly sliced
1 cup water
3/4 cup sugar (plus 1 tablespoon for sprinkling on crust)
1/4 cup cornstarch
1/2 teaspoon nutmeg
1/2 teaspoon cinnamon
1/2 teaspoon allspice

1/4 cup honey (local honey if you can get it)
1 tablespoon lemon juice
1/4 cup butter
whipped cream, ice cream, or cheddar cheese (optional)
a little nutmeg for garnish (optional)

PREHEAT OVEN to 425°. Fit one crust into a 9-inch pie plate. Set aside. Combine the pears and water in a saucepan over high heat. Bring to a boil. Reduce the heat and simmer for 5 minutes. Drain, saving 1/2 cup of the liquid. Set the pears and liquid aside. Combine the sugar, cornstarch, and spices. Separately, combine the reserved pear juice, honey, and lemon juice. Add the liquid to the sugar mixture. Add the cooked pears, stirring well to coat. Pour the pears into the prepared piecrust. Add the top crust. Trim, seal, and flute the edges. Cut slits in the top to allow steam to escape as the pie bakes. Brush the top of the pie evenly with melted butter and sprinkle with 1 tablespoon of sugar. Bake for 30 to 35 minutes. If edges brown too rapidly, cover them with foil. (Put the shiny side out so that it will reflect the heat away from the edges of the pie.) Serve warm or cool, with whipped cream and nutmeg, ice cream, or cheddar cheese.

Serves 6 to 8

Lemon Custard Pie

EMMALINE GEDDIE, Cumberland County

"I grew up near Stedman," Emmaline Geddie told me. "I was raised on a farm. On the first day of May we went barefooted. You see I'm barefooted right now. We raised cotton and beans and a little tobacco, and we had a huge garden. We raised butter beans, green peas, collards, turnips, beets, anything you could grow around here, okra. I used to go in the woods and pick blueberries. We had a cow; we had our own milk. My brothers would do the tending to the cow and all. I'd go out there and want to learn how to milk that cow and take my washcloth, you know, to do all that cleaning. 'Get away from here!' they'd say and squirt me with milk, and I'd have to come back to the house and wash my hair. If I'd had any sense, I wouldn't have wanted to milk that cow.

"My daddy would raise chickens and eggs and take the mule and wagon and drive to Fayetteville every Friday morning to deliver eggs to his customers. He'd be gone all day long. I looked forward to him coming home that afternoon, because I knew he'd bring me something. He'd bring me new shoes, and I'd wear them if they were too little and hurt my feet. He'd bring Johnny Cakes, cookies. I always knew I'd have a little something extra."

Emmaline learned to make lemon custard pie from simple ingredients typically on hand in the family cupboard. Wonderful long ago, this pie is still wonderful now.

1 baked 9-inch piecrust

Filling
1/2 cup all-purpose flour
1 cup sugar
2 cups milk
dash salt
3 egg yolks, beaten

grated zest of 1 lemon
juice of 1 lemon
1 tablespoon butter

Meringue
3 egg whites
1/2 teaspoon cream of tartar
1/2 cup sugar

PREHEAT OVEN to 350°. In a saucepan, combine the flour, sugar, milk, salt, and egg yolks. Cook over low heat, stirring constantly until the mixture thickens. Remove from heat. Add the lemon juice, lemon zest, and butter and mix until smooth; let it cool.

To make the meringue, beat the egg whites until stiff, then add the cream of tartar and sugar gradually. Pour the filling into the prepared crust. Spread the beaten egg whites over the top of the filling. Bake until the meringue is lightly browned, about 8 to 10 minutes. Remove from the oven and cool. Refrigerate any leftovers.

Serves 6 to 8

Lemon Meringue Pie
. . . .

KAY BAKER, Lenoir County

"This recipe means a lot to me," said Kay Baker of Kinston. "I had to pass a difficult chemistry class when I went to art school at East Carolina University during the 1970s. I was no good at chemistry, and I had to make a successful glaze to pass the course. There was a graduate student in the class who told me he would coach me if I would make him a lemon meringue pie like his mother made. I agreed. He said he liked it very lemony, and that was good because that's how my family made it. I went to the kitchen in what was then called New Dormitory, made the pie, and returned to the classroom with it. He ate the whole thing for lunch, helped me with my glaze, and I passed the course."

1 baked 9-inch piecrust

Filling
7 tablespoons cornstarch
1 1/2 cups sugar
1/2 teaspoon salt
1 cup boiling water
4 egg yolks
1/4 cup butter
1/2 cup lemon juice
1 tablespoon grated lemon zest

Meringue
1 teaspoon lemon juice
4 egg whites
4 to 5 tablespoons sugar, or to taste

COMBINE the cornstarch, sugar, salt, and lemon juice in a saucepan. Beat the egg yolks in a small bowl, then blend them into the cornstarch mixture. Stir constantly as you gradually add the water. Place the saucepan over medium heat. Cook, stirring for 8 to 10 minutes, until the mixture becomes thick and smooth and is too thick to continue stirring. Remove from heat. Stir in the butter and lemon zest. Cool to room temperature without stirring. Pour the filling into the prepared piecrust.

To make the meringue, preheat oven to 375°. Combine the lemon juice and the egg whites; beat with an electric mixer until soft peaks form. Add the sugar, one tablespoon at a time, beating until glossy after each addition. Spread the meringue lightly over the filling. Bake until lightly browned, about 6 to 8 minutes.

Serves 6 to 8

Lemon Chiffon Pie

SARAH SAWYER ALLEN, Lenoir County

The gelatin makes this dessert a bright, shimmering delight.

1 baked 9-inch piecrust
4 eggs, separated
1 1/2 cups sugar, divided
grated zest of 1 lemon
1/2 cup lemon juice
1 envelope unflavored gelatin
1/3 cup cold water

IN A DOUBLE BOILER over boiling water, combine the egg yolks, 1 cup sugar, lemon zest, and lemon juice. Stir constantly until the mixture thickens. Remove from heat. Soften the gelatin in the cold water. Combine the gelatin with the egg mixture, and then stir until smooth. Set aside. Beat the egg whites until soft peaks form. Add 1/2 cup sugar and continue beating until the sugar is well incorporated. Gently fold the egg whites and sugar into the hot mixture. Do not overmix. Pour the filling into the prepared piecrust and refrigerate. This pie is good served cold with a dollop of whipped cream.

Serves 6 to 8

PIES, COBBLERS, DUMPLINGS, AND A SONKER 123

Lemon Icebox Pie

KATHERINE SAWYER WARD, Bertie County

If there's a culinary heaven, lemon icebox pie must be in a prominent place there. It's a cool crowd pleaser that disappears quickly, so Katherine Sawyer Ward of Windsor says to make two.

2 9-inch graham cracker crusts
1 pint whipping cream
3/4 cup sugar
1 can (8 ounces) frozen lemonade, thawed
1 can (14 ounces) sweetened condensed milk
    (Katherine uses Eagle brand)
1 1/2 teaspoons fresh lemon juice

WHIP the cream until stiff peaks form. Continue whipping while gradually adding the sugar. Set aside. In a separate bowl, combine the lemonade, condensed milk, and lemon juice. Stir until well blended. Fold in the whipped cream. Divide the filling evenly between the prepared piecrusts. Chill before serving.

Serves 6 to 8

Affinity (Banana Cream) Pie

JACKI EPPERSON, Durham County

"The delicious pie will satisfy keen appetites. When used as a dessert it should be served as individual tarts or other small portions," reads a note introducing the pie section in a handmade cookbook Jacki inherited from her husband's grandmother, Leone Webb Epperson.

Called affinity pie in Leone's book, this is an old version of banana cream pie. I like to take it to new mothers.

Jacki Epperson with Leone Epperson's homemade cookbook

1 baked 9-inch, deep-dish piecrust

Filling
2 cups milk
3/4 cup sugar
1/4 cup all-purpose flour
1/4 cup cornstarch
1/4 teaspoon salt
2 egg yolks, beaten
2 cups milk
1 teaspoon grated lemon zest
2 bananas

Meringue
2 egg whites
1/2 cup sugar

HEAT the milk in a saucepan until it just comes to a boil. Remove it from the burner and blend in the egg yolks. Combine the sugar, flour, cornstarch, salt, and egg mixture in a double boiler over medium heat. Stir the mixture constantly until it becomes thick, about 20 minutes. Mix in the lemon zest. Chill for 1 hour.

To make the meringue, beat the egg whites on high speed until they peak. Blend in the 1/2 cup sugar.

To assemble the pie, preheat oven to 400°. Slice the bananas into the bottom of the prepared piecrust. Pour the custard evenly over the bananas. Spread the meringue over the bananas and custard. Bake for 8 to 10 minutes or until brown. Chill well before serving. Refrigerate any leftovers.

Serves 6 to 8

Strawberry Pizza Pie

MARIE BATCHELOR, Duplin County

I visited Marie Bachelor at her home near Beulaville on a fall day. The roses in Marie's garden were still blooming, and late tomatoes hung heavily on the vines. "I was born and raised in Rose Hill," Marie told me. "I love to grow stuff. I love to grow things from seed. When I was a child, strawberries were a big crop; they [the growers] had to go off to Wilson County to find someone to pick them. Strawberries and biscuits were our favorites I enjoy cooking for my family because it brings people together." Strawberry pizza pie is a great way to do just that.

Crust
1 1/2 cups all-purpose flour
1 1/2 sticks (3/4 cup) butter,
   softened
1/2 cup pecans, chopped
1 tablespoon sugar
1/2 teaspoon salt

Filling
1 cup cream cheese, softened
2 cups 10X powdered sugar
2 cups nondairy whipped topping
   or whipped cream
1 pint strawberries, cleaned,
   trimmed, and chopped

Topping
3/4 cup sugar
1/4 cup cornstarch
1/3 cup water
1 teaspoon almond extract
2 or 3 tablespoons of strawberry gelatin, to add color

PREHEAT OVEN to 350°. Mix all the crust ingredients together and press into the bottom of a 9 × 13-inch baking pan. Bake for 15 minutes. Remove and let cool.

To make the filling, blend the cream cheese and sugar together until smooth. Add the whipped topping and spread the filling over the crust. Spread the strawberries over the filling.

For the topping, put all the ingredients in a saucepan and cook over medium heat until thick. Cool slightly and pour over the berries. Chill before serving.

Serves 6 to 8

Pineapple Pie

ELIZABETH LOWDER, Iredell County

Elizabeth's pineapple pie conveys a satisfying taste contrast between the sweet dairy center and the lemon juice mixed with pineapple.

1 9-inch graham cracker (or other cookie) crust
1 to 2 tablespoons lemon juice (to taste)
1 can (14 ounces) sweetened condensed milk
   (Elizabeth prefers Eagle brand)
1 cup cream cheese, softened to room temperature
1 can (20 ounces) crushed pineapple, drained, or equivalent
   amount of fresh, crushed pineapple

MIX the lemon juice with the condensed milk. Blend in the cream cheese. Add the pineapple and mix well. Pour the filling into the graham cracker crust; chill until firm. Refrigerate any leftovers.

Serves 6 to 8

Pineapple Coconut Pie

ELIZABETH SANDERLIN, Currituck County

I met Elizabeth Sanderlin one warm June day at her home near Shawboro. She was a North Carolina Home Demonstration agent from 1951 to 1969. In 2006, in recognition of her work, an auditorium was named in her honor in the Currituck Center for the North Carolina Cooperative Extension Service.

Neighbors came and went as we sat on Elizabeth's screened-in porch overlooking a cornfield. Known as Miss Currituck, Elizabeth was born in 1904 in Moyock. "[My father] had a general merchandise store," she told me. "That means he had everything in there from medicine, dried goods, candy, nuts, and bolts. Country stores at that day and time carried everything; they weren't specialized. We lived beside my father's store. Oftentimes he would send them [local people] over to eat, and we never knew how many folks there were going to be, because there wasn't a place in Moyock to eat. A lot of them came up a creek in a boat from Gibbs Woods and other places, and they'd have to have some meal; so he'd send them to the house.

"[One] thing they made a lot of was pies. You'd make the pies the day before. Every Sunday you'd have to have pies made. We used a lot of pumpkin, lemon pies, and then chocolate. We had whipped cream to go on the pumpkin pie," she continued. "My cousin, Elizabeth Reed, served this when I visited her once," said Elizabeth of her pineapple coconut pie recipe.

1 unbaked 9-inch piecrust
1 can (20 ounces) crushed pineapple, drained
1/2 cup flaked coconut
1 cup sugar
1 stick (1/2 cup) butter, softened
4 eggs
1 teaspoon vanilla extract

PREHEAT OVEN to 350°. Combine the pineapple, coconut, sugar, butter, eggs, and vanilla extract and blend well. Pour the filling into the prepared piecrust. Bake for about 35 to 40 minutes, or until the pie is firm in the center. It will be pretty and brown when done.

Serves 6 to 8

Coconut Pie

CARRIE CATHERINE BYRD, Swain County

Carrie Catherine Byrd's coconut pie is made from a nourishing milk-and-egg custard. Add the coconut and flavoring, and you have a time-honored dessert.

1 baked 9-inch piecrust
3 cups milk
1 cup sugar
1/4 cup all-purpose flour
1/4 cup cornstarch
1/8 teaspoon salt
2 egg yolks
3 tablespoons butter or margarine
1/2 teaspoon vanilla extract
1 cup flaked coconut
whipped cream for garnish (optional)

IN A DOUBLE BOILER, bring 1 1/2 cups of the milk to a boil. In a separate bowl, combine the sugar, flour, cornstarch, salt, egg yolks, and remaining milk. Gradually stir this into the hot mixture. Cook until thick. Remove from heat; add the butter, vanilla extract, and coconut and stir until the butter is melted and the coconut is well incorporated. Pour the filling into the prepared piecrust. Chill before serving. Garnish with whipped cream, if desired. Refrigerate any leftovers.

Serves 6 to 8

Impossible Coconut Pie

MRS. ALMA ROUNTREE, Camden County

"This has been around a long, long, long time, and I've used it a lot," says Alma Rountree of South Mills. "It's a good recipe. The self-rising flour is what makes the crust. That's the reason why they call it impossible coconut pie. So you don't have to put in a separate crust."

4 eggs, well beaten
1 3/4 cups sugar
1/2 cup self-rising flour
2 cups milk
1 teaspoon vanilla extract
1/2 stick (1/4 cup) butter, melted
1 cup flaked coconut

PREHEAT OVEN to 350°. Grease two 9-inch pie plates. Mix all the ingredients together. Divide the filling evenly between the two pans. Bake for 30 to 40 minutes.

Makes 2 pies, 6 to 8 servings each

Coconut Butterscotch Pie

RUTH SMITH GREENE, Caldwell County

"I had one sister that baked pies, and one that baked cakes, and one that made cookies," said Ruth Smith Greene, a retired teacher from Granite Falls. "We always had company; we always boarded the teachers; and all the preachers stayed at our house especially during evangelistic crusades. If my daddy saw someone passing the road, we didn't know who'd be coming through to the dining room. He'd just say 'just come on in' and there'd be plenty.

"I brought four of my friends home from Appalachian College in 1932 when I was a freshman there," Ruth continued. "They just loved this. We used delicious homemade pastry, butter and whole milk. It's a pretty pie, and it's good."

1 baked 9-inch piecrust

Filling
2 cups milk
1/2 cup all-purpose flour
1 cup brown sugar
1/4 teaspoon salt
3 egg yolks, slightly beaten
1/2 stick (1/4 cup) butter
1 teaspoon vanilla extract
3/4 cup flaked coconut

Meringue
3 egg whites
1/2 cup sugar
1/4 cup flaked coconut

PREHEAT OVEN to 425°. Combine the milk, flour, sugar, and salt in a saucepan. Warm the mixture over medium heat, stirring constantly, until it thickens. Add some of the hot mixture to the beaten egg yolks. Stir this warmed egg mixture back into the saucepan. Continue cooking over medium heat until custard forms. Remove from heat. Add the butter, vanilla extract, and coconut. Mix well and pour the filling into the prepared piecrust.

Make the meringue by beating the egg whites until stiff. Continue beating while gradually adding the sugar. Spread the meringue over the pie filling. Sprinkle with coconut. Bake until golden brown, about 8 to 10 minutes. Chill before serving.

Serves 6 to 8

German Chocolate Pie

PHYLLIS MCNEIL, Hoke County

This scrumptious German chocolate pie, like many other heirloom recipes contained in this collection, uses canned milk. Evaporated milk was invented in the 1880s and used extensively during the early twentieth century as a safe alternative to fresh milk, which spoiled quickly. Since household refrigerators became widely used during the 1930s and 1940s, evaporated milk has mainly been used to add rich taste and smooth texture to desserts.

1 unbaked 9-inch piecrust
1 cup sugar
dash salt
1/4 cup cocoa
1/2 cup evaporated milk
1/2 teaspoon vanilla extract
1 egg, well beaten
3 tablespoons butter, melted
3/4 cup flaked coconut
1/3 cup chopped nuts

PREHEAT OVEN to 350°. Combine the sugar, salt, and cocoa. Add the milk, vanilla extract, egg, and butter. Blend well. Stir in the coconut and nuts. Pour the filling into the prepared piecrust. Bake for 40 minutes or until the edges are set. Cool completely before serving.

Serves 6 to 8

Mama's Christmas Pie

GERRY MAYO BEVERIDGE, Cartaret County

"I'm sharing my mother's Christmas pie," Gerry Mayo Beveridge of Beaufort told me. "Some people call this Japanese fruit pie. The only time we ever saw a coconut when I was a child was when Mama and Daddy would buy one at Christmastime, and we'd crack it, and drink the milk out of it, and grind it up. We had raisins at Christmastime, and we had a pecan tree in the backyard; so we had the three main ingredients. Living on a farm, we had plenty of lard for the pie pastry and plenty of butter for the pie filling. Of course, the sugar had to be bought, which might have been traded for some chickens or some eggs that Mama took to the store."

1 unbaked 9-inch piecrust
1 cup sugar
1 stick (1/2 cup) butter, softened
pinch salt
2 eggs, beaten
1 tablespoon cider vinegar
1/2 cup flaked or shredded coconut
1/2 cup pecans or walnuts, chopped
1/2 cup seedless golden raisins

PREHEAT OVEN to 325°. Mix the sugar, butter, salt, eggs, and vinegar in a mixing bowl. Add the coconut, nuts, and raisins. Mix well, then pour the filling into the prepared piecrust. Bake for approximately 40 minutes. Cool before serving.

Serves 6 to 8

Betsy's Pecan Pie

KATHERINE SAWYER WARD, Bertie County

"This is my daughter, Betsy's, recipe," my cousin Katherine Sawyer Ward of Windsor told me. The gooey, crunchy texture and sweet taste will make Betsy's pecan pie a cherished dessert generation after generation.

1 unbaked 9-inch piecrust
1 cup dark corn syrup
1/2 cup sugar
3 eggs, beaten
1 tablespoon butter
1 tablespoon all-purpose flour
1 teaspoon baking powder
1/2 teaspoon salt
2 teaspoons vanilla extract
1 cup pecans, chopped

PREHEAT OVEN to 350°. Mix the corn syrup, sugar, and eggs in a saucepan over medium heat. When well blended, add the butter. When the butter is melted, remove the saucepan from the heat; set aside to cool. Combine the flour, baking powder, and salt. Add the wet ingredients to the flour mixture. Add the vanilla and stir until smooth. Fold in the pecans. Pour the filling into the prepared piecrust. Bake for 45 minutes.

Serves 6 to 8

Pecan Raisin Pie

. . . .

MARTHA BARNES, Pitt County

Here's an old-fashioned rendition of pecan pie copied from one of the cookbooks my aunt Martha handwrote in the 1950s.

1 unbaked 9-inch piecrust
1 cup brown sugar
3 eggs, separated
1 tablespoon butter, softened
1 cup pecans, chopped
1 cup raisins, chopped
1/4 teaspoon cinnamon
1/4 teaspoon nutmeg
pinch salt
1/2 teaspoon vanilla extract

PREHEAT OVEN to 450°. Combine the sugar, egg yolks, butter, nuts, raisins, spices, and salt; set aside. In another bowl, beat the egg whites until soft peaks form. Add the vanilla extract, then fold in the sugar mixture. Pour the filling into the prepared piecrust. Bake for 10 minutes. Reduce heat to 350° and continue baking until a knife blade stuck in the center of the pie comes out clean, about 30 minutes.

Serves 6 to 8

Peanut Chess Pie

EDDIE LOU WEST, Northampton County

Eddie Lou West lives near Jackson in a historic house. "The house is known as Mowfield Plantation," she told me. "It was built in between 1790 and 1805. What really put it on the map was a race horse named Sir Archie, and he's the foundation sire for all American thoroughbred race horses today.

"I grew up on peanuts. All my life I have been more on peanuts than anything else, knowing how to cook them from when they were green until when you would roast them, and always wanting to learn how to do a good peanut pie that would sort of be a hit with all the families at reunions or church socials or things like that. I came up with one, and I call it peanut chess pie, but I like to make it in the little pies. It will freeze real well. If you don't want to put it in the little pie shells, it'll do two 9-inch pies; so that you can keep one for the family, and take one to someone if they're sick in the neighborhood, or someone that you know that likes your peanut pie."

16 3-inch tart pans lined with piecrust, the equivalent of 2 regular sized 9-inch piecrusts
1 stick (1/2 cup) butter, melted
1 1/2 cups sugar
1 tablespoon cornmeal

3 extra-large eggs
1 tablespoon vinegar
1 teaspoon vanilla extract
1 1/2 to 2 cups peanuts, roasted, skinned, and coarsely chopped

PREHEAT OVEN to 325°. In a mixing bowl combine the butter, sugar, and cornmeal. Mix well and set aside. In a separate bowl, beat the eggs slightly. Add the vinegar and vanilla extract. Blend well, then add to the sugar mixture. Blend in the peanuts. Spoon the filling into the prepared pastry shells. Bake for 30 minutes.

Makes 16 individual pies or 2 pies that serve 6 to 8 each

Peanut Butter Pie

BARBARA EVERETT ROBERSON, Beaufort County

Barbara Everett Roberson grew up in Little Washington but was living across the street from me near Garner, Wake County, when I met her. In 2001, my neighbor Donna Matthews Saad and I watched as out-of-state cars crowded into the Roberson's yard filled with friends and relations who were in town to attend the funeral of Barbara's husband. Donna and I cooked a meal for the bereaved family: roast turkey, gravy, rice, green beans, and pound cake. As fate would have it, Barbara soon reciprocated, crossing the street to my home with roast pork, corn, and peanut butter pie to comfort me after my father's death. These acts of compassion—expressed with food—led to a lasting friendship between Barbara and me. Not surprisingly, much of our friendship is spent in her kitchen or mine.

As the locals say, when Barbara cooks she really "puts her foot in it," meaning, of course, "it's really good!" This is a wholesome pie that can even be shared with friends who have diabetes.

1 9-inch graham cracker (or other cookie) crust
18-ounce package low-fat cream cheese, softened
1/4 cup peanut butter
1 small package (4-serving size) sugar-free vanilla pudding,
*   regular or instant*
1 cup skim milk
1 teaspoon vanilla extract
1/4 to 1/2 cup sugar-free nondairy whipped topping

BEAT TOGETHER the cream cheese, peanut butter, pudding mix, and milk. The resulting mixture will appear lumpy, but do not overbeat. Stir in the vanilla extract. Pour the filling into the prepared piecrust. Chill until set, usually about 3 hours. Garnish with whipped topping.

Serves 6 to 8

Cousin Elizabeth's Chocolate Pie

HARRIET GUYTON, New Hanover County

"My cousin, Elizabeth Townsend, was renowned in Onslow County for her chocolate pie," Harriet Guyton of Southport told me. "The ingredients for it were staples in her kitchen like bread and milk would be in mine. It was always expected if there was a bake sale or a church or family gathering, that Elizabeth would bring her chocolate pie. My father was the youngest of twelve children, so you can imagine that family reunions were quite large. On arrival at such a reunion, I quickly scouted out the dessert table to make sure I got a coveted slice of her pie."

The last time Harriet saw her, Elizabeth was in her seventies and terminally ill, but she had prepared a pie for Harriet and her mother; they devoured every morsel as soon as they reached home.

1 baked 9-inch piecrust	**Filling**
	2 cups sugar
Meringue	*11 tablespoons flour, sifted*
3 egg whites	*6 tablespoons Hershey's cocoa*
6 tablespoons sugar	*3 cups water or milk*
	3 egg yolks, beaten
	1 stick (1/2 cup) butter
	1 teaspoon vanilla extract

PREHEAT OVEN to 325°. To make the filling, combine the sugar, flour, and cocoa in a saucepan. Add the water or milk and egg yolks. Cook over medium heat, stirring constantly, until the mixture thickens. Remove from heat and add the butter and vanilla extract. Pour the filling into the prepared piecrust.

To make the meringue, beat the egg whites until stiff. Gradually add sugar, beating until smooth. Pile lightly on top of the filling. Bake until lightly browned, about 15 minutes.

Serves 6 to 8

Chocolate Chess Pie

MARIANNE PORTER ABSHER, Bladen County
RUTH SCRUGGS PORTER, Rutherford County

The Porter family of Bladen County traces roots to Mary
Anne Bush and Preston Porter, who married in 1898 and
set up housekeeping on their farm in the White Oaks section of the county near Kelly. Preston farmed, ran a saw-
mill, trapped animals for their pelts, met the local ferry
to haul freight up the river, and picked up mail for the
Kelly area. Sadly, both Preston and Mary Anne died young,
Preston in 1928 and Mary Anne in 1935, but not before
they produced eight children. Some of the Porter children
remained on the family farm after their parents' deaths;

*Marianne Absher (right)
and Vicki Little introduce
Ella Little to water from
the family well at the
Porter houseparty*

others relocated to Georgia and Florida in order to find jobs. The children
married and moved away, but they kept close ties with home and the Kelly
area and visited as often as they could. As the families expanded, so did
their need for a place to stay when they came home. In 1941, they moved
the event to White Lake, where the reunion has been held annually ever
since during the third week of July. The local family brought plenty of
farm-fresh food, and the tradition of gathering each summer was born.

I was fortunate to visit the family in 2006 when 149 Porters moved
into the Future Farmers of America camp on White Lake for the entire
week to hold the annual Porter houseparty. They had gathered from nine
states. The menu schedule is posted all year on their website so that everyone can creatively prepare dishes to share. Kitchen helpers range in
age from toddlers to folks in their sixties.

The Friday I was there, the entire clan was going to the family farm for
a hayride that snaked past pastures of grazing cows. At the end of the trail
we stopped at a rustic cabin to enjoy watermelon. The cabin was sited on
a little pond where one of the eight-year-old boys got dunked to cool him
off after he got a little bit out of the family behavioral boundaries. The
cabin does not have electricity but does have a pump, where I saw one-

year-old Ella Little being informally baptized by her grandmother and aunt, Marianne Porter Absher.

"Mother's full name is Ruth Scruggs Porter," Marianne Porter Absher told me. "She was born in Rutherford County but has lived in Bladen County since she married into the Porter family in 1941. This pie is a family icon at the Porter houseparty we hold every summer at the Future Farmers of America camp on White Lake."

1 unbaked 9-inch piecrust	*2 eggs*
1 1/2 cups sugar	*1 teaspoon vanilla extract*
3 tablespoons cocoa	*3 ounces evaporated milk*
1/2 stick (1/4 cup) butter, softened	

PREHEAT OVEN to 350°. Lightly beat together the sugar, cocoa, butter, eggs, vanilla extract, and evaporated milk. Pour the filling into the prepared piecrust. Bake for 45 minutes or just until the filling is set. Cracks on the surface of the pie are not unusual. Top a slice with whipped cream or ice cream and be prepared to enjoy it with a large glass of cold milk.

Serves 6 to 8

Chocolate Amaretto Pie

MARTHA BLAINE WOODS, Macon County

"My mother, Nell Cabe, first enjoyed this pie in a restaurant near here where she pestered the chef until he gave her the recipe," Martha Blaine Woods of Franklin told me. "She made it her own by changing some of the ingredients and adding the amaretto."

Crust
1/3 cup water
1/3 cup vegetable oil
1 to 2 cups all-purpose flour
1/4 cup graham cracker crumbs

Filling

1 cup sugar

1/2 cup cornstarch

1/4 cup cocoa

2 cups milk, divided

3 eggs yolks, beaten

1/2 stick (1/4 cup) butter

1 teaspoon vanilla extract

1/4 cup amaretto liqueur

Meringue

3 egg whites

1/2 cup sugar

1/4 teaspoon baking powder

TO MAKE the crust, preheat oven to 375°. Combine the water, oil, and enough flour to thicken to a working consistency. Roll the dough out on a floured pastry board or cloth. Sprinkle and gently pat the graham cracker crumbs into the pastry. Carefully transfer the dough to a 9-inch pie pan and press it into place. Bake for 8 to 10 minutes.

To make the filling, combine the sugar, cornstarch, and cocoa. Warm 1 cup of the milk over medium heat until it is almost boiling; then stir in the sugar mixture and egg yolks. Stir constantly as the mixture quickly thickens. Continue to stir as you gradually add the remaining milk. As soon as the mixture is thick and smooth, remove it from the heat. Stir in the butter, vanilla extract, and amaretto. Blend well. Pour the filling into the prepared piecrust.

Make meringue by beating the egg whites. When they become frothy; continue beating while adding the sugar very slowly, making sure all the sugar dissolves. Add 1/4 teaspoon baking powder and continue beating until the egg whites are stiff. Spread the meringue on top of the filling and bake at 350° until golden brown, about 8 minutes.

Serves 6 to 8

Blender Chocolate Pie

ELIZABETH LOWDER, Iredell County

"This is one of my daughter's recipes. Everyone wants her to bring this pie to a covered-dish supper," said Elizabeth Lowder of Mooresville.

1 unbaked 9-inch piecrust
1 cup evaporated milk
2 eggs
1 cup sugar
1/4 cup all-purpose flour

3 tablespoons cocoa
1/2 stick (1/4 cup) butter, softened
pinch salt
1 teaspoon vanilla extract

PREHEAT OVEN to 400°. Combine the milk and eggs in a blender and blend until smooth and light. In a separate bowl, combine the sugar, flour, cocoa, butter, and salt. Add one-half of this mixture to the blender. Blend until smooth. Add the rest of the mixture and the vanilla extract. Blend. Pour the filling into the prepared piecrust. Bake for 20 to 25 minutes or until the center rises.

Serves 6 to 8

Fudge Pie

HELEN COCHRANE, Guilford County

Chocolate and pecans make a delectable combination in Helen's fudge pie.

1 unbaked 9-inch piecrust
1 stick (1/2 cup) butter, softened
1/4 cup cocoa
1/4 cup all-purpose flour

1 cup sugar
1/4 teaspoon vanilla extract
2 eggs
pecans, chopped (optional)

PREHEAT OVEN to 350°. Combine the filling ingredients and mix well. Pour the filling into the prepared piecrust. Bake for 25 minutes. Good served warm with whipped cream.

Serves 6 to 8

Grandma's Quick Chocolate Pie

RON JOHNSON, Franklin County

Grandma's pie is as comforting as a cup of hot chocolate on a cold day, but you don't have to wait for winter to enjoy it.

1 baked 9-inch piecrust

Filling
1/2 cup sugar
1/2 cup all-purpose flour
5 tablespoons Nestle Nesquik
3 egg yolks
1 3/4 cups milk
1/4 cup margarine, softened

Meringue
3 egg whites
1/2 cup sugar
1/2 teaspoon vanilla extract

PREHEAT OVEN to 350°. Combine the sugar, flour, and Nesquik. In a separate bowl, combine the egg yolks and milk and beat well. Add the dry ingredients and the margarine to the egg yolk mixture; blend until smooth. Pour the mixture into a saucepan and cook over medium heat, stirring constantly, until thickened. Pour the filling into the prepared piecrust.

Make the meringue by beating the egg whites until stiff. Add the sugar and vanilla extract. Spread the meringue over the filling and bake until golden brown, about 8 minutes.

Serves 6 to 8

Refrigerator Pie

MONA DEAN CLARK, Bladen County

"When we were living in Wilmington, and my dad worked in the shipyard [during World War II]," said Mona Dean Clark of Elizabethtown, "we had two boarders that stayed with us. They were like big brothers. It was a bad time. I remember the excitement in Wilmington when it was announced that the war was over, and I was just a little girl, but I was amazed that people just went wild. The church bells were ringing all over the city. There was this man who was on the back of a truck with a load of lumber, and he was throwing the lumber off the truck as they went down the street and just waving and shouting! It was just amazing how delighted people were.

"I remember that we used to drive all the way from Wilmington to Dublin [Bladen County] to get meat, because you couldn't get it in Wilmington," she continued. "My grandmother on my father's side raised cows and pigs and a big garden, and so we never went without, because she did raise them. But now my husband's family has always raised their food, and they had ration tickets just like anyone else, but his mom had a big family, and so she cooked with molasses and corn syrup and things like that. They still had sweets. And he said he could remember sitting by the fire picking out hickory nuts, of all things, to go into a molasses cake. And I know down at my husband's family, we'd all gather down in the kitchen, and it was crowded because there were so many of us, but we didn't notice it because we were having such a wonderful time together.

"I was just looking at a recipe that my mother fixed during the war when we were staying in Wilmington and you know, during the war you couldn't find some of the ingredients you needed to cook with, and I thought, 'This is a great recipe for hard times.' My mom, Olive Kirby Hester, just called it refrigerator pie."

Mona Dean Clark

2 *cups crushed vanilla wafers (enough to line a 9-inch pie plate)*
1 *package (4-serving size) raspberry gelatin*
1 *can (12 ounces) evaporated milk, refrigerated overnight*
   (Mona Dean prefers Carnation)
1 *can (8 ounces) crushed pineapple or equivalent of fresh pineapple*
1/2 *cup sugar*

LINE the bottom of a pie plate with the crushed vanilla wafers. Drain the liquid from the canned pineapple into a large measuring cup; add water to make 1 cup of liquid. Dissolve the sugar and gelatin in this liquid; chill the mixture, but do not let it congeal. In a large mixing bowl, beat the evaporated milk until stiff. Fold in the chilled gelatin mixture and the crushed pineapple. Pour the filling over the vanilla wafers, chill, and enjoy.

Serves 6 to 8

Sour Cream Pie

FOY ALLEN EDELMAN, Lenoir County

This is a great dessert for any season. For variety, you can use a graham cracker crust with half a cup of chopped pecans added instead of a traditional piecrust.

1 unbaked 9-inch piecrust

Filling
1 1/2 cups sour cream
1 cup sugar
1/4 cup all-purpose flour
2 egg yolks
3/4 cup raisins
1/2 teaspoon cinnamon
1/4 teaspoon cloves
1/4 teaspoon allspice
1/4 teaspoon nutmeg
1/4 teaspoon vanilla extract

Meringue
2 egg whites
1/4 cup sugar

PREHEAT OVEN to 350°. Beat the sour cream, sugar, flour, and egg yolks together until well blended. Stir in the raisins, spices, and vanilla extract. Blend well. Pour the filling into the prepared piecrust. Bake for 50 to 60 minutes. Remove the pie from the oven but leave the oven heated.

To make the meringue, beat the egg whites until they form peaks. Gradually add 1/4 cup sugar. Spread the meringue over the filling. Bake 8 to 10 minutes or until the meringue turns golden brown. Remove from oven. Cool. Enjoy. Refrigerate any leftovers.

Serves 6 to 8

Grandma Davis's Blueberry Biscuits

PEGGY LANIER, Onslow County

"I grew up in rural Onslow County. When I was a child, my invalid grand-mother lived with us, so our house was a hubbub of family activity surrounding her. People came to visit all the time. Sundays were especially busy. My parents were members at a small Primitive Baptist church where several pastors rotated between its three different locations. The churches had originally been built in different communities to accommodate members back in the horse and buggy days. By the time I was growing up, people rode in cars and could get to any of the three churches. On the first Sunday in the month, the preachers held services at the church in our community, and afterwards lots of members came to Sunday dinner at our house. People from Wilmington (forty-five miles away) came to services at our church, and it wasn't unusual for them to come to our house for dinner and to spend the afternoon. When dinner was ready, the men ate at the table first, next the adult women ate, and finally the children. My mother had many people to feed, but she would always set aside food for me, making sure I always got something I liked even though I had to wait for the children's turn to eat. I have such happy memories of gathering around the table and enjoying good food. I can still smell the food, hear the laughter and the heartfelt singing of hymns on those wonderful Sunday afternoons.

Blueberry biscuits were then and still are a special family favorite. My mother, Minnie Davis, told me that she learned to make them from her mother. Mama would go out around the fields where wild blueberries grew. She remembers gathering them and bringing them home for her mother to make biscuits. When I grew up, the recipe became a community favorite as well as a family favorite of all mama's four children and their children. Even as years passed, and the grown grandchildren married and moved further away, it was still a priority for all of us to gather at mama's house. As soon as one of the grandchildren would mention blueberry biscuits, mama's hands would be rolling out the dough. Blueberry biscuits seemed to become one of mama's favorite ways of saying to each of her children and grandchildren just how much she loved us."

5 cups self-rising flour
1 cup shortening
1 cup cold water
3 pints frozen blueberries
2 tablespoons sugar per biscuit

PREHEAT OVEN to 350°. Line a 9 × 13-inch baking pan with aluminum foil and coat the foil with nonstick cooking spray. Combine the flour, shortening, and water to make a stiff dough. With floured hands, divide the dough into 12 equal pieces. Knead each piece until very firm. Roll each piece of the dough out as thin as possible but thick enough that it won't tear when you pick it up. Lay the rolled out dough on your hand and place 1 cup of blueberries on it. Sprinkle the blueberries with 2 tablespoons of sugar. Pull the sides of the dough together tightly over the blueberries, and pinch them together to seal in the blueberries. Remove the excess dough. Repeat with the remaining dough. Place the biscuits, seal side down, in the prepared pan. Bake for 45 minutes. Serve hot with some of the syrup that has accumulated in the bottom of the pan poured over each biscuit.

Makes a dozen biscuits

Blackberry Dumplings

PAT CARROLL, Wake County

"These are good served hot with vanilla ice cream or whipped cream," Pat told me.

1 cup self-rising flour
1/4 cup shortening
enough milk to make a sticky dough
1/2 teaspoon salt

4 cups fresh blackberries

2 2/3 cups sugar

1 stick (1/2 cup) butter cut into 8 pats

PREHEAT OVEN to 375°. Grease a 9 × 13-inch baking dish. Wash the blackberries well and set aside. Combine the flour, shortening, milk, and salt to make the biscuit dough. When the dough is sticky but not wet, divide it into 8 equal portions and, on a floured surface, roll out each portion into a circle. To assemble the dumplings, place 1/2 cup of the blackberries onto each circle. Sprinkle 1/3 cup of sugar over the blackberries, and place a pat of butter on top. Fold the circles in half over the filling, using a fork to seal the dough. Arrange the dumplings in the prepared dish. Bake for 25 to 30 minutes.

Makes 8 dumplings

Lazy-Day Sonker

LISA TURNEY, Surry County

Northwestern North Carolina is famous for a unique pastry known as sonker. Lisa Turney is from the Brown Mountain Community. I visited her at Horne Creek Living Historical Farm State Historic Site, where she is the site director. Dedicated to the study, preservation, and interpretation of North Carolina's agricultural heritage, the former Hauser family farm is being used to show what "typical" family farm life was like in North Carolina's Northwest Piedmont region in the first decades of the twentieth century. Buildings are being renovated or reconstructed; heirloom varieties of fruits, vegetables, and field crops are being grown; and livestock is being raised in ways that produce representative breeds, many of which are now classified as rare and endangered.

When I asked Lisa if sonker is anything like cobbler, she referred me to the publication "Sonkers . . . Surry Style," published by the North Carolina Cooperative Extension in Surry County. It states, "Sonker is another name for a cobbler that can be made in several different variations."

Lisa explained, "Many of the older sonker recipes began by lining a deep dish with a layer of pastry and baking it. Then, a layer of fruit was added, followed by another later of pastry, and it was baked until golden brown. Today's cooks, however, often do not have a lot of time to spend in the kitchen. So, someone modified a sonker recipe down to its basic components. What follows is a recipe that is so simple there is no need to write it down. It can be quickly committed to memory. It's called a Lazy Day Sonker, but almost everyone who has eaten it would agree that it tastes like a lot of effort went into it. It's just wonderful." If you take a shine to this special dish, you can attend the Sonker Festival held each fall in nearby Dobson.

1 stick (1/2 cup) butter
1 cup self-rising flour
1 cup milk
1 1/2 cups sugar, divided
2 to 4 cups fresh fruit (strawberries, blueberries, peaches,
    cherries, blackberries)

PREHEAT OVEN to 350°. Wash and drain the fruit and set aside. Put the butter in a 1- or 1 1/2-quart casserole dish and place it in the oven. Remove when the butter is melted. Combine the flour, milk, and 1 cup sugar to form a smooth batter. Pour the batter over the melted butter. Do not stir. Spread the fruit evenly over the batter and sprinkle the remaining 1/2 cup sugar over the fruit. Bake for 30 minutes or until golden brown on top. Serve hot with fresh cream, whipped cream, or ice cream.

Serves 4 to 6

Cookies, Bars, and Teacakes

Old-Fashioned Teacakes

Butter Cookies

Alice's Wonderful Sugar Cookies

Soft Sugar Cookies

Peanut Butter Sugar Cookies

Melt-in-Your-Mouth Shortbread Cookies

Oatmeal Crispies

Jellies

Granny Helton's Chocolate Chip Cookies

Fudge Squares

Chocolate Macaroons

Old-Fashioned Molasses Cookies

Moravian Molasses Cookies

Smithville Duffy Cakes

Apple Tart Roll-Ups

Hazel's Cinnamon Cookies

Cinnamon Sticks

Ginger Snaps

Gingerbread Bars

Mannie's Butterscotch
   Cookies

Coconut Melt-Aways

Old-Fashioned Gingerbread
   Men with Royal Icing

Hermits

Nut Cookies

Nutty Fingers

Crumb Nut Bars

Crunchy Bran Drops

Almond Crescents

German Sweet Cakes

Butter Pecan Cookies

Chess Bars

Date Pinwheels

Peanut Cookies

Cheesecake Bars

Cream Cheese Clouds

Fruitcake Cookies

Krisan's Sour Cream Cookies

Rocks

Lemon Squares

Date Loaf

Caramel Squares

Chew Bread

Jet-Age Brownies

Brownies in a Jar

Angel Food Drop Cookies

S'more Crispy Squares

Fry Bread

Fastnachts

Bourbon Christmas Cookies

E DITH HEARD, our neighbor on Highland Avenue in Kinston in the early 1950s, made especially good peanut butter cookies. One day, when my older brother Will was five, she offered him a cookie still warm from the oven. He stuffed it in his mouth and gobbled it down. My mother said, "Will, what do you say to Mrs. Heard?" Without hesitation, he looked up at Mrs. Heard's face and answered, "Give me another one." And who doesn't want another one? These small bites of pure pleasure are easy to make; they fill a house with tantalizing aromas and call everyone to the kitchen to sit down and enjoy them with a glass of milk or cup of coffee.

During the 1600s the Dutch settlers who came to New York City handed out *koekjes*, "little cakes," on New Year's Day as a special snack. By the 1800s Americans called them cookies and had developed many varieties including jumbles, rocks, and teacakes. Today North Carolinians make a diverse assortment, from old favorites like molasses cookies to rich treats like cream cheese clouds. Some easy recipes include angel food drop cookies from Mecklenburg County, crunchy bran drops from Davidson County, and coconut melt-aways from Orange County. Janet Manuel's nutty fingers are molded in the palm of the hand. During the holiday season you might try Carrie Blair's bourbon Christmas cookies or my mother's recipe for fruitcake cookies; or use your favorite cookie cutters on Mary Charles Pawlikowski's gingerbread men or Wanda Brooks's butter cookies, then decorate them with icing and colored sugar. Tammy Stoker's jet-age brownies and Donna Saad's chess bars are good when you're in the mood for very rich tastes. You may remember Dianne Lambert's caramel squares as butterscotch chewies or blondies.

Cookies are portable snacks. They fit nicely into lunch boxes, picnic baskets, and care packages that send a taste of home to a college student or a member of the military. I have happy memories from my student days of sharing cookies and conversation in Carroll Hall at North Carolina State University in Raleigh. Returning on Sunday nights from weekend trips home, my suitemates brought shirt boxes lined with waxed paper and filled with fresh, sweet, chocolate chip cookies. We got together to savor them as we traded tales about weekend adventures. Liberty Heath shares recipes for chocolate chip and sugar cookies, good for packing and mailing, great for anyone with the munchies.

By the way, I wasn't able to obtain Edith Heard's recipe, but Shannon Coleman's peanut butter sugar cookies are included; you might try making them to charm the children—big and small—in your neighborhood.

Tips for Baking Cookies

* Invest in nonstick insulated cookies sheets. These marvelous inventions bake cookies evenly and help to prevent burnt edges.

* If you have time, refrigerate cookie dough for an hour or so before baking. This makes the dough easier to roll out or drop. When you do bake the cookies, they'll keep their shape without running.

* Cooling cookies on a rack prevents moisture from making them soggy when they are stored.

Old-Fashioned Teacakes

PAT BULLOCK CARROLL, Wake County

"My parents were sharecroppers," Pat told me. "We lived on a farm near Wake Forest while I was growing up with my seven brothers and sisters. We didn't have a lot of fancy desserts, but my mom, Lyda Hamilton Bullock, would always make teacakes for our birthdays. We could have all we wanted. Sometimes she would pick out black walnuts to use for flavoring. We didn't get stockings at Christmas, but we did get oranges. My mother would save the peels and dry them. Then she'd wrap them in a muslin towel and beat them up into a tasty powder. When she didn't have any nuts, she would use the dried orange peel to flavor the teacakes. They were delicious."

Pat Carroll in her garden

2 cups sugar

1 stick (1/2 cup) butter, softened

2 eggs, beaten

1/2 cup buttermilk

2 teaspoons lemon extract or 1 1/2 teaspoons vanilla extract

3 cups self-rising flour

PREHEAT OVEN to 400°. Grease cookie sheets. Combine all the ingredients except the flour in a large mixing bowl. When well blended, add the flour a little at a time until it is well incorporated and a smooth dough is formed. Roll out the dough on a floured surface until it is about 1/2 inch thick. Cut out circles of dough using a small drinking glass and place on cookie sheets. Bake until edges are brown, about 10 to 12 minutes. Cool cookies on cookie sheets for 2 to 3 minutes before removing to wire racks. Cool completely before storing.

Makes 4 dozen

Butter Cookies

WANDA BROOKS, Stanly County

I was one of those children who liked to "help" in the kitchen. I remember being in the kitchen with Ida Mae and my mother in the winter back then. My job was to squish red, green, and yellow food coloring into granulated sugar with my fingers until I made colored sugar. Ida Mae would roll out vanilla colored dough until it was flat. I stood at the kitchen table on the red vinyl seat cover in a metal chair as we studiously cut out cookies with cutters shaped like reindeer, Christmas tree ornaments, and bells. My mother carefully lifted them onto baking sheets with a spatula. Then we decorated them with the colored sugars, baked them, and admired the results. My parents left some of these cookies in the living room on Christmas Eve with a Coca-Cola so that busy Santa would have a snack as he made his way around the world that night. I was always gratified when adults, especially Santa, enjoyed one of my culinary "creations." My first gift on Christmas Day was seeing the crumbs from those cookies. You can share this experience with children you know by using Wanda Brooks's butter cookies recipe, but you don't have to wait for Christmas.

Cookies

1 stick (1/2 cup) butter, softened (Don't substitute margarine.)
1/2 cup shortening
1 cup sugar
3 eggs
1 teaspoon vanilla extract
3 1/2 cups all-purpose flour
2 teaspoons cream of tartar
1 teaspoon baking soda

Colored Sugar

1 cup sugar
a few drops yellow, red, blue, and green food coloring

TO MAKE the cookies, cream the shortening and sugar. Add the eggs and vanilla extract and blend well. Combine the flour, cream of tartar, and baking powder and then blend it into the sugar mixture until well incorporated. Gather the dough together into a ball, wrap it in plastic wrap, and chill it well in the refrigerator—about 2 hours. When you are ready to bake, preheat oven to 350°. Roll out the dough on a floured surface to 1/8-inch thickness. Cut with cookie cutters. Place on an ungreased baking sheet.

To make the colored sugar, divide the sugar among 4 small bowls. Squeeze a few drops of food coloring into each. With your fingers, rub the food coloring into the sugar until it is evenly distributed. Sprinkle the cookies with the sugar. Bake for 8 to 10 minutes or until golden brown. Immediately remove from baking sheets and cool on racks.

Makes 4 dozen

Alice's Wonderful Sugar Cookies

ALICE ALLEN-GRIMES, Craven County

"About 30 years ago I was visiting my college roommate in Burlington, N.C.," says my first cousin, Alice Allen-Grimes from New Bern. "One of her mother's friends brought over these cookies. They were wafer thin and had sugar crystals pressed into the tops; it made them shiny. She gave me the recipe; I've been making them ever since. You can use plain white granulated sugar, or you can purchase a bigger crystal sugar in various colors from a specialty-baking store. If I make them around Easter or for a baby shower, I use a little colored sugar to make them yellow or pink. They're also pretty when they're white. During the holiday season I sprinkle them with red and green sugar. Twenty-year-old friends that I've known since they were children call me up begging to know when they'll be ready. I probably make 100 dozen each Christmas and put them in brown lunch bags that I've stenciled with decorations.

"The main tip is to keep the dough fluffy. My secret is to whip the sugar and butter by hand with a wooden spoon. I call them wonderful sugar cookies."

2 sticks (1 cup) butter, softened
1 cup 10X powdered sugar
1 cup granulated sugar
2 eggs
1 cup canola or other vegetable oil
2 teaspoons vanilla extract
4 1/4 cups all-purpose flour
1 teaspoon baking soda
1 teaspoon salt
granulated sugars in various colors (optional)

USE A WOODEN SPOON to cream the butter until fluffy. Continue beating with a spoon while adding in the sugars. When well blended, add the eggs, one at a time, beating well after each addition. Continue beating until the batter is creamy and light. Add the oil and vanilla extract. In a separate bowl, combine the flour, baking soda, and salt. Add the dry ingredients to the creamy mixture and blend until a smooth dough forms. Wrap the dough in waxed paper; refrigerate for several hours.

When you are ready to bake, preheat oven to 350°. Prepare the cookie sheets for baking by lightly spraying them with a nonstick cooking oil like Pam. Form the dough into balls about 3/4 inch in diameter. Place the balls on a cookie sheet 2 inches apart. Using a small drinking glass dipped in sugar slightly flatten the balls. Bake for 10 to 13 minutes. As you remove each batch of cookies, wipe any sugar from the cookie sheet with a paper towel. You will *not* need to re-spray them, as they will retain enough oil to keep the cookies from sticking.

Makes 5 to 6 dozen

Soft Sugar Cookies

LIBERTY HEATH, Caldwell County

"This makes a very creamy, buttery, soft sugar cookie," said Liberty. "For variety, I make my cookies a little smaller, 1/2 teaspoon at a time, and frost them so they make sugar cookie sandwiches. You can then dip them in melted chocolate and dress them up even more."

Cookies
3 cups all-purpose flour
1 teaspoon cream of tartar
1/2 teaspoon baking soda
1/4 teaspoon salt
2 1/4 sticks (1 1/8 cups) butter,
    softened
1 cup sugar
2 large eggs
3 tablespoons buttermilk
2 teaspoons vanilla extract

Frosting (optional)
1/3 cup butter
1 1/2 teaspoons vanilla extract
2 cups 10x powdered sugar
1/4 cup milk

PREHEAT OVEN to 375°. Combine the flour, cream of tartar, baking soda, and salt, then set aside. In another bowl, cream the butter until light. Add the sugar and beat until fluffy. Add the eggs, one at a time, beating well after each addition. Add the buttermilk and vanilla extract and blend well. Add the dry ingredients and blend dough until smooth. Chill the dough for at least 20 minutes. Drop by teaspoon 1 inch apart onto ungreased cookie sheets. Bake for 9 to 12 minutes, or until the edges of the cookies are golden brown. Remove immediately from cookie sheets to a cooling rack. Frost, if desired.

To make the frosting, combine all the ingredients and blend until smooth. Spread onto the cooled cookies.

Makes 4 to 5 dozen

Peanut Butter Sugar Cookies

REBECCA SHANNON COLEMAN, Cherokee County

"This is from my grandmother," said Rebecca Shannon Coleman of Murphy. "The recipe originated in the Old Mountaineer Bakery over thirty-five years ago. My grandmother was a baker there. We would go up and stay with my grandmother for vacations and after school and she would always make them."

Rebecca Shannon Coleman

3/4 cup white sugar
3/4 cup brown sugar
2/3 cup creamy peanut butter
2/3 cup lard or shortening
3/4 cup all-purpose flour
1 egg

PREHEAT OVEN to 350°. Cream the sugars, peanut butter, and shortening until fluffy. Add the egg and blend well. Add the flour and blend until smooth. Roll the dough into 1-inch balls and place on ungreased cookie sheets. Gently flatten the balls with a fork to form a crisscross pattern on top of the cookies. If the fork sticks in the dough, wet it between cookies. Bake the cookies for approximately 10 to 15 minutes or until golden brown.

Makes about 4 dozen

Melt-in-Your-Mouth Shortbread Cookies

MARY CHARLES PAWLIKOWSKI, Nash County

"I give these as Christmas gifts," said Mary Charles. "Folks get very ornery if I skip a year."

2 to 2 1/2 sticks (1 to 1 1/4 cups) butter, softened
1/2 cup sugar
2 1/2 cups all-purpose flour
1/4 teaspoon salt

PREHEAT OVEN to 375°. Cream 1 cup butter and the sugar until light and fluffy. Gradually add the flour and salt. If the dough is too stiff to roll out at this point, add more butter, a little at a time until the dough is pliable enough to roll out. Roll out the dough on a lightly floured surface to 1/2-inch thickness. Cut it into 1-inch squares. Place the squares on ungreased cookie sheets and prick each square in several places with a fork. Bake for 12 to 18 minutes or until they are a pale golden color. Remove immediately from cookie sheets and cool completely on wire racks. Store in an airtight container at room temperature.

Makes 6 1/2 dozen

Oatmeal Crispies

LUCIE LEA ROBSON, Mecklenburg County

You can omit the walnuts and dates from this recipe if you prefer a simpler oatmeal cookie. Either way, they hit the spot with a glass of milk or iced tea or a cup of coffee and are a great side item for ice cream or sherbet.

1 cup shortening (Lucie Lea prefers Crisco)
2 eggs, beaten
1 cup light brown sugar
1 cup white sugar
1 1/2 cups all-purpose flour
1 teaspoon salt
1 teaspoon baking soda
1 teaspoon vanilla extract
3 cups quick-cooking oatmeal
1/2 cup walnuts and dates, chopped

CREAM the shortening and sugars until fluffy; add the eggs and beat well; combine the flour, salt, and baking soda and add to the creamed mixture. Blend until smooth. Add the vanilla extract, oatmeal, and nuts and/or dates, if desired. Continue blending until well mixed. Divide the dough in half and, using waxed paper, form each half into a log approximately 1 1/2 inches in diameter. Chill the logs until firm. To bake, preheat oven to 350° and grease baking sheets. Slice the dough into 1/2-inch-thick rounds and arrange the rounds about 1 inch apart on the prepared baking sheets. Bake for 10 minutes. Remove immediately from cookie sheet to cooling rack.

Makes 5 dozen

Jellies

MARIE SOLOMON KAHN, New Hanover County

"My mother, Louise Fick Solomon, used to make butter cookies," Marie Solomon Kahn of Wilmington told me. "We call them jellies, because they're little round cookies about an inch and a half in diameter with a depression in the middle where you put a dab of jelly. They're real short, butter cookies, very good."

3 sticks (1 1/2 cups) butter, softened
3 egg yolks
1 cup sugar
3 cups self-rising flour, more if needed
1 teaspoon vanilla extract
jelly

PREHEAT OVEN to 375°. Grease and flour cookie sheets. Cream the butter and sugar until very light. Add the eggs and flour and blend well. With floured hands, form the dough into 1 1/4-inch balls and arrange them on the prepared cookie sheets 1 inch apart. Using your thumb, make a depression in the middle of each. Fill with jelly. Louise suggests red currant or mint jelly at Christmas, but any flavor will do. Bake for 10 to 15 minutes or until golden brown.

Makes 4 dozen

Granny Helton's
Chocolate Chip Cookies

LIBERTY HEATH, Caldwell County

"You can make the dough and freeze it for later so you can have home-made cookies in a pinch," says Liberty Heath of her grandmother's cookie recipe. "I freeze mine in a log shape so I can cut off the number of cookies we want to eat and put back the rest for later. These cookies are good to make and use the base for chocolate chip cookie ice cream sandwiches."

1/2 cup shortening (Liberty prefers butter-flavored Crisco)
1 stick (1/2 cup) butter
1/4 cup white sugar
1 1/4 cups brown sugar
1/2 teaspoon baking soda
2 eggs
1 1/4 teaspoons vanilla extract
2 1/2 cups all-purpose flour
1 1/2 cups milk chocolate chips
1/2 cup semisweet chocolate chips
1 1/2 cups black walnuts (optional)

PREHEAT OVEN to 375°. Using an electric mixer, beat the shortening and butter on medium to high speed for 20 to 30 seconds. Add the sugars and baking soda. Beat until smooth, scraping down the sides so that all ingredients mix well. Add the eggs one at a time, beating well after each addition. Add the vanilla extract. Add the flour 1/2 cup at a time until all is incorporated and the dough is smooth. Don't overbeat; the more you work the dough the tougher the cookies will be. Fold in the chocolate chips and nuts, if desired. Drop by teaspoon 1 inch apart on ungreased baking sheets. Bake for 8 to 10 minutes. Remove immediately from baking sheets and cool on racks.

Makes 5 dozen

Fudge Squares

MARGUERITE HUGHEY, Buncombe County

Marguerite recorded a note at top of this recipe: Mrs. Van Dyke, 1949. These no-bake squares are light and delicious.

2 squares (2 ounces) unsweetened baking chocolate
1 cup evaporated milk
2 cups sugar
1/4 teaspoon salt
1 tablespoon butter
24 marshmallows
1 teaspoon vanilla extract
3 cups graham cracker crumbs
1 cup English walnuts, chopped

GREASE a 9 × 13-inch baking pan. Combine the chocolate and evaporated milk in a saucepan over low heat. When the chocolate is melted, add the sugar, salt, and butter and stir until the sugar is dissolved and the butter is melted. Cook until the mixture reaches the soft ball stage, about 230° on a candy thermometer. Remove the saucepan from the heat. Stir in the marshmallows, vanilla extract, graham cracker crumbs, and nuts. Mix well. Press the batter into the prepared pan and chill overnight. Cut into squares.

Makes about 30 squares

Chocolate Macaroons

JACKIE EPPERSON, Durham County

"I got this recipe for a wedding gift from a church friend of my late mother-in-law," Jacki told me. "It came originally from Mattie Belle Powell of Durham." You can use brown wrapping paper to line the cookie sheet. These freeze well.

2 egg whites
1/2 teaspoon salt
1/2 cup sugar
3/4 cup semisweet chocolate chips
1 teaspoon vanilla extract
1/2 cup shredded coconut

PREHEAT OVEN to 325°. Line a cookie sheet with brown or parchment paper. Grease the paper. Beat the egg whites until foamy. Add the salt. Add sugar gradually, beating until the mixture stands in stiff peaks. Melt the chocolate chips; let cool slightly. Fold the chocolate, vanilla extract, and coconut into the egg whites until they are well incorporated. Drop by teaspoon 1 inch apart onto the prepared cookie sheet. Bake for 20 minutes. Cool before removing from paper.

Makes 2 dozen

Old-Fashioned Molasses Cookies

MYRTLE AND RICHARD FREEMAN, Montgomery County

Old-fashioned or not, the molasses, spices, sugar, and lemon in these cookies make a flavor combination that never goes out of style.

4 cups all-purpose flour
2/3 teaspoon baking powder
1 teaspoon ginger
1/3 teaspoon cinnamon
1/2 teaspoon nutmeg
1/2 teaspoon salt
3/4 cup shortening
1 1/2 cups brown sugar
3/4 cup molasses
2 eggs
2/3 teaspoon baking soda
1/2 cup hot water
1 tablespoon lemon juice

PREHEAT OVEN to 375°. Lightly grease cookie sheets. Combine the flour, baking powder, spices, and salt; set aside. Cream the shortening and sugar until creamy and soft. Add the molasses and gradually beat in the eggs. When well blended, add the flour mixture a little at a time, mixing well after each addition. Combine the hot water and lemon juice and whisk in the baking soda; work the liquid into the dough until it has a smooth consistency. Drop by teaspoon 1 inch apart onto the prepared cookie sheets. Bake for 8 minutes. Cool on racks. Store the cookies in an airtight container.

Makes about 70 to 85 cookies

Moravian Molasses Cookies

BRENDA MALONE ZIMMERMAN, Rowan County

"When I was a child, my family lived in Greensboro," Brenda Malone Zimmerman of Salisbury told me. "One of our next-door neighbors was a Moravian. We called her Granny Atchison. She kept these fine, thin wafers in her cookie jar."

1 cup dark molasses
1/3 cup lard or shortening
1 tablespoon butter
1 cup dark brown sugar
1 1/2 teaspoons baking soda
1 tablespoon cold water

1 1/2 teaspoons cloves
1 1/2 teaspoons cinnamon
1 1/2 teaspoons ginger
1 1/2 teaspoons allspice
4 cups all-purpose flour

COMBINE the molasses, lard, and butter; mix well. Add the sugar. Beat well. Wisk together the baking soda and water and stir briskly into the molasses mixture. Add the spices and flour and stir until well incorporated. Wrap the dough well and refrigerate for 24 hours before baking. When ready to bake, preheat oven to 350°. Lightly grease cookie sheets. Roll out the dough as thin as possible on a generously floured surface. Cut into desired shapes (circles, stars, gingerbread men). Bake until golden brown, about 10 minutes. Do not overbake. Store in air-tight containers. Dough may be frozen for later use.

Makes 5 to 6 dozen

Smithville Duffy Cakes

SUSAN CARSON, Brunswick County

"In 1839 Mrs. Mary Duffy of Smithville was operating an 'eating house' on the water skirts [i.e., the waterfront]—we do not know exactly where," said Susan Carson, a cook, historian, and resident of Southport. "This was a very popular place with residents and visitors alike. She liked children and kept them supplied with little teacakes or sugar cookies which the children called Duffy cakes.

"The actual recipe for these came to me from my great aunt, who called it Grandma's teacakes. It is almost identical to one that I found in an old English cookbook that my daughter brought me from London. Since so very many of the early settlers in our area were English, I feel that this recipe is authentic. I have baked these cookies for many people, and they are always liked. Daddy told me that Aunt Babe, his mother's sister, used to bake these for him and the other children when they were growing up. He was born in 1889."

1 stick (1/2 cup) butter, softened
1 cup sugar, plus 1/2 cup for sprinkling
1 egg
1/4 cup milk or cream
1 teaspoon vanilla extract
2 cups all-purpose flour
1/2 teaspoon salt
1 teaspoon baking soda
1/2 cup raisins

PREHEAT OVEN to 375°. Grease a cookie sheet. Combine the butter, sugar, egg, milk or cream, and vanilla extract. Beat until light and fluffy. In a separate bowl, combine the flour, salt, and baking soda, then stir the dry ingredients into the creamed mixture. Blend until smooth. Chill the dough at least two hours. Roll out small portions of the dough on a lightly floured surface to the desired thickness. Cut out cookies with a 3-inch cookie cutter and place on the prepared cookie sheets; sprinkle the cookies with sugar, and press one or two raisins into the center. Bake about 8 minutes or until lightly browned. Cool and store in a tightly covered container.

Makes about 4 dozen cookies

Apple Tart Roll-Ups

FLOSSIE JOHNSON, Wilkes County

"I live seven miles from where I was born in Wilkes County up near the racetrack," Flossie told me. "I haven't wanted to go anywhere else. I love to travel and to go to places, but I'm always happy when I come home." She is a well-known hostess in the area where she lives and the author of two cookbooks, *Flossie's Favorites* and *Flossie's Favorites Too*. "I learned how to cook from Mama and Grandma," she said. "I knew how much seasoning and what to put into things. I still have a garden now. I remember my grandmother, Alice [pronounced Elsie] Williams [born about 1870], on my mother's side well. Her house was always immaculate. She cooked on a fireplace. She hung the pots over the fire. Grandma always had the most delicious food. She made homemade pies. She made what we called cake, but Grandma called it sweetbread. She would make big pans and bake it in the stove and when it was ready, cut it out in little squares and, when it was cool, put it in a crock container that kept it fresh. She had what she called a springhouse where she put her milk. She made her own butter, and put it down in the springhouse in little jars to keep it cool. When we were little, we'd go to see grandma and she'd go get the sweetbread and glasses and we'd go to the springhouse and she'd pour us a glass of that cold milk and we'd have the cake.

"My mother, Courtey Williams, was born in 1901," Flossie continued. "[When I was growing up] we had a wood stove. Everybody had wood floors with the linoleum on them. We used lamps, wood stoves to cook on, wood fireplaces and stoves to heat the house. We didn't have power. I remember that my dad had a Delco [battery] that we operated off. Mama had a washing machine that operated off of that. It was comfortable. I think the winters were colder then. We used to set water out. It would freeze; then we'd have ice to keep things cold. Daddy bought an icebox. If we had fresh meat, we put it in the icebox. Mama always had some kind of dessert. We always had honey and jelly or molasses, we called it 'something sweet.' Most of the time Mama had some kind of pie made, apple pie, peach pie, peach cobbler. Mama used to make something like a tart."

enough pie dough for 2 crusts

3 cups fresh apples, peeled, cored, and chopped

1 cup sugar

1 teaspoon cinnamon

1 teaspoon ginger

1 stick (1/2 cup) butter, cut into small pats

PREHEAT OVEN to 350°. Grease a 9 × 13-inch baking pan. Roll out the pie dough on a floured surface into a rectangle, approximately 12 × 24 inches. Evenly distribute the apples across the dough. Combine the sugar, cinnamon, and ginger and sprinkle over the apples; then dot with the butter pats. Roll up the apples into the dough lengthwise to form into a log. Using a sharp knife, slice the log into 1 1/2-inch-thick roll-ups. Place the roll-ups in the prepared baking pan. Bake for 25 minutes or until golden brown.

Makes 18 roll-ups

Hazel's Cinnamon Cookies

BRENDA MALONE ZIMMERMAN, Rowan County

Brenda Malone Zimmerman is the director of activities and volunteer services at the Lutheran Home at Trinity Oaks in Salisbury. "In 1990, Lutheran Home Resident Council sponsored a cookie project for the people who were in Desert Storm," she told me. "We asked volunteers to bring in cookies. We had residents baking cookies, and we sent about sixty dozen overseas. While we were doing that, one of the participants, Hazel Lyerly, was going to be out of town; so she brought a package of cookies by my office early, and I set the box on top of my file cabinet. About two weeks after we mailed the rest of the cookies, I found the box. I had forgotten they were there. Not knowing how they would be, I went ahead and opened them. I served some to the residents, and now they're one of my favorite cookies. You can make the dough up ahead of time.

You roll the cookie dough into balls about the size of a large marble. You can freeze the dough, yank it out of the freezer, and bake them when you have company. It makes a really crisp cookie."

2 3/4 cups all-purpose flour	2 eggs
2 teaspoons cream of tartar	1 cup shortening
1 teaspoon baking soda	1 teaspoon vanilla extract
1/4 teaspoon salt	1/4 cup cinnamon
1 3/4 cups sugar, divided	

COMBINE the flour, cream of tartar, baking soda, salt, and 1 1/2 cups sugar; set aside. Separately, beat the eggs with the shortening and vanilla extract. Add the flour mixture and blend until smooth. Refrigerate the dough until stiff. In a small bowl mix 1/4 cup sugar with the cinnamon. When ready to bake, preheat oven to 350°. Roll the dough into 1/2-inch balls and then roll the balls in the cinnamon sugar. Place on ungreased cookie sheets and bake for 12 to 15 minutes or until lightly browned.

Makes 4 dozen

Cinnamon Sticks

. . . .

MARIE SOLOMON KAHN, New Hanover County

"Max's [Marie's husband's] aunt used to make cinnamon sticks," Marie, of Wilmington, told me. "They were kind of like a macaroon. She was a maiden lady. Her name was Stella Shrier. She was the Clerk of Court here for years. She was real particular about who she would give them to. You kind of had to beg if you wanted some of Aunt Stella's cinnamon sticks. I'm not sure how she determined it, but they were good." The original recipe says to wax the baking pan with beeswax.

3 egg whites, beaten stiff	1 3/4 cups 10X powdered sugar
2 heaping teaspoons ground cinnamon	2 cups ground almonds

PREHEAT OVEN to 350°. Grease and flour cookie sheets. Fold the cinnamon into the egg whites. Combine the egg whites with the sugar and almonds. Form the dough into 2-inch-long crescents and place them on the prepared cookie sheets. Bake for 10 minutes.

Makes 4 dozen

Ginger Snaps

LUCIE LEA ROBSON, Mecklenburg County

The fragrance of the spices fills up your home when you bake ginger snaps. You can use cookie cutters like gingerbread men or just circles. The cookies remain crunchy when stored in an airtight container. If you want to draw faces on the cookies, Wanda Brooks suggests the decorator icing found in the Icings, Fillings, and Sweet Sauces chapter.

1 cup shortening	*4 cups all-purpose flour*
1 cup brown sugar	*1 teaspoon baking soda*
1 egg	*1 teaspoon salt*
1 cup dark molasses	*4 teaspoons ginger*
1 tablespoon white sugar	*1/2 teaspoon cinnamon (optional)*
	1/2 teaspoon cloves (optional)

PREHEAT OVEN to 350°. Grease a cookie sheet. Cream the shortening and brown sugar together in a mixing bowl until fluffy. Add the egg, molasses, and white sugar. Mix until smooth. In a separate bowl, combine the flour, baking soda, salt, ginger, cinnamon, and cloves. Combine the wet and dry ingredients. Blend together until smooth. Roll out the dough on a floured surface to 1/4-inch thickness. Cut out the dough with cookie cutters and place on the prepared cookie sheet. Bake for 8 minutes.

Makes 5 dozen

Gingerbread Bars

HELEN COCHRANE, Guilford County

Gingerbread bars are delectable treats that are easy to take along for a sweet snack in the car or to share with friends.

3/4 cup shortening or canola oil
2 cups all-purpose flour
1 cup sugar, plus 1/4 cup, reserved
2 teaspoons baking soda
1 teaspoon cinnamon
1/2 teaspoon cloves
1/2 teaspoon ginger
1/2 teaspoon salt (optional)
1/4 cup molasses
1 egg

PREHEAT OVEN to 375°. Grease a 10 × 15-inch jellyroll baking pan. Melt the shortening in a large saucepan. Cool for 5 minutes and stir in 1 cup sugar. In a separate bowl, combine the flour, baking soda, spices, and salt, if desired. Add the flour mixture to the wet ingredients and blend well. Press the dough into the bottom of the prepared baking pan. Sprinkle with the remaining 1/4 cup sugar. Bake for 10 to 12 minutes. Remove from the oven and let cool for 5 minutes. Cut into bars. Cool completely.

Makes 48 to 54 bars

Mannie's Butterscotch Cookies

MARGARET BARNES FAHRINGER, Robeson County

"Mannie is my maternal grandmother, Margaret Shaw Barnes MacNeill, for whom I am named," said Margaret Barnes Fahringer. "She was born in 1886 in Maxton. My mother, Mary MacNeill Fahringer, was born in 1922, and I was born in 1953. In my mom's notebook she calls them 'Mother's Butterscotch Cookies,' but all my life we called them 'Mannie's Butterscotch Cookies.'

"The diameter and thickness really affect the hardness and softness, so you have to learn to perfect this just right," Margaret continued. "For crisp, almost biscuitlike tea cookies, slice them slightly less than 1/4 inch thick. For softer cookies that are crisp around edges and softer in the middle, slice about 1/2 inch thick. I recommend trying various thicknesses to see how you like them. Do not overcook, but just turn the bottom barely brown."

1 1/2 sticks (3/4 cup) butter	*3 1/2 cups all-purpose flour*
2 cups brown sugar	*2 teaspoons baking powder*
2 eggs, beaten	*pinch salt*
	1 teaspoon vanilla extract
	1 1/2 cups pecans, chopped

IN A MEDIUM SAUCEPAN, melt the butter. Add the sugar and blend well. Add the eggs, mixing until smooth. Combine the flour, baking powder, and salt and add to the wet mixture, stirring until well incorporated. Add the vanilla extract and blend until the dough is smooth. Stir in the pecans. Chill the dough until it is stiff. Form the dough into logs approximately 1 3/4 inches in diameter. Refrigerate the dough until ready to bake. When ready to bake, preheat oven to 350°. Grease cookie sheets. Cut the logs into 1/4- to 1/2-inch-thick slices and place them on the prepared cookie sheets. Bake for about 10 minutes or until golden brown.

Makes 4 to 5 dozen

Coconut Melt-Aways

HARRIET ROBSON, Orange County

These yummy little bite-sized cookies disappear almost as quickly as you can make them.

1 stick (1/2 cup) butter, softened
1/2 cup shortening
3 tablespoons sugar
2 cups all-purpose flour

1 cup flaked coconut
approximately 2 cups of 10x
    powdered sugar, for dipping

CREAM the butter, shortening, and sugar. Add the flour and blend until smooth. Stir in the coconut. Divide the dough into two equal parts and form each piece into a log approximately 1 inch in diameter. Wrap each log in waxed paper. Chill at least an hour and a half in the freezer. When you're ready to bake, preheat oven to 375°. Cut each log into 3/4-inch-thick slices and place them on ungreased cookie sheets. Bake approximately 15 minutes or until they are very light brown. While the cookies are still warm, coat both sides with the confectioners sugar and then let cool.

Makes 3 dozen

Old-Fashioned Gingerbread Men with Royal Icing

MARY CHARLES PAWLIKOWSKI, Nash County

"You can bake Christmas ornament hooks into the cookies for hanging on your tree," Mary Charles Pawlikowski told me. "If you want to decorate them, use raisins for the eyes, nose, etc. Bows and other clothing details can be made with colored icing. I use Royal Icing for decorating the cookies. Of course, you can make the cookies in any shape you want. When I smell these cooking, I smell the holidays coming."

Cookies	Icing
2 cups sugar	*1 cup 10x powdered sugar*
1 cup shortening	*1 tablespoon butter, melted*
2 eggs	*a little milk*
1/2 cup molasses	
4 cups all-purpose flour	
1 teaspoon ginger	
1 teaspoon cloves	
1 teaspoon nutmeg	
1 teaspoon baking soda	
1/4 teaspoon salt	
2 teaspoons cinnamon	

CREAM the sugar and shortening until light and fluffy. Blend in the eggs and molasses until the batter is smooth. In a separate bowl, combine the flour, ginger, cloves, nutmeg, baking powder, salt, and cinnamon. Blend the two mixtures together. Wrap the dough tightly in waxed paper or plastic wrap and place in the refrigerator for several hours. When ready to bake, preheat oven to 325°. Roll out the dough on a floured surface to 1/8-inch thickness and cut into desired shapes. Bake for 10 to 12 minutes or until the edges of the cookies are light brown. Cool completely before decorating.

For the icing, blend the powdered sugar with the butter. Add enough milk to make a stiff icing. Fill a pastry bag or plastic ziploc bag (with one corner snipped off) with icing and pipe faces or designs on the cookies.

Makes 3 to 4 dozen, depending on size of cookies

Hermits

MARGUERITE HUGHEY, Buncombe County

Marguerite obtained this recipe from a Mrs. Brooks in 1957. The first ingredient on the list was Spry, a vegetable shortening developed by the Lever Brothers during the Great Depression when lard was in short supply. Spry quickly became a competitor to Crisco, another vegetable shortening developed in 1910. Spry was promoted by a nationally syndicated radio show called *Aunt Jenny's Real Life Stories* that ran from 1937 through 1956. Following the dramatic portion of the show, the Aunt Jenny character shared a recipe that used Spry shortening. Perhaps Mrs. Brooks listened to Aunt Jenny and copied down the ingredients for these delicious cookies. Since Spry is no longer available, you can use your favorite shortening.

3/4 cup shortening
1 1/2 cups brown sugar, firmly packed
2 eggs, beaten well
1 tablespoon milk

2 1/2 cups all-purpose flour
1/2 teaspoon baking soda
3/4 teaspoon salt
1 teaspoon cinnamon
1/4 teaspoon cloves
1/2 cup nuts, chopped
1 cup raisins

PREHEAT OVEN to 350°. Grease a baking sheet. Cream the shortening and brown sugar until light. Add the beaten eggs and milk and blend until smooth. In a separate bowl, combine the flour, baking soda, salt, and spices. Add the dry ingredients to the creamed mixture and blend well. Fold in the nuts and raisins. Drop by rounded teaspoon 1 inch apart onto the prepared baking sheet. Allow to stand a few minutes, then flatten cookies slightly with the back of a fork. Bake for 12 to 15 minutes.

Makes 6 dozen

Nut Cookies

· ·

JEAN BALLANCE, Hyde County

You may think a cold December day is not a good time to go visiting in Hyde County, but you might feel very differently if you passed Lake Mattamuskeet, a breathtaking wildfowl sanctuary. "I live at Lake Landing about five miles from Englehard," Jean Ballance told me. "In the 1950s we had 100,000 geese here. They started flying at 4:00 P.M. The sky was black with them. I'd pull over and watch them. Local people, if they had a spare room, would rent it to hunters. They are still a boost here. The swans far outnumber the Canada geese now. They come right up to the backyard. We hear the owls when they have babies. They hunt at night.

"This was a nut cookie that Mother made. They're not teacakes, but they spread out."

1/2 cup sugar
1/4 cup shortening
2 eggs
1 tablespoon milk
1 cup all-purpose flour
2 teaspoons baking powder
1/2 teaspoon salt
1 teaspoon vanilla extract
1 cup nuts, chopped
pecan halves (optional)

PREHEAT OVEN to 350°. Cream the sugar and shortening together until smooth; add the eggs and milk and blend well. In a separate bowl, combine the flour, baking powder, and salt and add to the creamed mixture. Blend until smooth. Stir in the flavoring and nuts. Drop by rounded teaspoon onto ungreased baking sheets. Top each cookie with a pecan half, if desired. Bake for 12 to 15 minutes.

Makes 2 1/2 dozen

Nutty Fingers

Janet Haire Manuel, Martin County

Pecans grow in copious quantities in the northeastern counties of North Carolina. "My mother and aunt were always finding recipes and sharing them with each other," Janet Haire Manuel of Jamesville told me. "These bite-sized cookies were one of their favorite sweets. We often had them on holidays and other special occasions."

1 1/2 sticks (3/4 cup) butter, softened
6 tablespoons 10x powdered sugar, plus more for dusting
2 teaspoons vanilla extract
2 cups all-purpose flour
1 cup pecans, chopped

PREHEAT OVEN to 350°. Grease cookie sheets. Cream the butter and sugar together until fluffy. Add the vanilla extract and blend well. Gradually add the flour and blend until well incorporated. Stir in the nuts. Pull off small amounts of dough and roll into logs the width of a finger and 2 inches long. Place 1 inch apart on prepared cookie sheets. Bake for 10 to 15 minutes. Do not over bake. Let cool slightly, then roll in powdered sugar.

Makes 5 dozen

Crumb Nut Bars

MARGUERITE HUGHEY, Buncombe County

"Marguerite Hughey's personal cookbook indicates that Merrill Dill gave her this recipe in 1954," Mary Charles Pawlikowski of Nash County, the current owner of the cookbook, told me. At the top is a note, "Mrs. Sisk 1956."

1 1/4 cups all-purpose flour
1 1/4 cups brown sugar, divided
1 teaspoon baking powder
1/2 teaspoon salt
5 level tablespoons shortening
2 eggs, separated
1 cup nuts, chopped
1 teaspoon vanilla extract

PREHEAT OVEN to 335°. Grease and flour a 9 × 11-inch baking pan. Work the flour, 1/4 cup brown sugar, baking powder, salt, and shortening together until mixture is smooth. Blend in the egg yolks. When well blended, pat the mixture evenly into the bottom of the prepared pan. Beat the egg whites until stiff. Fold in 1 cup brown sugar, the chopped nuts, and the vanilla extract. Spread over the flour mixture. Bake for 25 to 30 minutes. Remove the pan from the oven and set it on a damp dish towel for about 5 minutes. Meanwhile, spread a sheet of waxed paper onto a flat surface. Using a knife, loosen the bars from around the edges of the pan and turn the pan upside down onto the waxed paper. Cut into squares while warm.

Makes 30 squares

Crunchy Bran Drops

CARRIE BLAIR, Davidson County

You might wonder how anything made from bran can taste this good, but cinnamon, dried fruit, and nuts give these cookies a rich, satisfying texture and flavor.

1 1/2 cups brown sugar, firmly packed
2 sticks (1 cup) butter, softened
2 eggs
1 teaspoon vanilla extract
2 1/4 cups all-purpose flour
1 cup unprocessed bran
1 teaspoon baking soda
1 teaspoon cinnamon
1/2 teaspoon salt
1 cup dates or apricots, chopped
1/2 cup sunflower seeds or your favorite nuts, chopped

PREHEAT OVEN to 375°. Lightly grease cookie sheets. Beat the sugar and butter together until light and fluffy. Blend in the eggs and vanilla extract. Combine the flour, bran, baking soda, cinnamon, and salt and add it to the butter mixture. Blend until smooth. Stir in the fruit and nuts until well incorporated. Drop by rounded teaspoon onto prepared cookie sheets. Bake for 8 to 10 minutes or until golden brown.

Makes about 4 1/2 dozen

Almond Crescents

MARIE SOLOMON KAHN, New Hanover County

"A lot of the cookies we make are from my mother's family. Her name was Louise Solomon. She was born in 1893," Marie Solomon Kahn of Wilmington said. "My mother's family was from northern Germany, and my father's family was from Bavaria, which is further south. There are other people in the community who make these same cookies, because they have the same background." Almond crescents, one of Marie's family specialties, are pretty, white cookies.

2 sticks (1 cup) butter, softened
1/2 cup 10x powdered sugar (plus more for coating cookies)
1/2 cup almonds, ground
1 teaspoon vanilla extract
2 cups self-rising flour

PREHEAT OVEN to 350°. Cream the butter and sugar together. Add the almonds and vanilla extract. Blend in the flour until the dough is smooth. Divide the dough in half and form each half into a 1-inch-thick log. Cut the logs into 3/4-inch-long pieces, shape into crescents, and place 1 inch apart on ungreased cookie sheets. Bake for 10 to 12 minutes or until lightly browned, being careful not to overbake. Roll in powdered sugar while still warm.

Makes 4 dozen

German Sweet Cakes

DIANNE EASLEY LAMBERT, Cabarrus County

"I got this recipe from my cousin Marylyn when she gave me a kitchen bridal shower before I was married in 1974," said Dianne Easley Lambert of Concord. "Marylyn made these for one of the refreshments at the shower. She had bought a recipe box and asked the guests to bring a recipe for me. I always think of the people who came to the shower when I use one of the recipes in that box."

Cookies
enough whole graham crackers to line the bottom of a
  9 × 13-inch baking pan and to cover the filling
2 sticks (1 cup) butter
1/2 cup white sugar
1/2 cup brown sugar
1/2 cup milk
1 egg, beaten
1 cup pecans, chopped
1 cup shredded coconut
1 cup graham cracker crumbs

Topping
1/2 stick (1/4 cup) butter
1/4 cup milk
1 1/2 cups 10X powdered sugar

GREASE a 9 × 13-inch pan with butter. Line the bottom of the pan with whole graham crackers. In a double boiler, combine the butter, sugars, milk, and egg. Bring to a slow boil and cook until slightly thickened. Remove from heat and add the pecans, coconut, and crushed graham crackers. Pour the cooked mixture over the graham cracker–lined pan. Place another layer of graham crackers on top. Refrigerate until mixture cools.

To make the topping, combine the butter, milk, and sugar in a saucepan. Cook, stirring, over medium heat until the sugar is dissolved and the mixture is well blended. Spread over the graham crackers and refrigerate until serving time.

Makes 24 servings

Butter Pecan Cookies

MARGUERITE HUGHEY, Buncombe County

"Delicately browned, they'll be rich and short," states a typewritten note left by Marguerite. "Still browner, they'll be rich and crisp. I prefer to bake these the minimum amount of time, but you have to handle them carefully when first taking them off the baking sheet. They are so 'short' that they crumble easily. However, when completely cold, they are firm. They are attractive to serve, and are yum-yum good."

2 sticks (1 cup) butter, softened
2/3 cup brown sugar
1 egg yolk
2 cups all-purpose flour
pecan halves

PREHEAT OVEN to 375°. Thoroughly cream the butter and sugar; beat in the egg yolk. Add the flour and mix well. Chill slightly, about 20 minutes, for easier handling, but not too long or the dough will be brittle. With floured hands, form the dough into 1-inch-diameter balls. Place the balls on ungreased cookie sheets about 2 inches apart. Flatten the balls slightly with the back of a floured fork. Top each cookie with a pecan half. Bake for 12 to 15 minutes or until lightly browned. Remove from the pan while warm.

Makes from 4 to 5 dozen

Chess Bars

Donna Matthews Saad

DONNA MATTHEWS SAAD, Vance County

"I grew up on a farm until I was in the sixth grade. Then we moved to Henderson," says Donna Matthews Saad. "We still have Christmas in a log cabin on that farm. It didn't have any nails in it. The farm had horses and two ponds where we went fishing.

"This is one of my favorites if you love really rich desserts, which I do," Donna continues. "Anything with cream cheese is good."

1 stick (1/2 cup) butter, melted
3/4 cup shortening
2 cups sugar
3 cups self-rising flour
1 teaspoon vanilla extract
3 eggs
1 cup cream cheese
2 cups 10x powdered sugar

PREHEAT OVEN to 350°. For the first layer, combine the butter, shortening, sugar, flour, and vanilla extract, blending until smooth. Add 1 egg and beat well. Press the mixture into a 9 × 13-inch baking pan. For the top layer, combine the remaining 2 eggs with the cream cheese and powdered sugar and beat until smooth. Spread the mixture over the first layer. Bake 30 to 40 minutes or until golden brown. Cool and cut into bars.

Makes 12 to 16

Date Pinwheels

ARAMINTA PIERCE BLOWE, Halifax County

My aunt Araminta, from Weldon, was born in 1911. She belongs to historical organizations, a book club, and a bridge club and is a member of Weldon's Library Board, where she says date pinwheels are her favorite addition to the refreshment table.

2 1/4 cups dates, chopped
1 cup sugar
1 cup water
1 cup nuts, chopped
2 sticks (1 cup) butter, softened
2 cups brown sugar
3 eggs, well beaten
4 cups all-purpose flour
1/2 teaspoon salt
1/2 teaspoon baking soda

COMBINE the dates, sugar, and water in a saucepan. Cook over low heat until thick, about 10 minutes. Remove from heat, stir in the nuts, and cool. Meanwhile, in a mixing bowl, cream the butter, gradually adding the brown sugar. Add the eggs and beat well. In a separate bowl, combine the flour, salt, and baking soda and add to the creamed mixture, mixing well. Chill thoroughly. Divide the dough in half. On a floured surface, roll out each half separately into a rectangle approximately 6 × 12 inches and about 1/4 inch thick. Spread each with the date filling and, starting with the longer side of the rectangle, roll up the dough to form a log. Chill overnight. When ready to bake, preheat oven to 400°. Cut each log into 1/4-inch-thick slices and place on ungreased cookie sheets. Bake for 10 to 12 minutes or until lightly browned.

Makes 5 dozen

Peanut Cookies

JACKI EPPERSON, Durham County

"Because cookies keep satisfactorily for many days, large quantities may be made at a time. You will find them convenient for giving variety to desserts," reads a note over the cookie section of Jacki's heirloom cookbook. Peanut cookies are just one of the many recipes that were recorded in the early twentieth century.

1/2 stick (1/4 cup) butter, softened
1/2 cup sugar
1/4 cup milk
1 egg
1 cup all-purpose flour
1/4 teaspoon salt
2 teaspoons baking powder
3/4 cup peanuts, chopped fine

PREHEAT OVEN to 375°. Cream the butter and sugar; add the milk, egg, flour, salt, and baking powder. When well blended, fold in the peanuts. Drop by rounded teaspoon onto ungreased cookie sheets. Bake for 10 to 12 minutes. Remove from the cookie sheets immediately to cool.

Makes 2 dozen

Cheesecake Bars

HELEN COCHRANE, Guilford County

This is one of the delicious recipes Helen Cochrane, currently of Garner, has prepared for the Clara Craven Book Club, of which she has been a member since 1945. Each month the members meet to discuss a new book and share a bite to eat.

1 box (18 1/4 ounces) of your favorite yellow cake mix

1 egg

1 stick (1/2 cup) butter, melted

1 teaspoon lemon juice (optional)

1 cup cream cheese, softened

2 eggs

2 cups 10X powdered sugar

1/2 cup nuts, chopped

PREHEAT OVEN to 350°. Combine the cake mix, egg, butter, and lemon juice and mix well. Pat the mixture into the bottom of an ungreased 9 × 13-inch baking pan. Blend the cream cheese, eggs, and powdered sugar until smooth. Stir in the nuts. Spread over the cake mixture. Bake for 1 hour. Cool completely and cut into bars.

Makes 48 bars

Cream Cheese Clouds

. . . .

CARRIE BLAIR, Davidson County

Carrie Blair grew up on a tobacco farm right next door to her present address in Davidson County. When she was young, her family woke up between 3:00 and 5:00 A.M. to work on the farm. Homegrown food made up the bulk of their diet. Carrie's mother cooked wholesome meals completed by simple desserts. Carrie, however, is known locally for fancy desserts. "You can freeze cream cheese clouds overnight," Carrie told me, "then tear them apart, put them in a zip lock bag, and return to freezer. When you get ready to serve them, you can fill them with cherry or other pie filling and sprinkle with nuts. They're real easy to do. It's real nice to have on hand. If somebody comes in, and you want a quick dessert, you can just pull them out of the freezer."

1 cup cream cheese, softened
1/2 cup 10x powdered sugar
1/4 teaspoon vanilla extract
1 cup heavy cream
1 can (21 ounces) cherry pie filling
nuts, chopped (optional)

BLEND the cream cheese, sugar, and vanilla extract with an electric mixer at medium speed. Beating on low speed, gradually add the heavy cream, blending well. Whip the mixture until it thickens. Mound the mixture in 8 equal portions on a waxed paper–lined cookie sheet. Using the back of a spoon, shape each portion into a 3 1/2-inch shell. Freeze for at least 2 hours. When ready to serve, fill each cloud shell with cherry pie filling. Sprinkle with nuts if desired. Serve immediately.

Makes 8

Fruitcake Cookies

SARAH SAWYER ALLEN, Lenoir County

My mother, Sarah Sawyer Allen, lived in Kinston for almost sixty years, but she was born in Bertie County and never forgot it. This recipe came from one of Sarah's friends there, Annie May Cherry from Windsor.

3/4 pound raisins
2 cups candied cherries, chopped
2 cups dates, chopped
6 slices candied pineapple, chopped
7 cups pecans, chopped
1 1/2 cups all-purpose flour, divided
2 sticks (1 cup) butter, softened
1 cup brown sugar
1 teaspoon cinnamon
3 eggs, beaten

3 cups all-purpose flour
1 teaspoon baking soda
1/2 cup milk

PREHEAT OVEN to 300°. Grease cookie sheets. Combine the fruit and nuts in a large bowl. Toss the fruit and nuts with 1/2 cup flour and set aside. In a separate bowl, cream the butter, sugar, and cinnamon; blend in the eggs until smooth. Add the flour, baking soda, and milk. Blend until the batter is smooth. Add the fruit and nuts gradually, mixing well after each addition until they are well incorporated. Drop by teaspoon onto the prepared cookie sheets. Bake for 20 minutes.

Makes 10 dozen

Krisan's Sour Cream Cookies

HELEN COCHRANE, Guilford County

Krisan Gregson never has to worry about what to get her mother, Helen Cochrane, for her birthday. Krisan's scrumptious sour cream cookies are about as good a birthday gift as you can get. You can even freeze them, if you wrap them well, for happy remembrances of the actual day.

Cookies
1 stick (1/2 cup) butter, softened
1 cup brown sugar, firmly packed
1/2 cup sugar
2 eggs
1 cup sour cream
1 teaspoon vanilla extract
2 3/4 cups all-purpose flour
1/2 teaspoon baking soda
1 teaspoon salt

Glaze
1 stick (1/2 cup) butter, melted
4 cups 10x powdered sugar
1 teaspoon vanilla extract
1 1/2 to 2 teaspoons hot water

COMBINE the butter, sugars, eggs, sour cream, and vanilla extract. Mix well. Add the flour, baking soda, and salt. Blend until smooth.

Refrigerate the dough for 30 minutes. When ready to bake, preheat oven to 375°. Grease cookie sheets. Drop the dough by rounded tablespoon onto the prepared cookie sheets. Bake for 8 to 10 minutes, being careful not to let them brown. Remove immediately from cookie sheets. Cool on racks.

To make the glaze, combine the butter, sugar, and vanilla extract and blend until smooth. Add hot water as needed to keep the glaze soft enough to spread. The glaze will harden when spread on the cookies.

Makes 5 dozen

Rocks

MARGUERITE HUGHEY, Buncombe County

> 1 1/2 cups sugar
> 2 1/2 cups self-rising flour
> 1 teaspoon cinnamon
> pinch salt
> 2 sticks (1 cup) butter, softened
> 3 eggs
> 2 pounds English walnuts, chopped
> 3 cups raisins, chopped

PREHEAT OVEN to 375°. Combine the butter and eggs. Combine the sugar, flour, cinnamon, and salt and add to the butter mixture. Blend well. Fold in the walnuts and raisins until evenly distributed. Drop by rounded teaspoon onto ungreased cookie sheets. Bake for 12 to 15 minutes. Store in an airtight container.

Makes 4 dozen

Lemon Squares

SARAH SAWYER ALLEN, Lenoir County

Baking lemon squares gives the house a buttery, sweet aroma that has welcomed visitors to social gatherings for as long as I can remember. Bridal showers, bridge parties, and family reunions are not complete without a golden tray of these tangy delicacies. I cover a serving plate with a doily before arranging the powdered squares on top, which gives them a pretty, lacy appearance. The Candy chapter has a recipe for candied orange and grapefruit peel. These make a contrasting and delicious garnish for the serving plate.

Crust	Topping
2 sticks (1 cup) butter, softened	4 eggs, slightly beaten
1/4 teaspoon salt	1/2 cup lemon juice
1/2 cup 10x powdered sugar	grated zest of 1 lemon (optional)
2 cups all-purpose flour	2 cups sugar
	1/2 cup all-purpose flour
	1/4 cup 10x powdered sugar
	for dusting

PREHEAT OVEN to 350°. Grease a 9 × 13-inch baking pan. Make the crust by blending the butter, salt, powdered sugar, and flour together until smooth. Press the crust evenly into the bottom of the prepared pan. Bake for 25 minutes. While the crust is baking, prepare the topping by beating the eggs, lemon juice, lemon zest (if desired), sugar, and flour together until smooth. Pour over the baked crust. Reduce oven temperature to 325° and bake for 25 more minutes. Do not overcook. Dust with powdered sugar when cool and cut into squares. Store in refrigerator or other cool place.

Makes 48 squares

Date Loaf

WANDA BROOKS, Stanly County

Wanda Brooks of Richfield remembers helping her mother make date loaf when she was so small that she had to stand on a chair to reach the counter.

2 cups vanilla wafers, crushed, divided
1 pound English walnuts or pecans, chopped
2 cups dates, chopped
1 package (10 ounces) marshmallows
1/2 cup milk

COMBINE the nuts, dates, and 1 cup of the vanilla wafer crumbs. In a saucepan over low heat, combine the marshmallows and milk and cook until the marshmallows are melted. Remove from heat and add the nut mixture. Mix well. Divide the mixture in half and shape each half into a log approximately 12 inches long and 2 inches in diameter. Trim the ends so they are flat, then roll the logs in the remaining cookie crumbs. Chill in the refrigerator until the logs are firm. Cut into 3/4-inch-thick slices.

Makes 30 slices

Caramel Squares

DIANNE EASLEY LAMBERT, Cabarrus County

"I'm from Concord," Dianne Easley Lambert told me. "This is one of my mother's recipes. My mother was a basic cook, very good, and earthy. Most everything was made from scratch. We ate from the garden during the summer. Now we call this gourmet food; we ate fresh food from the earth. We usually ate at the kitchen table.

"We almost always had something sweet. We had pecan trees. We gathered them and shelled them. That would be something we'd do in the wintertime. Caramel squares are made from typical ingredients that you just have in your cabinet. They have a crusty top when you make them. You can whip them up and have them just like they are or with ice cream. I don't remember a time when we didn't have this recipe. I find that the recipes that you go back to are the more simple things."

1 stick (1/2 cup) butter
1 cup brown sugar
1 egg
pinch salt
1 cup all-purpose flour
1 cup pecans, chopped
1 teaspoon vanilla extract
1 teaspoon baking powder

PREHEAT OVEN to 350°. Grease an 8-inch-square baking pan or dish. Combine the butter and sugar in a saucepan and stir over medium heat until the butter is melted. Remove from heat and cool. Add the egg and blend well. Add the remaining ingredients; stir until well blended. Pour the batter into the prepared pan. Bake for 20 to 25 minutes. Cool and cut into 2-inch squares.

Makes 16 squares

Chew Bread

....

SALLY GULLY, Gaston County

"I was born in 1928 so I grew up during the Depression," Sally Gully said. "My father was a Baptist minister. We lived in Cramerton, a little mill village, and when the mill closed, the people in the church couldn't pay a salary. So we got lots and lots of 'poundings' when people would bring a surprise to your house. They would bring all this food, a pound of sugar and a pound of butter, and that's where it got its name, canned goods and all kinds of things. So we never went hungry. My father was a hunter and a fisherman. That put game and fish on our table all during the Depression—fish, squirrels, rabbits, all kinds of things. My mother was a wonderful cook. She got up early on Sunday morning to get dinner started. Next she'd go across the street where the church was and teach Sunday school. She'd rush home between Sunday school and church with her hat on, put on her apron, and she would roll out the biscuits for dinner, take off her apron, and then run back across the street to church. This is a recipe that our six children remember. It's a chewy kind of a brownie. These are memories of growing up poor but rich."

2 cups brown sugar
1 stick (1/2 cup) butter, melted
3 eggs
2 cups self-rising flour
1 teaspoon vanilla extract

PREHEAT OVEN to 325°. Grease a 9 × 13-inch baking pan. Blend the brown sugar, butter, and eggs together until smooth. Beat in the flour and vanilla extract. Pour the batter into the prepared pan. Bake for 30 minutes. The bars will sink in on themselves as they cool. Cut into squares.

Makes 24 squares

COOKIES, BARS, AND TEACAKES

Jet-Age Brownies

TAMMY STOKER, Nash County

Tammy Edwards Stoker is from the small Nash County town of Spring Hope. She remembers the smell of rich, chocolate brownies permeating the house where she grew up with four siblings. Tammy's mother, Geraldine, must have hypnotized the children into behaving perfectly by rewarding them with her jet-age brownies. These brownies were so popular and easy to make that the older children quickly learned to take over the baking when their mother went outside the house to work. These brownies are moist, chewy, and nearly intoxicating.

1 stick (1/2 cup) butter
2 squares (2 ounces) unsweetened chocolate, melted, or
    2–3 tablespoons cocoa (Tammy uses Hershey's brand)
3/4 cup white sugar
3/4 cup light brown sugar
2 eggs
1 teaspoon vanilla extract
1 cup self-rising flour
1 cup nuts, chopped

PREHEAT OVEN to 325°. Grease an 8-inch-square pan. Melt the butter and chocolate in the top of a double boiler. Remove from heat and add the sugars, blending well. Add the eggs and beat well. Add the vanilla extract and flour and stir until well blended, then fold in the nuts. Pour the batter into the prepared pan. Bake for 30 to 35 minutes. Do not overcook. Let the brownies cool and "cave in" on themselves before cutting into 2-inch squares.

Makes 16 brownies

Brownies in a Jar

MARGUERITE HUGHEY, Buncombe County

You can fill a jar with the dry ingredients for Marguerite's luscious brownies, attach an index card listing the remaining ingredients and cooking instructions, then tie a bow around the jar for a practical gift for chocoholics or busy parents.

Fill a 1-quart jar with

1 1/4 cups self-rising flour
2/3 teaspoon salt
1/2 cup chocolate chips
2/3 cup brown sugar
2/3 cup white sugar
1/3 cup cocoa
1/2 cup flaked coconut
1/2 cup nuts, chopped

When ready to bake

3 eggs
2/3 cup vegetable oil
1 teaspoon vanilla extract

PREHEAT OVEN to 350°. Grease and flour a 9 × 13-inch baking pan. Shake the jar to mix the ingredients and empty the contents into a bowl. Blend well with the egg, oil, and vanilla extract. Pour the batter into the prepared baking pan. Bake for 27 to 32 minutes. Cool and cut into squares.

Makes 12 brownies

Angel Food Drop Cookies

LUCIE LEA ROBSON, Mecklenburg County

Angel food drop cookies are heavenly, as pretty and light as angel food cake.

4 egg whites
dash salt
1/2 teaspoon cream of tartar
1/2 cup sugar, divided
1/2 cup all-purpose flour
1/2 teaspoon vanilla extract
1/2 teaspoon almond extract

PREHEAT OVEN to 350°. Line a baking sheet with parchment or brown paper. In a small bowl, sift together the flour and 1/4 cup of sugar; sift the mixture 3 more times; set aside. Beat the eggs and salt until frothy; add the cream of tartar and the remaining 1/4 cup of sugar and beat until stiff. Add the flavorings and beat until well blended. Fold the flour and sugar into the egg mixture a little at a time. The mixture will be sticky and stiff. Drop the dough by rounded teaspoon about 1 to 1 1/2 inches apart on the prepared baking sheet. Sprinkle the cookies with a little sugar. Bake for about 20 minutes or until cookies just begin to brown.

Makes about 2 dozen

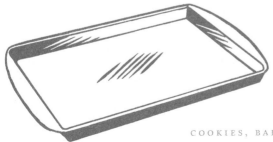

S'more Crispy Squares

LAL JOHNSON, Anson County

You don't need a campfire to enjoy this version of the out-door favorite, S'mores.

1/2 stick (1/4 cup) butter
1 package (10 ounces) marshmallows
1 teaspoon vanilla extract
6 cups crunchy rice cereal
2 milk chocolate bars (approximately 1.5 ounces each)
 or more to taste

Lal Johnson

GREASE a 9 × 13-inch baking pan. Place the butter and marshmallows in a large saucepan over low heat and stir until completely melted. Remove from heat and add the vanilla extract. Stir in the rice cereal until well incorporated. Use a buttered spatula to press the mixture into the prepared pan. Melt the chocolate bars and drizzle the chocolate over the top. Cool and cut into squares.

Makes 18 to 24 squares

Fry Bread

BETTY OXENDINE MANGUM, Robeson County

Betty Oxendine Mangum, a Lumbee, is originally from Robeson County. As I crossed North Carolina collecting recipes and trying new foods, I attended several powwows. Seeing members of all ages enter a central dance floor wearing colorful regalia and moving to the rhythms of tribal drums is a truly captivating experience. Native foods are always available at the powwows. I sampled a drink made from sassafras and this delicious sweet.

4 cups all-purpose flour
1 tablespoon baking powder
1 teaspoon salt
1/4 cup powdered milk
1 1/2 cups warm water
1 cup lard or shortening
cinnamon and 10x powdered sugar for dusting (optional)
honey (optional)

COMBINE the flour, baking powder, salt, and milk; mix thoroughly. Add the warm water and blend until the dough is soft. Heat the lard or shortening in a frying pan over medium heat. With well-floured hands, divide the dough into 24 equal pieces and shape each piece into a flat circle. Begin frying the dough when a small piece of dough dropped in the oil makes a low crackling noise. Brown the dough on both sides, then remove from the oil and drain on paper towels. Fry bread is best when served warm. It can be sprinkled with cinnamon and/or powdered sugar or drizzled with honey.

Makes 24

Fastnachts

BRENDA MALONE ZIMMERMAN, Rowan County

"My daughter and I are fifth- and sixth-generation residents of Rowan
County. We belong to a Lutheran Church here. This is a traditional German
pastry served on Shrove Tuesday as we prepare for Lent," said Brenda
Malone Zimmerman of Salisbury. "This is one of my grandmother's recipes. Fastnachts was so hard to say that somewhere, way before my time,
our family began calling them tangle britches, and that's how they were
written in my Mam-maw's cookbook. She often made them on a rainy day
just to break the boredom. She served them hot, dusted with confectioner's sugar or dipped them into Karo syrup. Sometimes she served them
with home canned pie fillings. A superstition is that if you eat Fastnachts
before Lent, you wouldn't be bothered with gnats during the summer."

4 cups all-purpose flour

2 teaspoons baking powder

1 teaspoon salt

1/3 cup sugar

3 tablespoons shortening

3/4 cup milk

3 large or 4 medium eggs

1 teaspoon vanilla extract

vegetable oil for frying

COMBINE the flour, baking powder, salt, and sugar. Cut in the shortening until the mixture resembles course meal. Add the milk, eggs, and
vanilla extract and mix until smooth. Roll out the dough on a floured
surface until it is a little thicker than a piecrust. Meanwhile, heat the
vegetable oil in a frying pan over medium heat. Cut the dough into
4-inch squares, then cut 3 slits into each one. Lift them up, "tangling"
up the strips of dough formed by the slits. Drop into very hot oil. Fry
until golden. Remove, drain, and dust with powdered sugar. Store any
leftovers in an airtight container.

Makes 48 cookies

Bourbon Christmas Cookies

CARRIE BLAIR, Davidson County

"They're not hard to make. I got the recipe from a man at my office at least twenty years ago," said Carrie Blair of Thomasville. "It was before 1980." She's still making these festive cookies, so you know they're good.

Carrie Blair

3 cups raisins
1/2 cup bourbon whiskey
1 1/2 cups all-purpose flour
1 1/2 teaspoons baking soda
1 1/2 teaspoons cinnamon
1/2 teaspoon nutmeg
1/2 teaspoon cloves
1 stick (1/2 cup) butter
2 eggs
1/2 cup light brown sugar, packed
1 pound pecan halves
1/2 pound candied cherries

SOAK the raisins in the bourbon for 1 hour. Preheat oven to 325°. Grease a cookie sheet. Combine the flour, baking soda, cinnamon, nutmeg, and cloves; set aside. Cream the butter, eggs, and brown sugar together until smooth. Add the raisins and mix well. Add the dry ingredients, mixing well. Fold in the pecans and cherries. Drop by teaspoon onto the prepared cookie sheet. Bake for 15 to 20 minutes, checking frequently to make sure they do not overcook.

Makes 4 dozen

Puddings and Custards

I N NORTH CAROLINA, the term "pudding" might mean a creamy blend of milk, eggs, and flavoring, or a cake, or even a bar. "Well, I have to explain puddin' first," Rhonda Bond, of Bertie County, told me as she introduced her mother's recipe for sweet potato puddin'. "I grew up in Kelford . . . and in Kelford, if you said something was a puddin', you didn't say pudding, you said *puddin'*, and that means that something is dessert. It doesn't mean that it's like a Jell-O thing with milk and cream. It could be a cake, it could be a pie, it could be any of that. It's puddin'." The recipes in this chapter definitely qualify as "puddin's"!

Thrifty cooks in England originally made puddings from leftovers that were bundled up in cheesecloth and boiled for hours until they gradually developed a smooth, uniform texture. This technique grew a sweet, American identity with Hasty Pudding, prepared in a similar way using cornmeal, molasses, and spices. In North Carolina we call this Indian pudding, and you can try Betty Oxendine Mangum's recipe for it. As time went by, more elaborate concoctions became popular. Plum pudding is a heavy yuletide cake. Traditionally, it contained silver charms or coins that bestowed good luck to the persons who found them in their serving[s]. Susan Carson of Southport, known to her friends as Miss Susie, says her recipe for Mrs. Jones's plum pudding is derived from English ancestors who immigrated to the southeastern coast of North Carolina. Bread pudding is still enjoyed today, as it was when Miss Susie's mama made it during the frugal days of the Great Depression. Ruth Bickett's po' folks pudding is a light dessert that can be served with cake.

In the far west corner of North Carolina, Lucille Wolfe of Cherokee County makes an unusual dessert called kanuchi out of sweetened hominy and pinto beans. Mary Deal of Rowan County contributed egg custard to this collection. Egg custard is one of the most popular desserts in the south central Piedmont region. Puddings that include bananas range from basic to sophisticated: Madelyn Long prepares a version that requires no eggs and no cooking; Grandma Scott's banana pudding is the customary sweet custard poured over bananas and then covered with golden meringue; Marie Solomon Kahn's banana custard is very light; and Kate Herold's bananas supreme is a cheesecake-style dessert.

Finally, chocolate puddings are passionately loved and widely varied. My great-aunt Martha's easily made chocolate pudding is cool, thick, and delicious. Lucie Lea Robson's chocolate sponge is a much lighter but no less satisfying dessert. Very experienced cooks might try making Duchess of Windsor coffee chocolate pudding, an elegant custard-type dessert that makes a sophisticated last course for late-night gatherings and candlelit dinners.

If you're looking for an unusual sweet or one especially comforting on a cold night or during an illness, try a pudding or custard.

Tips for Making Successful Puddings and Custards

* For puddings cooked on the stove, use a double boiler. This method gives you control over how fast egg yolks and milk are heated, thus preventing the eggs from curdling and the milk from scorching. If you don't have a double boiler, you can improvise by using two saucepans, one just small enough to fit into the other.

* You might want to purchase a silicone spatula. This handy modern device is great for scraping the sides of saucepans and can be plunged into foods heated to temperatures up to 500° without harm.

* Any recipe that calls for a pudding mix refers to those that contain sugar, not those that are sugar-free.

Mary Deal's Egg Custard

MARY DEAL, Rowan County

"This was my grandmother's recipe," said Mary Deal of Salisbury. You can make it plain or pour the scrumptious egg custard over fresh fruit before you bake it. It's good alone and excellent served with cake.

3 eggs
1 cup sugar
1/2 cup milk
1 tablespoon all-purpose flour
dash salt
your favorite flavoring—vanilla, almond, or rum extract

PREHEAT OVEN to 450°. Place an ovenproof pan or dish with about 1 to 1 1/2 inches of water in the oven. Butter 4 to 6 custard cups. Beat the eggs until well blended. Stir in the sugar, milk, flour, salt, and flavoring. Continue stirring until the mixture is smooth. Pour the mixture into the prepared custard cups. Carefully place the filled custard cups in hot water in the ovenproof dish. Bake for 15 minutes or until the custard has set.

Serves 4 to 6

Old-Time Bread Pudding
Like Mama Made

SUSAN CARSON, Brunswick County

Her neighbors and friends know Susan Carson as Miss Susie. She was born in Southport and has resided there most of her eighty-plus years. She is a well-known local historian who regularly contributes columns to the *Wilmington Morning Star* and is the author of two nonfiction books about the history of the area, *Joshua's Dream* and *Joshua's Legacy*. Miss Susie remembers the town's diet changing during the 1930s from one that frequently included red meat and pork to one that focused on fish, chicken, and starches. Young boys met the shrimp boats each day and were given the fish that were caught in the nets. The boys walked through town in the afternoons selling fish for twenty-five cents a string; their catch would find its way onto many tables at suppertime. In the 1930s Mrs. Carson's mother often fixed deviled eggs, buttermilk biscuits, candied sweet potatoes, cornbread dressing, cornmeal dumplings, cornbread, stewed potatoes, and this bread pudding. These typical dishes provided hard-won sustenance in those days, but they still grace Brunswick County tables today. "When Mama had left-over cooked fruit, such as apples or pears," Miss Susie told me, "she often added that to the pudding mixture before baking."

2 eggs	1 teaspoon vanilla extract
1 cup milk	4 cups bread, cubed
1/2 cup sugar	1 cup raisins
1 teaspoon cinnamon	butter sauce (optional)

PREHEAT OVEN to 350°. Grease a 1-quart casserole dish. Beat the eggs and milk together with the sugar, cinnamon, and vanilla extract. Stir in the bread cubes until well moistened. Fold in the raisins. Pour the batter into the prepared baking dish. Bake for 40 minutes or until set. Serve warm with butter sauce (see the Icings, Fillings, and Sauces chapter) or ice cream.

Serves 6 to 8

Sweet Potato Puddin'

RHONDA BOND, Bertie County

Rhonda Bond

"This is my mama's recipe for sweet potato puddin'," said Rhonda Bond. "You start with sweet potatoes, and we usually ate it in the fall and the winter because, I don't know how much you know about raising sweet potatoes, but that's when they come off. So we ate it in the fall and the winter, for Christmas dinner and Thanksgiving dinner and other times too.

"You start with about a pound of sweet potatoes for a pretty big puddin'. Get a nice, big, firm round one, and I actually like it better with the white sweet potatoes if you can get those. You need a little pinch of allspice, a teaspoon of nutmeg and cloves, and you need a teaspoon and a half of cinnamon. You need the cinnamon; the rest of that, you use what's in your cabinet. If you're missing the allspice, go for it. Don't not make this, because you don't have the allspice. I make it using evaporated milk. You can make it using half-and-half, but it's not as authentic, because we didn't have half-and-half in Bertie County in 1965. I like to make it with three or four tablespoons of molasses, but I have made it with brown sugar instead. I like the molasses; it gives it a darker kind of flavor. It's just a good dessert to have."

1 pound firm, white (if available) sweet potatoes
3/4 cup sweetened flaked coconut
2 cups sugar
1/2 cup all-purpose flour
pinch allspice (optional)
pinch nutmeg (optional)
pinch cloves (optional)
1 1/2 teaspoons cinnamon
1/2 cup evaporated milk or
half-and-half
1 1/2 teaspoons vanilla extract
3 to 4 tablespoons molasses or brown sugar
1 large egg
1/2 stick (1/4 cup) butter,
cut into chunks

PREHEAT OVEN to 350°. Grease and flour a 9 × 13-inch baking dish. Grate the sweet potatoes either by hand or in a food processor. In a large bowl, combine the grated potatoes and coconut. Add the sugar, flour, and spices and blend well. Add the evaporated milk or half-and-half, vanilla extract, and the egg and blend until the batter is smooth and muddy looking. Stir in the butter and pour the mixture into the prepared pan. Cover the pan with aluminum foil and bake for 20 to 25 minutes. Remove foil and continue baking for another 20 to 25 minutes or until the pudding is reddish brown and fragrant. Cool to room temperature before cutting.

Serves 8 to 10

Po' Folks Pudding

RUTH BICKETT, Warren County

"This came down to me from my great-grandmother Green," says Ruth Bickett. "Great-Grandmother Ruth Green lived in a large house with nine children and also kept boarders who came to Female Academy, a girls' school in Warrenton. She was overwhelmed in the kitchen and had a cook named Vic, not through luxury, but out of necessity. Vic and Grandmother Green concocted this po' folks pudding for the family and the boarders and apparently everyone was well fed, and no one ever starved to death that I'm aware of.

"It was a very large and, a bit rambunctious, family," Ruth continued. "My grandmother was married in 1926, and, at her wedding breakfast, my great-grandmother had fried chicken. Grandma Ruth commented that it was the first time she ever realized that chickens had a breast. She had never had a chicken breast before; she was the middle child. This is the one recipe that I have kept and treasured and kept making it after I moved to Raleigh. My roommate and I made it in college, and served it to everyone we knew, and it was a big hit."

1 cup water
1/2 cup sugar
2 teaspoons flour
2 teaspoons salt
1/3 cup butter
1 teaspoon vanilla extract

IN A SAUCEPAN, combine the water and sugar and boil until the sugar is completely dissolved. Turn to a slow boil. Combine the flour with a little water then add it to the water and sugar mixture. Add the salt and blend until smooth. Remove the pan from the heat and add the butter and vanilla extract. Stir until smooth. Serve warm over cake.

Makes 1 1/2 cups

Grandma Scott's Banana Pudding

DAWN SCOTT, Alamance County

"My mother couldn't pass in Rex Nursing School in the 1940s until she was able to make lump-free egg custard," said Dawn Scott of Burlington. "The custard is delicious as it is—just wait until it blends with the bananas and vanilla wafers. Banana pudding is best the longer it sits, if you can wait.

"Egg custard can now even be made in the microwave," Dawn continued. "The key is cooking for small amounts of time and stirring regularly until it becomes the right consistency."

> *3/4 cup sugar (but Dawn says you can use as little as 1/4 cup)*
> *1/4 cup flour*
> *2 cups milk*
> *1/4 teaspoon salt (optional)*
> *2 eggs, separated*
> *1 teaspoon vanilla extract*
> *3 bananas*
> *1 box of your favorite vanilla wafers (Dawn says that fat-free*
> *   wafers don't work as well)*
> *1/4 cup sugar (sugar substitutes can be used)*

IN A LARGE glass measuring cup, combine the flour and sugar. Set aside. Heat the milk in a double boiler until scalded. Beat the egg yolks and salt slightly and gradually add them to the hot milk, stirring constantly until the yolks are thoroughly absorbed into the hot milk. Slowly pour the hot milk and yolk mixture into the sugar and flour, stirring constantly so that no lumps will develop as the two mixtures blend. When completely blended, slowly pour the mixture back into the double boiler. Keep stirring and cooking for about 15 minutes or until the mixture becomes a custard. For a thicker custard, continue cooking for another few minutes.

When the custard has reached the desired consistency, remove from heat and let cool. Stir occasionally to prevent a film from forming on top. When cool, add the vanilla extract.

To assemble the pudding, peel and slice the bananas. In a 2-quart, oven-safe dish, place a layer of vanilla wafers; top with a layer of banana slices and then custard; repeat layering until ingredients are used up.

Preheat oven to 400°. Beat the egg whites until stiff. Add 1/4 cup of sugar and beat a few more minutes. Spread the meringue over top of the pudding. Bake until the meringue peaks are golden brown, about 5 to 7 minutes. Be sure to refrigerate leftovers—if there are any!

Serves 4 to 6

Banana Custard

MARIE SOLOMON KAHN, New Hanover County

"My father was born in 1890. This was my grandmother's cookbook," Marie Solomon Kahn told me one Indian summer day in Wilmington. "It's fascinating to read. Her name was Ida Lyon Solomon. We had banana custard any time anybody had anything wrong with them. I had my tonsils out when I was two and a half or three, and I remember my grandmother bringing banana custard, because that was what you got when you didn't feel well."

You can prepare this fluffy custard using pieces of hot milk sponge cake from the Cakes chapter.

4 cups milk
1 cup sugar, divided
4 eggs, separated
3 tablespoons cornstarch
1 teaspoon vanilla extract

1/2 teaspoon almond extract
3 bananas
lady fingers or hot milk sponge
*   cake*
whipping cream (optional)

SCALD the milk with 1/2 cup sugar; remove from heat. Separately, cream the egg yolks with the remaining sugar. Add the cornstarch and blend well. Gradually add the milk mixture. Blend well. Return the mixture to the heat and cook until thickened. Remove from heat and cool slightly. In a separate bowl, whip the egg whites until stiff and fold them and the flavorings into the thickened milk mixture.

To put the trifle together, line a pretty bowl (with at least a 2-quart capacity) with lady fingers or slices of hot milk sponge cake. Add a layer of custard and a layer of sliced bananas. Repeat layering to fill the bowl. Top with whipped cream, if desired.

Serves 10 to 12

Banana Trifle

MADELYN LONG, Perquimans County

Madelyn Long of Hertford has won cooking awards for more than a decade. "I prepare this the day before," says Madelyn. "It gives the pudding and the other ingredients more time to mellow." You can adapt this recipe for diabetics by using fat-free milk, sugar-free pudding mix, and fat-free vanilla wafers.

> *2 packages (4-serving size each) of your favorite instant*
> *vanilla pudding mix*
> *1 can (12 ounces) evaporated milk, refrigerated overnight*
> *1/2 cup water*
> *1 cup sour cream*
> *3 bananas*
> *1 box (12 ounces) of your favorite vanilla wafers*
> *whipped topping for garnish*

BEAT the pudding mixes, milk, and water together until smooth and thick. Add the sour cream. Blend until smooth. Line the bottom of a trifle dish or 2-quart glass dish with vanilla wafers. Arrange the slices of 1 banana over the wafers; spread a third of the pudding over the bananas. Repeat layers two more times. Refrigerate. Garnish with topping when ready to serve.

Serves 6 to 8

Bananas Supreme

. . . .

KATE HEROLD, Henderson County

Kate Herold of Hendersonville told me, "This is the best banana dessert you'll ever eat." Its rich dairy ingredients make an irresistible combination of flavors that almost tastes like a cheesecake, but without baking.

2 cups crushed vanilla wafers, divided
2 boxes (6-serving size each) instant vanilla pudding mix
1 cup cream cheese, softened
1 can (14 ounces) sweetened condensed milk
1 tablespoon vanilla extract
2 cups sour cream
2 cups whipping cream
1 1/2 cups milk
4 bananas

EVENLY DISTRIBUTE 1 1/2 cups of crushed vanilla wafers in a 9 × 13-inch casserole dish. Reserve 1/2 cup of crushed wafers for top garnish. With an electric mixer on low speed, blend the vanilla pudding mixes, cream cheese, condensed milk, and vanilla extract until smooth. Add the sour cream and whipping cream and beat well. Slowly add the milk with the mixer on low speed. Blend until smooth. Spread half of the pudding mixture over the crumbs in the baking dish. Slice the bananas on top of the pudding and carefully spread the remaining pudding mixture on top. Sprinkle the remaining 1/2 cup crushed wafers around the edges to garnish. Chill for at least 1 hour before serving.

Serves 10 to 12

Persimmon Pudding

VADA BECK, Davie County

"I live on Cana Road," says Vada Beck. "This is one of my mother's recipes. In the fall of the year this was kind of a favorite, because she always made such good persimmon pudding, and, of course, the persimmons don't ripen until late in the fall. We had a lot of trees around. We would go out and gather them. We brought them in, and she would wash them and cap them and mash them up, and then we ran them through a sieve. We all had a hand in gathering, but my mother was the one who made the pudding. It was so special at Thanksgiving and Christmas. After we were married and moved away and our husbands and all came back, we loved that persimmon pudding. I can remember her stirring it up and mixing it together. After it was baked she would set the pan out on the porch to cool. She would cut it into squares to serve, take it out of the pan, and put it out on her serving dish. Then she would sprinkle fresh, grated coconut on top. She probably put two or three layers, and let that set for a while, and it would absorb all the juice from the pudding, and that made it good and very, very special. My mother was a person who cooked by 'a little bit of this and a little bit of something else,' and for a long time, we didn't have a recipe. We kept saying 'Mom, please write this down so we can make it later.' And she did, and I have made quite a few. I can't say they were always as good as Mom's. You want a persimmon that's kind of firm but still mellow, soft-like. You have to be careful in gathering them. If not, they get squishy."

> about a half-gallon of whole, ripe persimmons
>   (enough to yield 2 cups of pulp)
> 1 1/2 cups brown sugar
> 1/4 cup white sugar
> 2 eggs, beaten
> 1 1/2 sticks (3/4 cup) butter, melted

1 3/4 cups all-purpose flour
2 teaspoons baking powder
1/2 teaspoon salt
1/2 teaspoon cinnamon
1/2 teaspoon allspice
1/4 teaspoon cloves
1/4 teaspoon nutmeg
2 cups milk
Grated coconut (optional)

PREHEAT OVEN to 325°. Grease and flour a 11 × 13-inch baking pan. Both enamel and ceramic oven dishes work well. Wash, cap, and mash the persimmons. Press the mashed fruit through a sieve until you have two cups of pulp. You can also use a blender or food processor to grind the pulp until it has a smooth, consistent texture. Mix the pulp with both sugars. Add the eggs and beat well. Add the butter and blend thoroughly. In a separate bowl, combine the flour, baking powder, salt, and spices. Add the flour mixture alternately with the milk to the pulp mixture, stirring well after each addition. Pour the batter into the prepared pan and bake for at least 1 hour and 15 minutes or until it sets. Remove from the oven, cool, and cut into squares. Arrange the squares on a serving dish or serve from the pan. If using coconut, place a layer of pudding squares on a serving dish, top with coconut. Then place a second layer of pudding squares on top of that. Top with more coconut. Repeat with a third layer of each. Let stand a few minutes before serving.

Serves 8 to 10

Indian Pudding

BETTY OXENDINE MANGUM, Robeson County

Betty Oxendine Mangum is originally from Robeson County and is a member of the Lumbee tribe. Betty is also a former teacher in Wake County. This sweet, pungent pudding is a recipe that she shared with her students. It's a typical Native American dish with a long history, as it is made from corn, molasses, and dairy products that were raised on farms in North Carolina for generations. I especially enjoy it when the weather turns cold.

2 cups milk
1/2 cup yellow cornmeal
3/4 cup light molasses, divided
1/4 teaspoon ginger
1/2 teaspoon cinnamon
1 egg (optional)
1 tablespoon butter or margarine

PREHEAT OVEN to 300°. Grease a shallow, 2-quart baking dish or ovenproof skillet. In a medium saucepan, heat the milk until bubbles form around the edges. Separately, combine the cornmeal and water and stir until smooth. If a firmer pudding is desired, beat the egg into the cornmeal mixture at this point. Add the cornmeal mixture to the milk along with 1/2 cup molasses, the ginger, and the cinnamon. Cook, stirring constantly, until thickened and smooth. Pour the pudding into the prepared baking dish. Bake, uncovered, until the pudding has set and has a golden crust on top—about 1 hour. Combine the remaining 1/4 cup molasses and the butter and spread over the pudding. Cool for at least 30 minutes before serving.

Serves 4 to 6

Kanuchi

LUCILLE WOLFE, Qualla Boundary

As I headed west I was fortunate to meet the Blankenship family, members of the Eastern Band of Cherokee Indians who live on the Qualla Boundary, a section of western North Carolina that spans parts of Swain, Haywood, Jackson, Clay, and Cherokee counties. Some people refer to the Qualla Boundary as the Cherokee Reservation. Not only did I receive a warm welcome from the Blankenship family, but the area is filled with spectacular natural wonders. I found many reasons to return. Laura Blankenship introduced me to Native American recipes like bean bread, and she mentioned a dessert made by a relative of hers, Lucille Wolfe. Lucille happily described a dish made from hominy. Hominy is derived from the inner kernel of maize (sweet corn). The word "kanuchi" actually refers to a tree stump that was once used to pound corn on before it was simmered into a rich, white pudding that can be eaten at least three different ways. First, the hominy can be eaten alone as a breakfast dish. Next, pinto beans can be added to make it a hearty base for a meal. Finally, crushed walnuts can be combined with hominy and pinto beans, chilled and sweetened to make this unusual dessert.

4 cups cooked hominy
1 1/2 cups pinto beans with liquid from cooking
1 cup black walnuts, crushed
sugar, to taste

COMBINE the hominy and pinto beans in a 3-quart saucepan and cook over medium heat until hot. Remove from heat. Gradually add the crushed walnuts, stirring until they are well incorporated. Let the mixture cool, then refrigerate. Before serving, add the sugar a little bit at a time, tasting to make sure the mixture does not get too sweet.

Serves 6 to 8

Mrs. Jones's Plum Pudding

SUSAN CARSON, Brunswick County

"Where are the plums?" you may ask when you scrutinize the ingredients for this famous dessert. Plum pudding dates back to the 1600s in England when the word "plum" referred to a dried fruit like a raisin. It's a heavy and spicy pudding often served during the late winter months. For many years, silver charms and coins were baked into the pudding; they were said to bring luck and prosperity during the coming year to those who found them in their serving. Susan Carson of Southport commented that an old Yorkshire, England, tradition says, "In as many homes as you eat plum pudding in the twelve days following Christmas, so many happy months will you have during the year."

2 cups all-purpose flour	2 eggs, beaten
1/3 cup sugar	2/3 cup molasses
1 teaspoon salt	1/3 cup milk
1 teaspoon baking soda	1 cup raisins
2 teaspoons ginger	1 1/2 cups mixed, diced glazed
1/2 teaspoon cinnamon	fruits
1/4 cup shortening, melted	1 1/2 cups nuts

PREHEAT OVEN to 275°. Grease and lightly flour a 10-inch tube pan. Place a rack in the bottom of a pot large enough to hold the tube pan (I use a turkey roaster). The pot should have a lid. Fill the pot with enough water to come halfway up its sides and place it in the oven uncovered. Let it heat while you prepare the batter.

To prepare the batter, sift together the flour, sugar, salt, baking soda, and spices into a mixing bowl. Make a well in the mixture and add the shortening, eggs, molasses, and milk. Blend until smooth. Stir in the fruit and nuts until thoroughly blended. Pour the batter into the prepared tube pan and cover the pan with aluminum foil or waxed paper secured tightly with twine. Place the tube pan inside the prepared pot in the oven. Cover the pot. Bake for about 3 hours, adding more water as needed to keep the pot filled halfway. When the pudding is dark brown and firm to the touch, remove the tube pan from the pot and let the pudding stand a few minutes. Unmold on a serving plate and serve with Miss Susie's Jonesy sauce (see the recipe in the Icings, Fillings, and Sauces chapter).

Serves 8 to 10

Mrs. Truman's Apple Pudding

LUCIE LEA ROBSON, Mecklenburg County

Lucie Lea Robson's mother-in-law, Harriet Robson of Chapel Hill, likely acquired this recipe between 1945 and 1953, when Bess Truman was First Lady. Mrs. Truman was from Independence, Missouri, where apple pudding is known as Ozark pudding.

1 egg
3/4 cup sugar
3 heaping tablespoons self-rising flour
1/8 teaspoon salt
1 cup apples, peeled, cored, and cubed or chopped
1 teaspoon vanilla extract
3/4 cup pecans, chopped
1 cup whipped cream or nondairy whipped topping

PREHEAT OVEN to 300°. Grease a 1-quart baking dish. Beat the egg slightly. Add the sugar, flour, and salt. Blend until smooth. Add the apples, vanilla extract, and pecans. Pour the batter into the prepared dish. Bake for 25 to 30 minutes. Serve immediately, topped with whipped cream.

Serves 4 to 6

Chocolate Pudding

MARTHA BARNES, Pitt County

You can pour this chocolate pudding into individual custard cups or leave it in a bowl and dish out individual servings.

3 tablespoons cornstarch
1 cup cocoa
1/4 teaspoon salt
1 cup sugar
2 cups milk
2 cups whipping cream
1 teaspoon vanilla extract

COMBINE the cornstarch, cocoa, salt, sugar, and milk in the top of a double boiler. Bring the mixture to a boil and cook, stirring constantly, until the mixture becomes a thick, delicious pudding, about 20 minutes. Remove from heat. Whip the cream until soft peaks form. Add the vanilla extract. Fold the warm mixture into the whipped cream until well incorporated. Refrigerate and enjoy.

Serves 4 to 6

Duchess of Windsor
Coffee Chocolate Pudding

HARRIET ROBSON, Orange County

Lucie Lea Robson's mother-in-law, Harriet Robson, and Wallis Warfield Simpson lived in China at the same time. The recipe was recorded on onionskin paper using a manual typewriter. Perhaps it is named for Mrs. Simpson, a divorced American who became the Duchess of Windsor in 1936 when she married the English king Edward VIII. The couple traveled around the world and lived a life of genteel ease. You'll feel royal, too, when you enjoy this luxurious dessert.

3/4 cup white sugar
3/4 cup all-purpose flour
2 teaspoons baking powder
1/8 teaspoon salt
1-ounce square unsweetened
*   baking chocolate*
1/4 cup butter

1/2 cup milk
1 teaspoon vanilla or rum extract
1/2 cup brown sugar, packed
1/2 cup white sugar
1/2 cup cocoa
1 cup strong, cold, black coffee

PREHEAT OVEN to 325°. Grease a 1-quart baking dish. Sift together the sugar, flour, baking powder, and salt into a large bowl. Set aside. Combine the chocolate and butter in a double boiler and stir until melted. Add the chocolate mixture to the dry ingredients and blend well. Add the milk and flavoring and stir until smooth. Pour the batter into the prepared baking dish. Combine the sugars and cocoa and sprinkle over the batter in the baking dish. Pour the coffee gently over all. Bake for 40 minutes. Cool to room temperature and serve with sweetened whipped cream, if desired.

Serves 4 to 6

Chocolate Sponge

LUCIE LEA ROBSON, Mecklenburg County

"My mother-in-law, Harriet Robson, was a librarian," Lucie Lea Robson told me. "That's why her recipe for chocolate sponge is written on the back of an old library index card dated 1933." It's good alone, or you can serve it with sweetened whipped cream, crisp wafers, or salted almonds for a divine, light dessert that's pretty garnished with raspberries or strawberries.

1 1/2 teaspoons unflavored gelatin
1/4 cup cold water
3/4 cup boiling water
4 eggs, separated
1 cup sugar
1 1/2 ounces unsweetened baking chocolate, melted

STIR the gelatin into the cold water until it dissolves; add the boiling water and let it set for 30 minutes. Combine the egg yolks and sugar in a double boiler over medium heat and cook, stirring, until the mixture thickens into a smooth paste. Add the chocolate. Stir and continue cooking until the mixture is smooth. Remove from heat and stir in the gelatin. Beat the egg whites until very stiff and carefully fold them into the chocolate mixture until well incorporated. Do not over blend. Pour the pudding into a 1-quart dish and chill.

Serves 8

Lemon Mist

. . . .

GRACE REA, Moore County

"This recipe was served by my mother, Pearl Martin Preslar, for family get-togethers such as birthdays and holidays," Grace told me. "It was the family's favorite dessert. She always served it in a creamy yellow, enamel pan. I never remember ever using that pan for anything else. My mother died in December of 2003 at the age of ninety-six. When everything was distributed, we realized we hadn't found that pan. We didn't know what happened to it. The extended family dinner in 2007 was in our home, and we prepared lemon mist for one of the desserts. I had gone out to yard sales and found another identical pan, and I thought I might find out who had my mother's pan. I didn't say anything; I just served the lemon mist in that pan. My brother from Washington, N.C., came for the dinner, and asked me how I got his pan; so I found out where it was."

1 cup vanilla wafers, crushed
1 package (14-serving size) lemon Jell-O
1 cup boiling water
juice of 1 lemon
1 can (12 ounces) evaporated milk, refrigerated overnight
1/4 cup sugar
1/3 cup light corn syrup

THIS RECIPE is best prepared if the mixing bowl and beaters are chilled. Sprinkle the crushed wafers into the bottom of a 9 × 13-inch pan. Add the Jell-O to the boiling water and stir until dissolved; add the lemon juice and allow it to cool to room temperature. Whip the evaporated milk with an electric mixer until it is light and fluffy. Continue mixing as you slowly add the sugar and corn syrup. When the mixture is smooth, add the Jell-O and mix well. Pour the pudding over the crushed cookies in the pan. Chill at least 2 hours or until the pudding sets.

Serves 8 to 10

Macaroon Sherry Custard

LUCIE LEA ROBSON, Mecklenburg County

"This recipe is written on a sheet of notepaper from Joe Hardison's business in Raleigh," Lucie Lea told me. "Joe was my mother-in-law's brother. The note looks like it was written by Joe's cook, Rena Belle. I think this is one of her recipes."

1 cup of your favorite macaroons
6 eggs, separated
3/4 cup sugar, divided
1 cup sherry
4 ounces shaved almonds

PREHEAT OVEN to 400°. Cover the bottom of a 1-quart casserole dish with whole macaroons. Beat the egg yolks until lemon colored. Continue to beat while you slowly add 1/2 cup sugar and the sherry. When the mixture is smooth, pour it into a double boiler. Cook over medium heat, stirring constantly until it thickens into a custard consistency. Be careful not to turn up the heat too high or the eggs will curdle. Remove from heat. Pour the custard over the macaroons. In a clean bowl, beat the egg whites until peaks form. Blend in 1/4 cup sugar. Pour the mixture evenly over the custard. Sprinkle with shaved almonds. Bake until the meringue is brown, 5 to 8 minutes. Serve hot or cold. Store in the refrigerator.

Serves 6

Mimmie's Wine Jelly

MARY CHARLES PAWLIKOWSKI, Nash County

"This is a good special occasion dessert," Mary Charles Pawlikowski told me. "Maybe the wine jelly helped my great-grandmother, Mimmie, live to be over one hundred."

1 envelope (1 ounce) unflavored gelatin
2 cups cold water
1 quart (4 cups) boiling water
3 cups sugar
juice of 3 lemons
1 cup blackberry or other homemade wine

DISSOLVE the gelatin in the cold water. Add the boiling water and sugar and stir until the sugar is dissolved. Add the lemon juice and wine and stir well. Pour the liquid into a 2-quart ceramic dish. Refrigerate until the gelatin sets. Serve topped with whipped cream.

Serves 8 to 10

Granny's Syllabub

MARY CHARLES PAWLIKOWSKI, Nash County

English immigrants brought syllabub to America. The name comes from the words 'Sille,' a French wine, and 'bub,' short for bubbly. It is an easy dessert that is especially good when served in the coldest part of winter. Instead of the lemon zest for garnish, you might try grated nutmeg. "This always made us tipsy at Grandmother's Christmas table," Mary Charles Pawlikowski told me. "Now I know why—you can't stop eating it!"

1 cup heavy cream
1/2 cup 10x powdered sugar
1/4 cup red wine
grated zest of 1 lemon

WHIP the cream for 3 to 4 minutes. Keep whipping while you gradually add the sugar. When the cream begins to thicken into peaks, blend in the wine and zest. Spoon into glasses for serving.

Serves 6 to 8

Icings, Fillings, and Sweet Sauces

Seven-Minute Icing

Simple Chocolate Icing

Buttermilk Glaze

Microwave Chocolate Icing

Aunt Winnie's Chocolate Gravy

State Fair Biscuits

Hot Fudge Sauce

Chocolate Coffee Icing

Caramel Icing

Decorator Icing for Cookies

Seafoam Icing

Cake Filling

Orange Filling

Good Lemon Filling

Coconut Filling

Lemon Sauce

Pineapple Filling

Butter Sauce

Tootie Fruitie

Jonesy Sauce

Hard Sauce

Sauce Superb

Whipped Cream

G ROWING UP, I had relatives who set elegant tables when our family was invited for lunch on Sunday. I could smell the lemon furniture polish as I sat down to a pretty plate set on top of a lacy placemat or linen tablecloth. Sweet, fresh iced tea in fancy glasses accompanied every dinner then. We often had ham and sweet potatoes or chicken and rice with seasonal vegetables. The meals were good but actually very basic, as weekends were busy times. The way the cook made Sunday dinner special was with the dessert. It was easy to turn a basic yellow or white cake into something rich and different by adding a scrumptious icing, filling, or sauce, then garnishing it with a piece of fruit or a sprig of mint. This chapter contains some practical yet unusually tasty ways to enhance desserts and put the icing on your cake.

Try making a one-two-three-four cake and filling the layers with Juanita Hudson's coconut filling or my aunt Martha's pineapple filling. Wanda Brooks of Stanly County transforms plain vanilla ice cream into a crowd-pleasing sundae with her hot fudge sauce. Susan Carson of Southport in Brunswick County enhances the taste of her mother's bread pudding by adding Jonesy sauce. Carrie Blair of Davidson County covers cakes with fabulous caramel icing that makes all her guests cry for seconds. If you're a novice in the kitchen or in a hurry and want an icing that's a sure success, make Harriet Robson's chocolate coffee icing.

You may think that because Fay Kemp grew up in Dare County her grandmother's recipe for seafoam icing is unique to the Tidewater, but it isn't. As the name implies, it is a glossy, smooth, light icing. My mother used to make it for birthday cakes and other special occasions. If you've never had it, be sure to try it.

You can count on a happy ending to any meal when you add these North Carolina favorites to your collection of favorite desserts.

Tips on Making Successful Icings, Fillings, and Sweet Sauces

* Like puddings, many cake icings require use of a double boiler.

* Powdered, confectioner's, and icing sugars are basically identical. Powdered sugar is used to make icing because it dissolves immediately and produces beautiful, smooth icings. If you run out of it and need more immediately, you can make it by putting white sugar into a blender on high speed for a few minutes until it is reduced to smaller crystals. Store-bought powdered sugar contains a small amount of cornstarch to keep it from lumping. You do not need to add cornstarch to the sugar if you are planning to use it right away, but if you are going to store the fine sugar, add 1 tablespoon of cornstarch to every cup of white sugar.

Seven-Minute Icing

MAVERINE BAKER, Johnston County

Shiny, light, and fluffy, seven-minute icing is a beautiful covering for a layer or sheet cake. You can substitute brown sugar for the white in this recipe to get caramel icing. Maverine is a diabetic and uses only 1/2 cup sugar for this icing.

1 cup sugar
1/4 cup light corn syrup
1/4 cup water
2 egg whites
1 teaspoon vanilla extract

THERE ARE two ways to prepare this icing, one directly on a burner, the other in a double boiler. The first way is to bring to a boil the sugar, corn syrup, and water in a saucepan over low to medium heat. Let the mixture boil rapidly until it becomes hot syrup and when a spoon pulled out of it spins a 6- to 7-inch thread, about 230° on a candy thermometer; this usually takes about 7 minutes. Remove from heat. Beat the egg whites in a mixing bowl until they stand in peaks. Pour the hot syrup over the egg whites and continue beating until icing stands in very stiff peaks. Blend in vanilla extract.

The second way to prepare the icing is to combine the sugar, corn syrup, water, and egg whites in the top of a preheated double boiler. Use an electric mixer to beat the egg mixture on high for 7 to 10 minutes. Remove from heat. Blend in the vanilla extract. Spread on cake layers.

Makes enough to ice a 2-layer (9-inch) cake

Simple Chocolate Icing

MARGUERITE HUGHEY, Buncombe County

1 stick (1/2 cup) butter
*2 squares (2 ounces) unsweetened
    chocolate*
1 egg, beaten
1 1/2 cups 10x powdered sugar

pinch salt
1 teaspoon vanilla extract
1 teaspoon lemon juice (optional)
1 cup chopped nuts (optional)

MELT the butter and chocolate in a saucepan over low heat. Stir in
the egg, sugar, salt, vanilla, and lemon juice. Cook the mixture, stirring,
until it becomes smooth and thick. Mix in the nuts or sprinkle them on
top of the cake after spreading. Spreads best while still warm.

Makes enough to ice a 2-layer (9-inch) cake

Buttermilk Glaze

IMOGENE TOMBERLIN, Yancey County

"Very good on sponge or pound cake," Imogene Tomberlin of Burnsville
told me.

1 stick (1/2 cup) butter
1 cup sugar
1/2 cup buttermilk
1/4 teaspoon baking soda

COMBINE the butter, sugar, and buttermilk in a 1-quart saucepan and
bring to a slow boil over medium heat. Boil, stirring constantly, for 2
minutes. Remove from heat. Stir in the baking soda. Spread while still
warm.

Makes 1 1/2 cups

Microwave Chocolate Icing

WANDA BROOKS, Stanly County

Wanda Brooks of Richfield is a practical cook who serves delicious desserts. Here is a simple chocolate icing that is made in one dish.

1 stick (1/2 cup) butter
1/4 cup cocoa
1/4 cup milk
2 cups 10X powdered sugar
1 teaspoon vanilla extract

COMBINE the butter, milk, and cocoa in a microwave-safe dish. Microwave on medium-high heat until the butter melts, about 30 to 60 seconds. Watch carefully so you don't overcook. Remove from microwave. Beat in powdered sugar until well blended. Add vanilla extract. Beat until smooth. Spread while still warm.

Makes enough to ice a 2-layer (9-inch) cake

Aunt Winnie's Chocolate Gravy

PAT WILLINGHAM, Ashe County

Pat Willingham, now of Cleveland in Rowan County, smiled the entire time that she talked about her aunt Winnie, who wore a traditional bonnet and long sleeves when she worked outside. "My mom is from Ashe County," Pat told me. "Aunt Winnie's chocolate gravy was her recipe. She was my mother's sister. She was born, reared, and died in Ashe County and, to her, it was the best place in North Carolina. We have fabulous memories of going to her house. She was an incredible mountain woman—strong. She and her husband lived in the same house from the time they were married for the rest of her life. My family has this house of hers now, between Todd and the Baldwin community. In her house she had a wood cookstove and an electric stove, and they sat side by side, and she cooked on both of them, but she only made her chocolate gravy in the black iron skillet on top of the wood cookstove. She baked fabulous biscuits in the wood stove, and you serve the chocolate gravy on the biscuits. She never measured anything; so when I grew up and wanted to learn to make chocolate gravy, I had to watch her numerous times and calculate the measurements."

3 tablespoons butter	*1 1/4 cups sugar*
3 tablespoons flour	*1 1/4 to 1 3/4 cups milk*
3 to 4 tablespoons cocoa	

MAKING CHOCOLATE GRAVY is just like making milk gravy: melt the butter in an iron skillet over medium heat until it begins to bubble. Sprinkle the flour into the butter and stir until it begins to brown. Add the cocoa and sugar. Add the milk gradually, stirring constantly until a glossy, smooth consistency is reached. Serve over Betty Buchanan's hot state fair biscuits (recipe below).

Makes 2 cups

State Fair Biscuits

BETTY BUCHANAN, Wake County

Betty Buchanan's family has been cooking for visitors at the North Carolina State Fair for over seventy-five years. Generations of fairgoers enjoy eating annually at the fair's very first permanent booth, where a red neon sign reads "Hunnicutts." "It's tradition," Betty said at the fair booth as she prepared homemade biscuits. "We look forward to it all year. You have to love it, because you're on your feet for ten hours a day." Betty began helping fix food at the fair when she was about ten years old. "I was born in Wake County. We are probably the oldest family out here [at the state fairgrounds]. It's almost like it's in your blood now, part of the seasons. Our lifestyles are so different than the fair the rest of the year, and we really look forward to this. We were raised up with it. It's real tradition," she continued. "My father was a Raleigh policeman, and my mother was a nurse. My dad loved the restaurant style. I think probably years ago, he started out with a little bitty hot dog stand where you handed food out the window. Then they graduated to a big tent, and they would bring sawdust in and put it on the ground to make a floor for the tent. When they built these permanent booths, this was the first permanent booth, and I guess my dad had been here so long, until he got the first permanent booth. I think at first [they served] just the simple things like hot dogs and cold drinks, then they graduated up to the big kitchen and now they have plate lunches, fried chicken, country ham, barbecue. We love it ten days out of the year. We have met so many friends over the years that we only see during fair week that come in to eat with us. Some of the parents of the children came when my dad had it, and now they are coming with their children and some with grandchildren."

Now Betty makes biscuits all day during the ten-day fall run. "And I do love making homemade biscuits. It's very, very simple. I taught myself. My mother made a real dry biscuit, because that's the way my father liked them; she made hers with water and flour and shortening, because he liked a flat biscuit. My family likes a fluffy biscuit; so I use buttermilk and Crisco shortening and White Lily flour, and that combination to me makes the best, lightest biscuit. The less you touch the dough, the better. Very lightly, form your biscuit, and mash it lightly into the pan. And you will learn to pinch off a certain amount. My first biscuits were not successful. I had to try and try and try again; but I finally conquered it. So anybody can learn to make a biscuit. You might fail the first few times, but you will get the feel of it. And don't ever handle your dough real rough. Always handle it as if you were working with two feathers in your hand."

2 cups buttermilk
6 cups self-rising flour (Betty prefers White Lily)
a golf ball–size spoonful of shortening (about 2 tablespoons)
*   (Betty prefers Crisco)*

PREHEAT OVEN to 475°–500°. Combine all the ingredients in a wide mixing bowl and blend by squeezing the ingredients together with your hands. Mix thoroughly. If the dough is dry, add a little more buttermilk, but only a very little bit at a time; *the dough should be sticky but not wet.* Don't overhandle the dough or a tough biscuit will result. When just thoroughly mixed, sprinkle a little flour over the dough as you get ready to form it into biscuits. With floured hands divide the dough into 18 equal pieces, gently forming each into a biscuit, and then pat into a 9 × 13-inch baking pan. Bake for 10 to 12 minutes or until golden brown. Watch the biscuits carefully! You may have to experiment with your own oven to get the temperature right.

Makes 18 biscuits

Hot Fudge Sauce

WANDA BROOKS, Stanly County

Hot fudge sauce is sumptuous over ice cream or warm cake.

1 cup sugar
1/2 cup cocoa
3 tablespoons all-purpose flour
1/4 teaspoon salt

1 cup boiling water
1 tablespoon butter
1/2 teaspoon vanilla extract

COMBINE the sugar, cocoa, flour, and salt in a saucepan. Add the boiling water and butter. Cook over medium heat, stirring constantly, until the mixture thickens. Remove from heat and add the vanilla extract. Serve hot. May be stored in the refrigerator and reheated as needed.

Makes about 1 cup

Chocolate Coffee Icing

HARRIET ROBSON, Orange County

Lucie Lea Robson's mother-in-law, Harriet Robson, was serving chocolate coffee icing long before coffeehouses popularized the use of the caffeinated beverage in sweets. This icing is smooth and rich, but be careful—it will keep you awake.

2 squares (2 ounces) unsweetened baking chocolate, melted,
    or 1/2 cup cocoa
1 teaspoon butter, softened
1/3 cup hot coffee
1 1/2 cups 10x powdered sugar

BLEND all the ingredients together until smooth. Spread immediately.

Makes enough to cover 1 layer of a 9-inch round cake

Caramel Icing

CARRIE BLAIR, Davidson County

Caramel icing can be made in just a few minutes. It has a fluffy texture and spreads easily. Try it over plain cake, cupcakes, or a one-two-three-four cake (see the Cakes chapter for recipes).

2 cups brown sugar
1 cup white sugar
1 stick (1/2 cup) butter
1 cup evaporated milk
pinch salt
1 teaspoon vanilla extract

COMBINE the sugars, butter, milk, and salt in a saucepan. Cook over high heat until the mixture begins to boil. Lower the heat to medium high. Continue cooking 6 or 7 minutes, or until when a small amount of the mixture dropped into cold water forms a soft ball. Remove from heat and add the vanilla extract.

You can use this icing as a base for chocolate icing as well; just add 2 squares of unsweetened baking chocolate, melted and cooled, with the vanilla extract.

Makes enough to ice a 2-layer (9-inch) cake

Decorator Icing for Cookies

WANDA BROOKS, Stanly County

Wanda Brooks of Richfield uses this icing for decorating gingerbread cookies and houses. You can also add color and use it for painting designs on sugar cookies.

2 egg whites
2 1/2 cups 10x powdered sugar

IN A LARGE BOWL, beat the egg whites until frothy and slightly thickened. Beat in the sugar, 1/2 cup at a time. Continue beating for about 5 minutes or until the egg whites are stiff.

Makes 2 cups

Seafoam Icing

Fay Kemp

FAY KEMP, Dare County

Fay Kemp grew up during the 1950s in the small village of Mann's Harbor next door to her grandmother, Florence Jones. Fay's uncle, Howard Jones, worked for the Coast Guard at their station on Harkers Island. Florence would make her son, Howard, a yellow cake and frost it with seafoam icing. Then she would go to the local store, where ice cream was sold in five-gallon cardboard drums with metal lids. The store manager saved the empty ice cream drum for her. Florence cleaned it, removed the lid, and cut it down to the size of the cake. She placed the cake inside and re-fitted the top. Mail at that time was delivered several times a day; so Florence paid postage for the cake, and gave the converted ice cream drum containing the cake to the mailman who delivered the cake to Howard on Harkers Island.

> 1 cup sugar
> 3/4 cup water
> 1/2 cup light corn syrup
> 1/2 stick (1/4 cup) butter
> 2 egg whites
> 1 cup raisins
> 1 cup pecans, chopped
> 1 cup walnuts, chopped

COMBINE the sugar, water, corn syrup, and butter in a double boiler. Bring to a boil, stirring constantly. Add the raisins and chopped nuts. In a separate bowl, beat the egg whites until stiff peaks form. Add them to the sugar mixture. Blend well. Remove from heat. Let cool for 3 minutes before spreading on the cake.

Makes enough to ice a two-layer (9-inch) cake

Cake Filling

SUSAN CARSON, Brunswick County

You can dress up a basic cake by adding this simple but tasty custardlike filling.

2 tablespoons sugar
1 tablespoon cornstarch
2 egg yolks
1 cup milk

COMBINE the sugar, cornstarch, and eggs in a double boiler and heat gradually, stirring constantly, until the mixture thickens; set aside. Heat the milk in a saucepan to almost boiling, stirring constantly. Add the sugar and egg mixture and let it just come to a boil. Remove the pan from the heat and stir the filling until it is cool.

Makes about 1 cup

Orange Filling

JACKI EPPERSON, Durham County

"Leone Webb Epperson's homemade cookbook is a family treasure," Jacki Epperson of Durham told me as she opened a small notebook decorated with colorful cutouts from magazines surrounding page after page of handwritten recipes. "You can talk about replaceable things like sterling silver, but this is irreplaceable. You can't find this anywhere else in the wide world. Leone was born in 1898 and died in 1969. She began compiling this book during the 1920s. I am thrilled to pieces to find this. We found it in a little ice chest that was packed up when a relative moved to a nursing home."

Orange filling is one of Leone's sweet heirloom recipes.

1/4 cup orange juice
1 tablespoon lemon juice
1/4 cup butter
1 cup sugar
1 egg, slightly beaten
1/4 cup cornstarch
grated zest of 1/2 orange

COMBINE the orange and lemon juices, butter, and sugar in a saucepan over medium heat. Stir until smooth. Pour a little of the hot mixture into the beaten egg. Keep stirring as you add the egg back into the saucepan. When the mixture begins to thicken, stir in the cornstarch and orange zest. The filling is ready as soon as the cornstarch dissolves and the mixture becomes smooth.

Makes about 1 cup

Good Lemon Filling

MARTHA BARNES, Pitt County

Aunt Martha's good lemon filling is absolutely scrumptious; it makes any basic cake even better.

1 cup sugar
1/2 stick (1/4 cup) butter
2 eggs, beaten
juice of 2 lemons
grated zest of 2 lemons

COMBINE the sugar and butter in a double boiler over medium heat. Add the eggs, lemon juice, and grated lemon zest. Stir constantly until the mixture thickens. Turn off the burner and leave the mixture over hot water for 15 minutes. Remove from heat; let cool before spreading.

Makes about 1 1/2 cups, enough to fill a 2-layer (9-inch) cake

Coconut Filling (with optional icing)

JUANITA OGBURN HUDSON, Harnett County

"This is an 1800s recipe a friend in the church, Mae Johnson Coats, gave to me in the 1950s," says Juanita Ogburn Hudson of Bailey's Crossroads. "She said it was her grandmother's and guessed it originated around 1870." You can simply fill the layers, leaving the sides of the cake bare, or, to "dress cake up," prepare the second icing recipe below to cover the sides of cake.

Filling
2 cups sugar
2 cups milk
1/2 to 1 cup freshly grated or packaged flaked coconut
(or more as needed)
1 to 2 tablespoons all-purpose flour, if needed

COMBINE the sugar and milk in a double boiler and heat to a simmer. Add about 1/2 cup or more of the coconut to thicken the mixture. If too thick, add a little water. If too thin, add a little flour. Spread while warm. Refrigerate cake.

Makes 2 1/2 cups

Icing for Sides (optional)

5 tablespoons water
1 tablespoon light corn syrup
1/4 teaspoon cream of tartar
1 cup sugar
2 egg whites
1 tablespoon 10X powdered sugar, or more as needed

MIX the water, corn syrup, cream of tartar, and sugar together in a double boiler over medium heat. Maintain a slow boil until the resulting syrup spins a thread when pulled with a spoon, about 240° on a candy thermometer. In the meantime, beat the egg whites stiff. Fold in 1 tablespoon powdered sugar. Pour the hot syrup over the beaten egg whites, and beat the icing until it is light and fluffy. Beat in 1 heaping teaspoon of powdered sugar if icing seems too thin.

Makes enough to ice a 2-layer (9-inch) cake

Lemon Sauce

MARGUERITE HUGHEY, Buncombe County

1 cup brown sugar
grated zest of 1 lemon
1/8 teaspoon salt
3 tablespoons cornstarch dissolved in 1/2 cup water
2 cups water
juice of 1 lemon
1 stick (1/2 cup) butter

COMBINE all the ingredients in a saucepan. Cook over medium heat until thick and smooth. Pour over gingerbread while still warm.

Makes 3 cups

Pineapple Filling

. . . .

MARTHA BARNES, Pitt County

What sauce could possibly be easier than this? You can pour pineapple filling over cake layers or ice cream when you want a little something extra.

1 can (20 ounces) crushed pineapple
1/4 cup cornstarch
1/4 cup sugar

DRAIN the pineapple into a saucepan. Reserve the fruit. Combine the cornstarch and sugar and add to the pineapple juice. Bring the mixture to a boil for a few minutes until thick. Remove from heat. Stir in the reserved pineapple. Spread while warm.

Makes 2 1/2 cups

Butter Sauce

. . . .

SUSAN CARSON, Brunswick County

Susan Carson of Southport, known as Miss Susie, says this is perfect for plum pudding (see Susan Carson's recipe in the Puddings and Custards chapter). You can also pour it over gingerbread (see Juanita Bailey's recipe in the Cakes chapter).

Miss Susie suggests the following variations of butter sauce:

* Add freshly squeezed lemon juice.
* Substitute brown sugar for white and add crushed pineapple.
* Add coconut and a little fresh orange juice.
* Add raisins or blueberries.

1/4 cup butter

1/2 cup sugar

1/3 cup light cream (or evaporated milk)

COMBINE the butter, sugar, and cream in a saucepan and cook over low heat for 5 minutes.

Makes about 1/2 cup

Tootie Fruitie

· ·

NOLIE RIDENHOUR ZIMMERMAN, Rowan County

As I traveled to different regions, I heard many cooks talk about how they enjoyed tootie fruitie. Nolie Ridenhour Zimmerman of Salisbury found this recipe in one of her old, handwritten cookbooks.

2 1/2 cups raisins

1 cup pecans, chopped

1 3/4 cups flaked coconut

1 cup coconut juice (also called coconut milk)

2 cups sugar

GRIND TOGETHER the raisins, pecans, and coconut. Heat the coconut juice in a small saucepan. Add the sugar and bring the mixture to a boil. Remove from heat; add the fruit, nuts, and coconut. If the filling is too dry to spread, add a little more coconut juice or some water. Cool slightly and spread.

Makes 4 cups

Jonesy Sauce

SUSAN CARSON, Brunswick County

Miss Susie suggests pouring jonesy sauce over gingerbread, apple pie, cake, or dumplings. It's also good over plum pudding.

1 cup sugar
1/2 stick (1/4 cup) butter
1 egg, beaten
1 tablespoon vinegar
juice of 1 lemon

BLEND the sugar and butter in a saucepan over low heat. Add the egg, vinegar, and lemon juice and beat until just thickened. Serve hot.

Makes about 1 cup

Hard Sauce

JACKI EPPERSON, Durham County
KAY BAKER, Lenoir County

"Good over [plum] pudding," reads a note in Leona Epperson's handwritten cookbook. Kay Baker of Kinston has been enjoying hard sauce since she was a little girl. "Sometimes I just eat it on bread," Kay confided. Similarly, my grandmother used to make my younger brother, Reynold, sugar sandwiches out of white loaf bread spread with butter and sugar.

2 tablespoons boiling water
1 stick (1/2 cup) butter, softened to room temperature
1 cup 10X powdered sugar
1/2 teaspoon vanilla extract, whiskey, brandy, or rum
1/2 cup chopped nuts (optional)

POUR the boiling water over the softened butter. Use a fork to mash the sugar into the butter just until combined. Add the flavoring and nuts and stir until they are well incorporated. Refrigerate until the sauce hardens.

Makes about 1/2 cup

Sauce Superb

LUCIE LEA ROBSON, Mecklenburg County

You can pour this over ice cream, pudding, or cake. It's fabulously rich.

1/2 cup blanched almonds
1/2 cup brown sugar, firmly packed
1/4 cup apricot or other brandy
1/2 cup bourbon
1/2 cup flaked coconut, toasted

IN A BLENDER, grind the almonds to a coarse consistency. Add the sugar, brandy, and bourbon and blend until smooth. Pour the mixture into a bowl. Add the coconut and mix well.

Makes 2 cups

Whipped Cream

WILL ALLEN, Wake County

Will Allen in his kitchen

"Making whipped cream is very simple," Will told me. "It only has three ingredients. The heavier the cream, the sooner it will whip. Mix the sugar in while the cream is still soft. If you wait until the cream is thick, the sugar won't dissolve. We use it on fresh berry medley, like blueberries, strawberries, blackberries, or my grandmother's recipe for hot milk sponge cake."

> *2 cups (1 pint) heavy whipping cream*
> *1 to 1 1/3 cups sugar, to taste*
> *1 tablespoon vanilla extract*

BEAT the cream with an electric mixer on low speed. After a minute and a half, gradually add the sugar. Turn the mixer up to medium high. When the sugar is well incorporated, add the vanilla extract. Continue beating on medium-high speed until stiff peaks form.

Makes 2 cups

Ice Cream and Frozen Desserts

Vanilla Ice Cream

Homemade Freezer Ice Milk

Easy Ice Cream Surprise

Peach Ice Cream

Coffee Ice Cream

Lemon Ice Cream

Harvey's Bristol Cream

    French Apple Ice Cream

Caramel Ice Cream

Pineapple Sherbet

Orange Icebox Cake

Frozen Strawberry Pie

Snow Cream

MY SOUTHERN sweet tooth likes nothing better than to savor a cold dessert like homemade ice cream or sherbet. Smooth, rich, cool, and creamy, these frozen delights are particularly suited to taking advantage of flavors from each season's natural gifts. Once you master Marguerite Hughey's vanilla ice cream or Amy Van Benton's homemade freezer ice milk, you can dress them up by adding fruit, nuts, or other flavorings—try fresh strawberries, peaches, or pecans. Or just add a scoop of one of these frozen treats to half a cantaloupe or a dish of blueberries, like my father used to do.

Cold desserts have been well liked in America since colonial times. In 1809, Dolley Madison, born in Guilford County, North Carolina, wowed guests at the inauguration of her husband, James, with a complicated ice cream centerpiece. Ice cream is easy and fun to make at home now. Fans from one to one hundred years old make it the most popular dessert in the country. In a cone or cup, it is soothing, nutritious, and subtle. Place it beside your favorite cake for a double portion of flavorful decadence; add it to milk or a soft drink for a frothy float; or make a sundae by covering it with nuts, sauces, fruit, and whipped cream. My mother used to transform a simple scoop of vanilla ice cream into an elegant dessert by topping it with a little crème de menthe, garnishing it with mint leaves from our backyard, and serving it with a homemade cookie.

Churning ice cream or sherbet by hand is a nostalgic social event involving the guests, who take turns at the crank while anticipation builds for enjoying the cold, creamy reward. You can even have the pleasure of cold desserts without the exercise, if you like; many of the recipes included here do not require a special maker. Moreover, ice cream makers with small engines can do the work for you, and they are available at reasonable prices. If you crave the contentment of hand cranking, you can still find the old machines—maybe in the garage or attic of an elderly friend. However they're prepared, these luscious and refreshing treats lend themselves well to sharing with family, friends, and neighbors.

Note: Be sure to enjoy frozen desserts soon after you make them. Each time you remove a frozen dessert from the freezer to serve it and then refreeze it, ice crystals form that will compromise the taste. I recommend consuming them within one week at most.

Vanilla Ice Cream

MARGUERITE HUGHEY, Buncombe County

Vanilla ice cream is America's favorite dessert. Generation after generation has enjoyed this frozen treat, ever since Thomas Jefferson brought back a recipe from France in the early 1800s.

2 cups milk
3 eggs, beaten
2/3 cup sugar
pinch salt
2 cups heavy cream or half-and-half
1 tablespoon vanilla extract

HEAT the milk in a double boiler over boiling water. In a separate bowl, combine the eggs, sugar, and salt, and gradually add some of the hot milk, stirring constantly. Pour all back into the double boiler, and cook, stirring constantly, until the mixture thickens. Remove from heat and cool. Add the cream and vanilla extract. Freeze in an ice cream maker according the manufacturer's directions.

Makes about a quart

Homemade Freezer Ice Milk

AMY VAN BENTON, Perquimans County

"I was raised in Winfall. This is my mother's recipe. She was a birthright Quaker," Amy Van Benton told me. "My mother always made it on the Fourth of July. Mama made the custard, but Daddy froze it. We were young enough to beg to turn the crank, until we learned it was work."

Amy Van Benton of Winfall

2 large eggs
1 cup sugar
1 tablespoon all-purpose flour
1 quart milk
1 or 2 cans (12 ounces each) evaporated milk, chilled
vanilla extract or 1 cup of cleaned, peeled, chopped fruit

BEAT the eggs, sugar, and flour together until smooth. Heat the milk in a saucepan over low heat just until the boiling point. Quickly add the egg mixture and stir constantly until thick. Add 1 or 2 cans of evaporated milk, depending on how much ice milk you want. Add the flavoring or fruit. Freeze in an ice cream maker according to the manufacturer's instructions.

Makes 2 quarts

Easy Ice Cream Surprise

BRENDA ZIMMERMAN, Rowan County

"This is a recipe that I use to make people believe that I've spent a lot of time making a really good dessert when I haven't," said Brenda Zimmerman of Salisbury. "I have one friend who requests this for a birthday gift every year. I really prefer Breyers Vanilla Bean. I usually use pecans, but walnuts or almonds will do. I serve it with a little thin wafer cookie."

1/2 gallon of your favorite vanilla ice cream
1/2 cup chopped nuts
1/2 cup chopped cherries
1 cup dry sherry or amaretto

SOFTEN the ice cream in a bowl just enough to be able to insert a large spoon. Rapidly add the nuts, cherries, and sherry or amaretto. Blend well and refreeze.

Makes a little more than 1/2 gallon

Peach Ice Cream

MARGUERITE HUGHEY, Buncombe County

"Marguerite Hughey is now deceased," Mary Charles Pawlikowski of Nash County told me. "She used to live beside my husband's family in Raleigh. She was obsessed with recipes. I have nearly all of hers, given to me by her husband several years ago when we were there on a visit. Each recipe records the person who gave it to her and the year she obtained it. A friend named Mrs. Smathers gave her this one for peach ice cream in 1959."

1 cup mashed peaches
2 1/2 cups sugar, divided

1 egg, beaten

2 cups heavy cream

6 cups milk

1 teaspoon vanilla extract

COMBINE the peaches with 1/2 cup sugar; set aside. In a double boiler, blend the egg and 2 cups sugar until smooth. Stir in the cream. Heat the mixture until it begins to thicken. Remove from heat and stir in the milk. Blend until smooth. Freeze in an ice cream maker according to the manufacturer's instructions until the ice cream is mushy. Stir in the peaches and vanilla extract and return it to the ice cream maker until the ice cream thickens.

Makes 2 quarts

Coffee Ice Cream

MARTHA BARNES, Pitt County

Coffee ice cream is a great pick-me-up on a hot summer day.

1 package (4-serving size) chocolate pudding mix

1 1/2 cups milk

1/2 cup strong coffee

1/4 cup sugar

1 cup whipped cream

COMBINE the pudding mix, milk, and coffee and beat well. Add the sugar. Stir until dissolved. Separately, whip the cream until it forms soft peaks. Fold in the chocolate mixture. Place the bowl in the freezer for about 30 minutes and then whip the mixture well. Pour the mixture into an 8-inch-square casserole or other freezer-proof dish. Freeze it for at least 3 hours before serving.

Makes 1 1/2 pints

Lemon Ice Cream

AMY VAN BENTON, Perquimans County

"Mama used to make this back before you had twist plastic ice trays or ice makers," said Amy Van Benton of Winfall. "We had metal ice trays with a cube maker that sat down in it, and you pulled a handle to release the cubes. She would just take the cube maker out and put the cookie crumbs and then the custard in the empty ice tray." You can still use an ice cube tray without the liner as well as the pie plate suggested below.

1 cup crushed vanilla wafers, divided
2 eggs, separated
1 cup sugar
juice of 2 lemons
3/4 cup evaporated milk, refrigerated overnight

SPRINKLE 3/4 cup of vanilla wafer crumbs into a pie plate. To make the custard, heat the egg yolks, sugar, and lemon juice in a saucepan over low heat until thick; remove from heat and let cool. In a separate bowl, whip the evaporated milk until thick. Set aside. Beat the egg whites until stiff and combine them with the egg yolk mixture. Add the whipped evaporated milk to the egg mixture, and stir until the custard is well blended. Pour the custard into the prepared pie plate. Sprinkle the top with the remaining 1/4 cup of vanilla wafer crumbs. Freeze.

Serves 6 to 8

Harvey's Bristol Cream
French Apple Ice Cream

JANE SHERRILL LASLEY, Iredell County

"This is to-die-for ice cream!" Jane Sherrill Lasley told me. "To make it even richer, use another pint of heavy cream instead of the evaporated milk. Any good cream sherry will do, but Harvey's is by far the best. The only way to make this better, if you think your heart can take the excitement, is to serve it on freshly baked, homemade, warm apple pie."

Notes from Jane: You can omit the eggs entirely if you wish. Just mix sugars with applesauce and add to freezer can. Do not use reduced-fat or fat-free half-and-half or evaporated milk. Each half-cup serving contains a teaspoon of sherry. Because of the alcohol in the sherry, this ice cream will never get rock-hard. If using an electric ice cream maker, follow the manufacturer's directions.

> *2 pasteurized eggs or 1/2 cup Egg Beaters*
> *1 cup white sugar*
> *1/2 cup brown sugar, packed*
> *2 cups of applesauce (Jane prefers the White House brand)*
> *1 cup heavy whipping cream*
> *2 cups half-and-half*
> *1 can (15 ounces) evaporated milk, less 1/3 cup*
> *1/3 cup Harvey's Bristol Cream Sherry or your favorite cream sherry*
> *1 teaspoon vanilla extract*
> *a "good sprinkle" of nutmeg, cinnamon, and allspice or*
>   *1/2 teaspoon apple pie spice*

BEAT the eggs until light. Beat in the sugars. Add the remaining ingredients and stir until smooth. Pour the mixture into the freezer can of an ice cream maker. Crank until frozen. Serve immediately, or pack the freezer can in a mixture of ice and ice cream salt to harden.

Makes about 1/2 gallon

Caramel Ice Cream

MARGARET BARNES FAHRINGER, Robeson County

"Serve with chocolate cake for a wonderful bridge dessert or a sweet treat for any birthday party," Margaret Barnes Fahringer suggests.

1 cup sugar
5 cups milk (1 cup of which should be chilled)
1/4 cup all-purpose flour
pinch salt
2 cups heavy cream, whipped
1 teaspoon vanilla extract

BROWN the sugar in a saucepan over medium heat until it bubbles all over the bottom of the pan; add 4 cups of milk and stir well. Combine the flour, salt, and 1 cup cold milk and blend until smooth; strain the flour mixture into the hot milk mixture. Cook a few minutes over medium heat, stirring constantly, until the mixture thickens slightly. Remove from heat and chill. When cold, add the whipped cream and vanilla extract. Pour the mixture into a 9 × 13-inch pan or dish and freeze.

Serves 8 to 10

Pineapple Sherbet

JACKI EPPERSON, Durham County

"This was clearly a labor of love for Leone," Jacki told me as she looked over Leone Epperson's handmade cookbook. Leone lived in Durham most of her life, but she also had a house at Wrightsville Beach, where she must have enjoyed this tangy sherbet during hot weather.

3/4 cup sugar
3/4 cup water
juice of 6 lemons
2 cups crushed pineapple, drained
6 egg whites
4 cups heavy cream

BOIL the sugar and water together for 5 to 10 minutes, until a thick syrup forms. Remove from heat and stir in the lemon juice and pineapple. Freeze in an ice cream maker according to the manufacturer's instructions. When the mixture is partly frozen, beat the egg whites until stiff. Empty the contents of the ice cream freezer into a separate bowl and fold in the egg whites and cream. Return to the ice cream maker and continue churning until thick.

Makes about 6 cups

Orange Icebox Cake

. . . .

LUCIE LEA ROBSON, Mecklenburg County

Lucie Lea Robson's mother-in-law, Harriet Robson, lived in Chapel Hill during the 1940s when Harriet's husband, Charles, was a professor at the University of North Carolina. They lived at One Button Road, where the screen door opened and shut frequently as students, faculty, and friends visited. Air-conditioning didn't exist at the time, so cold desserts were popular during the hot, humid months. Harriet's recipe for old-fashioned orange icebox cake is simple to make but a party pleaser. It's a good way to end a heavy meal.

1 cup vanilla wafers, crushed
1 cup orange juice
1 tablespoon lemon juice
1 teaspoon grated lemon zest
24 marshmallows
1 cup heavy cream, whipped

SET ASIDE 1/4 cup of the crushed vanilla wafers. Line a 9-inch pie plate with the remaining 3/4 cup of wafers. Heat the orange and lemon juices, lemon zest, and marshmallows over low heat, stirring until the marshmallows melt and the mixture is well blended. Let cool, then fold in the whipped cream. Pour the mixture over the wafer crumbs in the pie plate. Sprinkle the reserved crumbs on top. Freeze, slice, and serve.

Serves 6 to 8

Frozen Strawberry Pie

SARAH SAWYER ALLEN, Lenoir County

In early April, signs appear on rural street corners of southern Wake County announcing "Miss Madison's Fresh Local Strawberries." Soon canopies, lawn chairs, and wooden tables sprout like buttercups behind the signs. This tells locals that the juicy, red berries are ripe and heralds the opening of fresh fruit season in North Carolina. Pick your own berries, buy them at your farmer's market, or grow them in your backyard. And be sure to save some for this refreshing pie.

Crust
1 cup all-purpose flour
1 cup nuts, chopped
1/4 cup brown sugar
1 stick (1/2 cup) butter, softened

PREHEAT OVEN to 350°. Combine all the ingredients until well blended. Press the mixture evenly into the bottom of a 9 × 13-inch cake pan. Bake for 20 minutes. Remove from the oven and let cool.

Filling
3 egg whites
1 cup sugar, divided
2 cups heavy cream
2 cups strawberries, cleaned, stems removed, and sliced
2 teaspoons lemon juice

BEAT the egg whites until peaks form. Add 1/2 cup sugar gradually. Set aside. In a separate bowl, beat the cream until stiff. Add 1/2 cup sugar gradually. Add the strawberries and lemon juice to the whipped cream and sugar. Fold in the egg whites and sugar. Spread over prepared crust. Freeze.

Serves 16

Snow Cream

. . . .

GRACE REA, Moore County

When you're snowbound, flurries that blow into the kitchen can turn into
a light dessert that's a satisfying distraction for children, young and old.
(If you aren't comfortable using real snow, this recipe can also be made
with shaved ice.) "I was born in 1935. I heard stories that it was snow on
the ground all winter," Grace Rea told me. "Here in Moore County, that's
unheard of. Maybe that's when my mother learned to make this." You can
substitute fresh milk for the evaporated milk if you wish.

> 8 to 10 quarts fresh, clean snow (or shaved ice)
> 1 1/3 cups sugar
> 1 can (12 ounces) evaporated milk
> 1 1/2 teaspoons vanilla extract
> 1/2 teaspoon lemon juice (optional)

IN A LARGE mixing bowl, combine the sugar, milk, and vanilla extract.
Add the snow (or shaved ice) gradually using a large spoon until the
mixture has the consistency of a milk shake. Pour the mixture into
cups and serve with a spoon and straw. Remember to enjoy snow cream
the day you make it! Like a snowy day in North Carolina, it doesn't last.

Serves 6 to 8

Candy

Fairy Kisses

Crystallized Grapefruit and
   Orange Peel

Aunt Martha's Burnt-Sugar
   Caramel Candy

Fats Marr's Potato Candy

Sugar-Coated Peanuts

Ruby Teague's Peanut Brittle

Peanut Butter Creams

Party Pecans

Pecan Kisses

Sherried Pecans

Pecan Divinity

Never-Fail Candy

Five-Minute Fudge

Mrs. Westbrook's Fudge

Quick Nut Fudge

Chocolate Coconut Mounds

Fudge Nut Ring

Peanut Butter Fudge

Martha Washington Candy

Date Roll

Uncooked Mints

Old-Fashioned Butter Mints

Bourbon Balls

Brandy Balls

Y OU CAN LEAVE a sweet taste in the mouths of your friends and family when you share some of the traditional candies from North Carolina's kitchens. If what you need is thick, rich fudge, you have several different recipes to choose from. Helen Cochrane from Greensboro in Guilford County recommends Mrs. Westbrook's fudge. Wanda Brooks of Richfield in Stanly County suggests quick nut fudge for people in a hurry who want a batch in less than an hour. Mary Henderson of Kinston in Lenoir County turns out a light peanut butter fudge that can be broken into pieces and stored for trips. My own recipe for fudge nut ring is filled with nuts and fruits, wonderful if you have a taste for something very rich and complex.

The winter holiday season is a great time to prepare candies for gifts and parties. Burnt-sugar caramel candy, date roll, or caramel squares make delectable Christmas presents. Lucie Lea Robson recommends sugared walnuts for parties.

I like to think of some of these confections as edible history. Fairy kisses, or meringue, a light candy made from whipped, sweetened egg whites, have been popular for over a hundred years. Martha Washington candy is a flavorful blend of chocolate and sweet cherries. Peanut brittle and divinity have been favorite southern treats for centuries. During the Great Depression of the 1930s, a clever cook in Brunswick County developed a recipe for candy made from potatoes. And I have vivid memories of wedding receptions in the 1950s where candy dishes brimmed with colorful mints and crystallized fruit peels.

Nita Jane Whitfield, an award-winning cook from Person County, shares her recipe for old-fashioned butter mints in these pages. Susan Carson's recipe for crystallized grapefruit and orange peel has a long personal history; it came to her from a friend, Mrs. Long, who got her recipe from a Mrs. Berg.

Cooks from across the state have a candy recipe that's right for you, whether you have years of cooking experience or you're brand new to the kitchen. If you're just getting started and think candy is way too hard for you to make successfully, think again and try Imogene Tomberlin's never-fail candy or uncooked mints. Once you begin to feel comfortable and your friends are crying for more, Mrs. Westbrook's fudge will offer more of a challenge. You can fill up your candy jar over and over again with a variety of rich, flavorful confections using these recipes.

Tips for Making Successful Candy

* The most complicated part of making old-fashioned candies like divinity and date roll is judging how long to cook the ingredients. The rule of thumb followed by most cooks whose recipes appear below is to test the hot, liquid candy every few minutes by dripping a small amount from a spoon into a glass of cold water. As soon as the liquid forms a ball in the cold water, it has reached "the soft ball stage," or 240° on a candy thermometer. When the liquid reaches this stage, you can remove it from the heat. You can purchase a candy thermometer at most grocery stores.

Fairy Kisses

HALIFAX COUNTY, Araminta Pierce Blowe

Fairy kisses are light, beautiful, fluffy, and easy to make. They absolutely deserve their name.

1 1/4 cups sugar
4 egg whites
pinch salt
1 cup chopped nuts
vanilla extract to taste

PREHEAT OVEN to 300°. Beat the sugar, egg whites, and salt for 15 to 20 minutes or until very stiff. Fold in the nuts and vanilla extract. Drop by teaspoon onto brown or parchment paper. Bake for about 30 minutes or until lightly browned and firm to the touch.

Makes 3 dozen

Crystallized Grapefruit and Orange Peel

SUSAN CARSON, Brunswick County

During the 1950s and 1960s, when I was growing up in the Inner Coastal Plain area of North Carolina, local people were frugal and careful of their possessions. Somebody who could make something out of an article that was seemingly useless, such as an empty soft drink bottle or an out-of-date license plate, was greatly admired. This strategy was also true of food, and is practiced today by cooks from all over North Carolina. Many recipes are cherished and shared not only because they are tasty but also because they make use of leftovers that would otherwise be thrown away. Bread pudding and watermelon rind pickles are examples.

The fruit peels in this recipe become delicious little candies that can be consumed alone or used as a colorful garnish on pound cakes and ice cream. The aroma they make while cooking fills the house with the fresh scent of citrus. According to Susan Carson of Southport, a Mrs. Long gave this recipe to her after a Mrs. Berg passed it to Mrs. Long.

1 grapefruit or 3 oranges
2 cups white sugar (plus more for coating the peels)
1 cup water

PEEL the grapefruit and/or oranges. Quarter the peel, then cut it into strips with scissors. Boil the peels in a quart of water for 30 to 60 minutes, changing the water a half a dozen times to get rid of the bitter taste. They're ready when you can pierce them easily with a fork. While the peels are boiling, make a syrup by boiling the sugar and water in a separate saucepan until it is thick and smooth. When the peels have cooked completely, drain and squeeze them lightly in a towel to remove any excess liquid but not hard enough to break them up. Add the peels to the sugar syrup and boil until the peels become transparent and the syrup is gone. Roll the peels in the extra sugar and spread them on waxed paper to dry. Store in an airtight container.

Yield depends on size of fruit

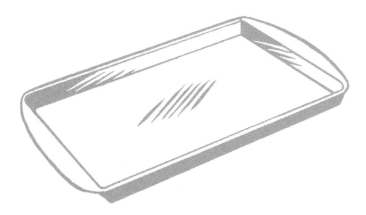

Aunt Martha's Burnt-Sugar Caramel Candy

MARTHA BARNES, Pitt County

When it came to candy, my father, an otherwise dignified lawyer, acted like a child. He loved candy. He liked hard fruit candy, chocolate bars, peanut brittle, caramels, candied fruit slices, pralines—almost any candy. I remember once seeing him stuff the entire top layer of a tin box of homemade candy into his mouth at one time to keep from having to share it. He looked like a chipmunk. But of all the candies he ate, this is the one my father eagerly awaited every Christmas of my childhood.

4 cups sugar, divided
1 tablespoon all-purpose flour
1/8 teaspoon salt
1 cup milk
1 tablespoon butter
2 cups nuts, chopped

BURNT SUGAR is basically caramelized sugar. To prepare it, place 1 cup of sugar in a saucepan over medium heat. Stir constantly until it turns into a thick amber-colored liquid.

Butter an 8-inch-square pan. Mix the sugar, flour, and salt together in a 2-quart saucepan. Add the milk and cook over low to medium heat until it boils. Add the burnt sugar slowly, stirring constantly. Add the butter and boil the mixture until it reaches the soft ball stage, about 240° on a candy thermometer. Let cool. Beat well and then fold in the chopped nuts. Pour the candy into the prepared pan, cool, and cut into scrumptious 1 1/2-inch pieces.

Makes about 25 pieces

Fats Marr's Potato Candy

SUSAN CARSON, Brunswick County

Susan Carson, Miss Susie to her friends, recalls that in Southport, her home, during the Great Depression of the 1930s, business and construction in the area came to a virtual halt. By 1933, the Red Cross was called in to distribute flour throughout the county. Farm produce provided some sustenance at home, though it often found no market. Southport residents were often poorly dressed and hungry. The Civilian Conservation Corps, a national program established in 1933 to provide work for unemployed Americans, moved a camp to Southport, where men lived in tents and worked on local utilities. Fats Marr was a cook for the facility. He created a recipe for candy made from potatoes. Miss Susie talked him into sharing it. I was assigned to make it when I joined her history class in Southport for a typical Depression meal.

1/2 cup unseasoned, well-mashed white potato (about 1 medium potato)
3 cups 10X powdered sugar
1 cup flaked coconut
1 teaspoon vanilla extract
2 squares (2 ounces) semisweet chocolate

BUTTER an 8-inch-square pan. While the potato is still hot, combine it with the sugar and coconut and beat well. Add the vanilla extract. Press the mixture into a lightly greased 8 × 8-inch pan. Meanwhile, melt the chocolate slowly over low heat, then spread it over top of the candy. Chill and cut into 2-inch squares. Keeps indefinitely refrigerated in an airtight container.

Makes 16 squares

Sugar-Coated Peanuts

....

GRACE REA, Moore County

"See how simple that is?" Grace Rea asked me as she pointed to her recipe for sugar-coated peanuts. "One caution to that," Grace's husband, Judd, added, "is that the moment all your moisture is dried out while you're cooking, it's time to put them on a sheet."

"These peanuts that I am using are sold by Eastern Star," Grace continued. Eastern Star is the largest fraternal organization in the world that includes both men and women. The organization gives approximately $1,500,000 a day to charities. "It's a fund raiser. Every year we sell two or three tractor-trailer loads. They're local North Carolina peanuts. We get them from Houston Peanut Company in Duplin County. I pass my recipe out with a bag. We generally raise $100,000 for Eastern Star. When they say, 'bring something for the refreshment table,' they know I'm going to bring them. Keep them airtight and they keep well. Be sure they're cold before you put them in your container." You can also find fresh North Carolina peanuts at farmers markets.

1 cup sugar
1/2 cup water
2 cups raw peanuts, shelled, skin on

PREHEAT OVEN to 300°. Heat the sugar and water in a saucepan over medium heat until the sugar dissolves. Add the peanuts and cook, stirring frequently, until the peanuts are completely coated and no syrup remains in the pan. Remove the pan from the heat and immediately pour the coated nuts onto an ungreased cookie sheet. Separate the peanuts with a fork. Bake approximately 30 minutes, stirring every 10 minutes.

Makes 2 cups

Ruby Teague's Peanut Brittle

. . . .

DAVID TEAGUE, Mecklenburg County

Be sure to store Ruby's peanut brittle in a sealed container so the candy stays crunchy and fresh.

2 cups sugar
1 cup dark corn syrup (David prefers Karo Blue Label)
1/2 teaspoon salt
1 cup warm water
1 1/2 cups raw or equivalent salted, roasted peanuts
1 tablespoon baking soda

GENEROUSLY butter a cookie sheet. Combine the sugar, corn syrup, salt, and warm water in a large saucepan. Heat until the temperature reads 250° on a candy thermometer. Stir in the peanuts. Continue cooking to 295°. Remove the pan from the heat. Add the baking soda and mix thoroughly. Spread the candy on the prepared pan to cool, then crack into pieces.

Makes about a pound

Peanut Butter Creams

. . . .

KAY BAKER, Lenoir County

"You need to use real butter, not margarine in this recipe," said Kay Baker of Kinston. "Melting a little paraffin with your chocolate will ensure that you coat the peanut cream well and seal up the soft interior of the candy. The paraffin keeps it nice and fresh. Store in a sealed container."

1/2 cup peanut butter
1 stick (1/2 cup) butter, softened
2 cups 10x powdered sugar

2 squares (2 ounces) unsweetened baking chocolate
2-inch square of paraffin

COMBINE the peanut butter and butter and blend until smooth. Gradually add the powdered sugar until the mixture holds together well and can be formed into balls. You may not need all the powdered sugar. In a saucepan, slowly melt the chocolate and paraffin together over low heat, stirring until they are thoroughly combined. Form the peanut butter dough into balls about 1 inch in diameter. Chill the balls for 30 minutes, then dip them into the chocolate and set them on a plate covered with waxed paper. Refrigerate the chocolate-covered balls until the chocolate hardens.

Makes about 3 dozen

Party Pecans

MARTHA BARNES, Pitt County

"They'll be crisp when cool," said a note on this recipe. "Keep in airtight jar."

1 egg white
1/4 cup cold water
1/2 cup sugar
1/4 cup cornstarch

1/2 teaspoon cloves
1/8 teaspoon salt
2 cups pecan halves

PREHEAT OVEN to 250°. Grease 2 cookie sheets. Combine the egg white with cold water. Sift the sugar, cornstarch, cloves, and salt into the egg mixture and mix well. Using tongs, dip each pecan into the mixture and place them on the prepared cookie sheets. Bake for 1 1/4 hours. Cool thoroughly.

Makes 60 to 80

Pecan Kisses

MARGUERITE HUGHEY, Buncombe County

3/4 cup brown sugar
1 teaspoon vanilla extract

1 egg white, beaten until stiff
2 to 2 1/2 cups pecans, chopped

PREHEAT OVEN to 250°. Grease a cookie sheet. Combine the sugar and vanilla extract with the beaten egg white. Mix until smooth. Fold in the pecans. Drop by teaspoon onto prepared cookie sheet. Bake for 1/2 hour, then turn off oven and leave cookies inside until oven is cold.

Makes 2 dozen

Sherried Pecans

MARGUERITE HUGHEY, Buncombe County

The pecan tree is indigenous to North America. Some folks call its tasty, brown nuts "pi-*kahns*," others say "pi-*kans*," and still others say "*pee*-kans." Alan Bundy of Sampson County raises the rich, golden nuts for a living. "North Carolinians are the only people who say '*pee*-kans,'" he told me. Whatever you call them, they're mighty good and even better when combined with candy.

1 pound light brown sugar
1/2 cup cream sherry

3 tablespoons butter
1 pound pecan halves

GREASE a sheet of aluminum foil. Combine the sugar, sherry, and butter in a saucepan. Bring the mixture to a boil and cook 4 minutes, stirring constantly. Remove the pan from the heat. Add the pecans. Stir until the sugar mixture clings to the pecans. Turn the pecans out onto the greased foil. Separate into clusters or individual halves and cool.

Makes 2 pounds

Pecan Divinity

ALAN BUNDY, Sampson County

Alan Bundy

Alan Bundy lives in Turkey, where he is the manager of Elizabeth's Pecans. The business is named for his daughter and features pecan candies and bags of the fresh, crunchy nuts gathered from 1,000 trees that Alan's father planted in 1981. The Bundys have deep roots in North Carolina: the pecan trees are located on forty-five acres that were originally owned by Alan's great-great-great-grandfather. The English general Lord Cornwallis slept in the family home in 1781 when he traveled through North Carolina during the Revolutionary War. Alan's uncle lives there today. This candy is just one divine way to enjoy the goodness of the nuts.

2 1/2 cups sugar
1/2 cup light corn syrup
1 teaspoon salt
3/4 cup water
2 egg whites
1 1/2 cups pecans, chopped
1 tablespoon vanilla extract

BUTTER a 9 × 13-inch baking pan. Cook the sugar, corn syrup, salt, and water in a saucepan over medium heat until a hard ball forms when a small amount of the syrup is dribbled into cold water, 250–260° on a candy thermometer. Remove the pan from the heat. Beat the egg whites in a separate mixing bowl until they form stiff peaks. Pour the hot mixture over the whipped eggs, beating constantly. When the mixture is smooth, add the pecans and vanilla extract. Continue beating until the mixture thickens into a mass and becomes heavy. Spread it into the prepared pan and cut when cool. Divine!

Makes 60 pieces

Never-Fail Candy

IMOGENE TOMBERLIN, Yancey County

For folks who are just starting to make candy, this is a great way to learn.

2 sticks (1 cup) margarine

1 can (12 ounces) evaporated milk
(Imogene prefers Carnation)

5 cups sugar

2 cups your favorite chocolate
chips

MELT the margarine in a double boiler. Add the milk and sugar and blend well. Boil the mixture for 5 minutes or until it reaches the soft ball stage, or about 240° on a candy thermometer. Remove the pan from the heat and stir in the chocolate chips until they are melted and the mixture is smooth. Pour the fudge out onto a large, greased platter that is at least 1/4 inch deep. Slice when cool.

Makes about 48 pieces

Five-Minute Fudge

FOY ALLEN EDELMAN, Lenoir County

I don't remember how many times I made this fudge recipe when I attended Grainger High School in Kinston during the 1960s. My friends and I gathered for dessert to celebrate anything—a birthday, holiday, Saturday, even a passing grade. Five-minute fudge is great for teenagers to try when they're learning to cook.

1/4 cup butter

2/3 cup evaporated milk

1 2/3 cups sugar

1/2 teaspoon salt

2 cups (4 ounces) miniature
marshmallows

1 1/4 cups semisweet
chocolate chips

1 teaspoon vanilla extract

1/2 cup nuts, chopped

GREASE an 8-inch-square baking pan. In a large saucepan over medium heat, combine the butter, milk, sugar, and salt. Heat until the mixture comes to a boil. Cook 4 to 5 more minutes, stirring constantly. Remove from heat. Add the marshmallows, chocolate chips, vanilla extract, and nuts and stir vigorously for 1 minute until the marshmallows melt and blend smoothly into the mixture. Pour the fudge into the prepared pan. Cool and cut into 2-inch squares.

Makes 16 pieces

Mrs. Westbrook's Fudge

HELEN COCHRANE, Guilford County

Mrs. Westbrook lived on Highway 50 near Garner in Wake County. Helen Cochrane and her daughter, Jean, have been making this recipe since 1963, when Jean married and she and her new husband rented a small apartment behind Mrs. Westbrook. This fudge gives them sweet memories of their first home.

4 1/2 cups semisweet chocolate chips
1 jar (7 ounces) marshmallow cream
5 cups sugar
2 sticks (1 cup) butter
1 can (12 ounces) evaporated milk
3 teaspoons vanilla extract
2 cups nuts, chopped

GREASE a 9 × 13-inch cake pan. Combine the chocolate chips and marshmallow cream in a large mixing bowl. Set aside. In a saucepan over medium heat combine the sugar, butter, and milk. Bring to a boil and cook for 8 minutes, stirring constantly. Pour the hot mixture over the chocolate chips and marshmallow cream and stir the mixture until the chocolate is melted. Add the vanilla extract and nuts, blending until the nuts are well incorporated. Pour the fudge into the prepared pan. Chill for an hour. Cut into squares and enjoy.

Makes 48 pieces

Quick Nut Fudge

WANDA BROOKS, Stanly County

"Quick and easy," said Wanda Brooks of Richfield. "This fudge is a good Christmas recipe."

2 cups 10x powdered sugar
1/2 cup cocoa
1/4 teaspoon salt
6 tablespoons (3/4 cup) margarine
1/4 cup milk
1 tablespoon vanilla extract
1 cup nuts, chopped

GREASE an 8-inch-square baking pan. Combine all the ingredients except the nuts in a microwavable bowl, placing the margarine on top. Cover the bowl with waxed paper, and microwave the mixture for intervals of 45 to 50 seconds, just until the margarine melts. This usually takes about 2 minutes. Remove the bowl from the microwave and stir the mixture until smooth. Fold in the nuts. Spread the candy evenly in the prepared pan. Cut into 2-inch squares when cool.

Makes 16 pieces

Chocolate Coconut Mounds

FOY ALLEN EDELMAN, Lenoir County

Mounds are just too good to enjoy alone. I fix them when I can share them with a friend who is in the mood for something chocolaty, creamy, and soothing.

1 square (1 ounce) unsweetened chocolate
1/2 cup sweetened condensed milk
1/2 teaspoon vanilla extract
1 1/3 cups flaked coconut

PREHEAT OVEN to 325°. Grease a cookie sheet. Combine the chocolate, condensed milk, and vanilla extract in a saucepan over low heat. Stir just until the chocolate has melted and the mixture is smooth. Remove the pan from the heat and quickly blend in the coconut. Drop by rounded teaspoon onto the prepared cookie sheet. Bake for 15 minutes. Remove the candies from the cookie sheet immediately and place them on waxed paper. Let cool.

Makes 24 pieces

Fudge Nut Ring

FOY ALLEN EDELMAN, Lenoir County

I need only about half an hour to make this beautiful confection. I like to arrange the nuts and maraschino cherries in a pattern on the top.

2 cups semisweet chocolate chips
2 cups butterscotch chips
1 can (14 ounces) sweetened condensed milk
1 cup walnuts or pecans, chopped
1/2 teaspoon vanilla extract
1 cup walnut or pecan halves
maraschino cherries (optional)
additional nuts for top (optional)

MELT the chocolate and butterscotch chips in a double boiler over medium heat. Add the condensed milk and stir until the mixture is well blended and begins to thicken. Remove the pan from the heat. Add the chopped nuts and vanilla extract. Blend well. Let cool until the mixture thickens, about an hour. Meanwhile, line the bottom and sides of a 9-inch pie pan with aluminum foil. Grease the foil and arrange 3/4 cup of the nut halves in the bottom of the pie pan, forming a 2-inch-wide ring around the edge of the pan. Spoon the chocolate mixture in small mounds on top of the nuts to form a ring. Decorate the top with additional nuts and maraschino cherries, if desired. Chill in the refrigerator until firm enough to slice.

Makes 16 slices

Peanut Butter Fudge

MARY AMYETTE HENDERSON, Lenoir County

Mary Amyette Henderson of Kinston was a young widow and mother of three children when I was a teenager. Her daughter, Jacki, was one of my best friends. I was sometimes fortunate enough to be asked to go to Atlantic Beach with her family for the weekend to stay in their Spartan Mansion trailer. Since we traveled in Mary's 1962 Volkswagen Beetle, we packed our weekend belongings in brown paper grocery bags that would crush together in the small luggage compartment at the front of the car. Mary also made this delicious fudge. "I never made this recipe by measuring ingredients until you asked me for it," she told me.

1 cup sugar
1 cup cocoa
1/2 cup evaporated milk
1/2 cup butter
1 teaspoon vanilla extract
3/4 cup peanut butter

COMBINE the sugar, cocoa, milk, and butter in a saucepan and bring the mixture to a boil over low to medium heat. Stir constantly, cooking until a candy thermometer reaches 240°. Turn off the heat and remove the thermometer but leave the pan on the burner. Stir in the vanilla extract. Quickly stir in the peanut butter, mixing until it is evenly distributed. Pour the fudge onto a buttered platter that is approximately 1/4 inch deep. Let cool completely and cut into squares.

Makes about 48 squares

Martha Washington Candy

LUCIE LEA ROBSON, Mecklenburg County

I associate this recipe with two significant dates in February: the 14th and the 22nd. You don't have to wait until then to make this candy, but it is a sweet way to remember your valentine and celebrate George Washington's birthday. Lucie Lea Robson attributes this recipe to her mother-in-law, Harriet Robson.

2 cups 10x powdered sugar
1 egg white
1 to 2 teaspoons vanilla extract
1 square (1 ounce) unsweetened baking chocolate
1/4 ounce paraffin
3/4 cup maraschino cherries (optional)
pecan halves (optional)

COMBINE the powdered sugar, egg white, and 1 teaspoon of the vanilla extract and blend well. The mixture should be firm but moist enough to form into balls about 1 inch in diameter; add more vanilla if the mixture is too dry. Chill the balls a few minutes in the refrigerator while you make the coating. Combine the chocolate and paraffin in a small saucepan over low heat; stir until the mixture is soft and well blended. Dip the sugar balls into the chocolate/paraffin mixture. Place a pecan half or a cherry on top while the balls are still warm, then cool them on waxed paper. You may also form the sugar balls around a cherry or pecan half before dipping them into the chocolate mixture.

Makes about 36 pieces

Date Roll

MARTHA BARNES, Pitt County

While I'm cooking, I often think of people who have given me recipes. This one reminds me of my great-aunt Martha Barnes. I was in the kitchen by age four or five with my mother and our housekeeper, Ida Mae Blount, so I also remember them when I cook, but it was Aunt Martha who copied her own personal recipes into a school notebook and gave it to me one Christmas. It was my first cookbook. The old, ragged notebook contains a tangible part of my family's history scratched out in Aunt Martha's hand with blue ink that came from a fountain pen. I have to keep it in a plastic sleeve now because it's so worn. But I still pull it out often, refreshing my memory as to exactly how much to measure for a recipe that I've been making since I was a child. I like to touch it and think of my ancestors who might have enjoyed the same family dishes that I do. Aunt Martha died a long time ago, but she remains a benevolent presence in my kitchen. This is another of her simple yet delicious recipes that even children can help make.

3 cups sugar
1 cup milk
1/4 teaspoon salt
1 tablespoon butter
1 cup chopped dates
2 cups nuts, chopped

COMBINE the sugar, milk, and salt in a saucepan and bring the mixture to a boil over medium heat. Cook, stirring, until a small amount of the mixture dropped into cold water forms a firm ball. Add the butter and dates and blend well. Remove the pan from the heat, add the nuts, and beat until stiff. Turn the candy out onto a sheet of waxed paper and form it into a log. With a sharp knife, cut the roll into thin slices. Cool the slices and store them in an airtight container.

Makes 48 slices

Uncooked Mints

IMOGENE TOMBERLIN, Yancey County

This is a simple recipe that doesn't even require a double boiler to make. "It keeps well in a covered metal can," Imogene Tomberlin said. "You can make it ahead and freeze it."

2 cups 10X powdered sugar
1/2 stick (1/4 cup) margarine, softened
3 tablespoons evaporated milk (Imogene prefers Carnation)
4 or 5 drops food coloring
10 drops peppermint oil

COMBINE the sugar and margarine in a mixing bowl. Add the milk, food coloring, and peppermint oil and work the mixture into the consistency of putty. Form the candy into 1/2-inch-thick ropes and cut the ropes into pieces. Let stiffen, then enjoy.

Makes 48 pieces

Old-Fashioned Butter Mints

. . . .

NITA WHITFIELD, Person County

Butter mints are a must-have at southern wedding receptions, bridge parties, and baby showers. Delicate and smooth, they are a pretty finger food made from four basic ingredients. This is a recipe for an experienced cook or anyone who enjoys a challenge in the kitchen. "Practice and persistence are all it takes to make butter mints," says Nita Whitfield, an award-winning candy maker. "They are a chemical process and when they mess up, you have to figure out why and correct it when you make the next batch. If you undercook a batch, you can put the candy back in the pot and cook it over. Add the same amount of water, and you will have to add the peppermint oil again as it will evaporate out when boiled. Ironically, a batch cooked over tastes even better."

Equipment

a professional candy thermometer (Nita uses a
  Wilton brand thermometer)
3-quart saucepan (Nita uses Revereware)
a slab of marble, polished and sealed, approximately
  14 × 26 × 1 inch
silicon spatula
metal spatula
scissors (no teeth) (Oxo brand all-purpose is excellent)
metal tin to store mints
waxed paper

Ingredients

1 cup water
1 stick (1/2 cup) butter
3 cups sugar
6 to 8 drops peppermint oil
food coloring

BEFORE you begin
1) Butter the marble slab.
2) Lay out your tools for easy access during mint preparation.

Make the Mints
1) Combine the water and butter in the saucepan and heat on low until the butter melts.
2) Blend in the sugar.
3) Clip a candy thermometer to the inside of the pan, being sure that the bulb does not touch the side or bottom of the pan.
4) Turn the heat up to medium high and then gradually increase the temperature until the mixture comes to a full, rolling boil.
5) After the candy cooks for about 5 minutes, the mixture will "settle" down in the pan some. It is chemically changing and thickening. At this

point, turn the heat up a small amount. Watch the thermometer as the temperature rises.

6) At between 8 and 10 minutes, the mixture will be thickening. Watch the temperature closely for it to reach 260°. The ideal temperature is between 263° and 265°. It's better to slightly undercook than overcook.

7) Remove the pan from the heat and, working quickly, with the silicon spatula in hand to scrape down the pan, pour the hot candy mixture up and down the length of the marble.

8) The hot candy will spread out into a very thin layer (about 1/8 inch thick) on the marble. The cold marble will cool the candy very fast. Add just a drop or two of food coloring (if desired) and the peppermint oil.

9) As the outer edges of the candy begin to cool and harden, use your hands to turn and press them into the center of the candy area, which will still be very hot. After about 30 seconds, continue to fold the candy in on itself, always shifting it to a cooler part of the marble, and pressing it out each time to about 1/4 inch thick. It will gradually become firmer as it cools, and you will have to press down hard to spread it out. You'll need to fold and move the candy about 6 times. Use a spatula to move the candy if it sticks to the marble.

10) When the candy has cooled, pick it up off the marble, and form it into a rope. Fold the rope over itself, *but not end to end* (the end being folded over should overlap the other end by an inch or so), then twist and stretch the rope out a small amount. Keep folding the rope over itself and twisting and stretching for about 5 to 6 minutes or until the candy gets glossy and harder to pull.

11) On a wide, flat surface (not on top of the marble) pull and twist out the candy into a long, thin rope (about 3/4 inch in diameter). Cut the rope into 3 or 4 equal segments. Stretch and twist each piece out to about 2 feet in length and then, using scissors, snip the candy into 1/2-inch-long pieces.

12) Layer the candy between sheets of waxed paper in a wide, flat cookie tin, letting it dry for at least 12 hours. If not eaten in one week, store the mints in the refrigerator. They also freeze really well.

Tips from Nita

* The most difficult task when you make butter mints is determining the correct temperature for cooking them. The temperature required to cook the candy will vary because of differences in elevation and humidity. You'll also get different temperature readings with different brands of thermometers. Nita cooks them to between 260° and 265°.

* If you undercook the candy mixture, it will be too stringy and soft in your hands when you start to pull it. If you overcook the candy, it will get hard on the marble way too fast.

* If you're a beginner, start with a half recipe so the candy will be easier to handle and pull—and if it doesn't come out right, you won't have wasted as much.

Bourbon Balls

KAY BAKER, Lenoir County

"This is my mother's recipe," Kay told me. "It's written in her own handwriting at the bottom of a page in the back of a cookbook called *Favorite Institute Recipes from Institute United Methodist Church*. Institute is located in Lenoir County near LaGrange. My daughters ask me to make these when they are coming to visit. You can freeze them if you want to make them ahead."

1 cup nuts, finely chopped
1/2 cup bourbon
1 stick (1/2 cup) butter, softened

2 cups 10X powdered sugar
8 squares (8 ounces) unsweetened baking chocolate

SOAK the nuts in bourbon for one hour. Melt the chocolate in a saucepan over low heat. Separately, combine the bourbon-soaked nuts, butter, and powdered sugar and blend well. Form the nut mixture into balls about 1 inch in diameter. Dip the balls into melted chocolate, and place them on a platter lined with waxed paper. Refrigerate until firm.

Makes 3 dozen

Brandy Balls

ARAMINTA PIERCE BLOWE, Halifax County

As my Aunt Araminta approaches her centennial, she does it in style, driving her 1986 Sedan Deville Cadillac around Weldon, where she is a well-known hostess.

5 cups vanilla wafers, crushed
2 cups 10X powdered sugar
1/2 cup cocoa
1 cup chopped nuts
1/2 cup brandy
1/2 cup light corn syrup
3/4 cup sugar

COMBINE the vanilla wafers, powdered sugar, cocoa, nuts, brandy, and corn syrup; mix until well blended. Form the mixture into balls approximately 1 1/4 inches in diameter. (If the mixture is too dry, add a little water.) Roll the balls in the sugar. Enjoy.

Makes 5 dozen

lemon custard pie, 120–21
lemon icebox pie, 124
lemon ice cream, 262
lemon meringue pie, 121–22
lemon mist, 227
lemon pound cake and icing, 64
lemon sauce, 248
lemon squares, 193
Lena Belle's seven-layer chocolate cake
    and icing, 36–37

Macaroon sherry custard, 228
Mae Wells's gingerbread, 26
Mama's Christmas pie, 133
Mannie's butterscotch cookies, 175
Marble cake, 40–41
Martha Washington candy, 288
Mary Deal's egg custard, 209
Melt-in-your-mouth shortbread cookies,
    161
Microwave chocolate icing, 237
Mimmie's wine jelly, 229
Mints
    old-fashioned butter mints, 290–93
    uncooked mints, 290
Miss Peach's sweet potato pie, 96–97
Miss Sadie's pound cake, 57
Molasses
    ginger snaps, 173
    gingerbread bars, 174
    Grandma's pie, 91
    Mae Wells's gingerbread, 26
    molasses cake, 29
    Moravian molasses cookies, 168
    old-fashioned molasses cookies, 167
    po' folks pudding, 213
Moravian molasses cookies, 168
Mrs. Jones's plum pudding, 222–23
Mrs. Truman's apple pudding, 223
Mrs. Westbrook's fudge, 283

Never-fail candy, 282
Nut cookies, 179
Nutty fingers, 180

Oatmeal
    lazy daisy oatmeal cake and icing, 30
    oatmeal crispies, 162
Old-fashioned butter mints, 290–93
Old-fashioned gingerbread men with
    royal icing, 17
Old-fashioned molasses cookies, 167
Old-fashioned teacakes, 155
Old-time bread pudding like Mama
    made, 210
Ole-timey egg custard pie, 94–95
$100 cake and icing, 81–82
One-two-three-four cake, 23–24
Open-face peach pie, 116–17
Oranges
    crystallized grapefruit and orange
        peel, 273–74
    orange filling, 245–46
    orange icebox cake, 266
    orange rum cake, 47–48

Party pecans, 279
Paul's feathery coconut cake and filling,
    45–47
Peaches
    open-face peach pie, 116–17
    peach and sour cream pie, 117
    peach ice cream, 260–61
    quick cobbler, 113
Peanut butter
    peanut butter creams, 278–79
    peanut butter fudge, 287
    peanut butter pie, 137
    peanut butter sugar cookies, 160
Peanuts
    peanut butter creams, 278–79